BEAST AND MAN IN INDIA

BEAST AND MAN IN INDIA

A POPULAR SKETCH OF INDIAN ANIMALS IN THEIR RELATIONS WITH THE PEOPLE

JOHN LOCKWOOD KIPLING, C.I.E.

GYAN

Published by

Gyan Publishing House
5, Ansari Road
Daryaganj, New Delhi-110002
Phone: 011-47034999, 9811692060
E-mail: books@gyanbooks.com

Distribution Network
gyanbooks.com
India, USA, Canada, UK, Australia, France

ISBN: 978-81-212-8901-6 (PB)
First Published,1891

2nd Impression 2023

Printed at: Gyan Press, Delhi.

BEAST AND MAN IN INDIA

AUTHOR: JOHN LOCKWOOD KIPLING

BEAST AND MAN IN INDIA

BEAST AND MAN
IN INDIA

A POPULAR SKETCH OF INDIAN ANIMALS
IN THEIR RELATIONS WITH
THE PEOPLE

BY

JOHN LOCKWOOD KIPLING, C.I.E.

WITH ILLUSTRATIONS

London
MACMILLAN AND CO., LIMITED
NEW YORK: THE MACMILLAN COMPANY
1904

I think I could turn and live with animals, they are so placid
and self-contained
I stand and look at them long and long.
They do not sweat and whine about their condition,
They do not lie awake in the dark and weep for their sins,
They do not make me sick discussing their duty to God,
Not one is dissatisfied, not one is demented with the mania
of owning things."

WALT WHITMAN.

TO THE OTHER THREE

CONTENTS

ILLUSTRATIONS

CHAPTER I

INTRODUCTORY

WHEN, on the 21st March 1890, under the auspices of the Hon. Sir Andrew Scoble, the Legislative Council of India passed an Act (XI. of 1890) for the prevention of cruelty to animals, some surprise was expressed in England that legislation should be necessary for a people who have long been quoted as an example of mercy. It was hinted that Orientals must have learned cruelty, as they have learned drunkenness, from brutal Britons. Those who know India need not be told that this insinuation is groundless, since both vices have for ages been rooted in the life of Eastern as of all the nations under heaven. The general conclusion of cultivated Europe as to the temper of Orientals towards animals is expressed by Mr. Lecky, in a clause of the sentence with which he concludes a survey of a growth of consideration for animals as an element of public morals, in his *History of European Morals from Constantine to Charlemagne*, and runs thus: "The Muhammadans and the Brahmans have in this sphere considerably surpassed the Christians."

There is enough truth in this statement to give

interest to an examination of it. The gulf that must exist between religious prescriptions that have earned a world-wide reputation for mercy and a practice which has led a Government, strongly adverse to unnecessary legislation, to frame an enactment for the prevention of cruelty, deserves looking into. We ought, perhaps, to distrust most of the compendious phrases which presume to label our complex and paradoxical humanity with qualities and virtues, like drugs in a drawer. At all events, it is better not to try to make another rule but to offer a few general considerations and details of actual fact, leaving the Christian to frame his summary for himself.

The wholesale ascription of tender mercy to India may not unfairly be held to be part of a wide and general misconception of Indian life and character, of which the administrator, the schoolmaster, and the missionary have reason to complain. They find on closer acquaintance that both Hindus and Muhammadans are more human and more like the rest of the world than the conventional pictures of Scholars, working from a dead and done-with literature, had led them to expect. Some of the most authoritative of these writers have never ventured to disturb their dreams by contact with the living India of to-day, and their gushing periods have, in consequence, as much actuality as Gulliver's Travels. For nearly all, the last few centuries of this era do not exist. To judge from their writings, the English power in India might have succeeded that of the Gupta kings. No mention is made of the horrible hole of the pit from which the country was digged; and the events that really shaped the character and habits of the people are ignored in favour of ancient lawgivers and forgotten Vedas. Nothing could be more scholarly, amiable, sentimental, or mistaken, and the plain result is a falsification of history which has more ill effects than are visible on the narrow horizon of an English study.

It is not a pleasant subject to dwell upon, but there is no more fitting adjective than "cruel" for the India of the late Mogul and the Pindāri. We may allow that through centuries of trouble the Hindu system availed to preserve Brahmanical ordinances, but these only affected a limited portion of the community. The masses of the people, who really have to do with animals, could not but be demoralised. So general precepts of mercy for the many shrank into ritual observances for the few. Moreover, such precepts as exist have been exaggerated in report.

Strictly speaking, the Parsee religious code alone, among those of Oriental races, directly enjoins a humane and considerate treatment of all animals during their life, as may be fully learned from the Book of Ardha Viraf, the Dante of the Zoroastrian *Inferno*. The Hindu worships the cow, and as a rule is reluctant to take the life of any animal except in sacrifice. But that does not preserve the ox, the horse, and the ass from being unmercifully beaten, over-driven, over-laden, under-fed, and worked with sores under their harness; nor does it save them from abandonment to starvation when unfit for work, and to a lingering death which is made a long torture by birds of prey, whose beaks, powerless to kill outright, inflict undeserved torment. And the same code which exalts the Brahman and the cow, thrusts the dog, the ass, the buffalo, the pig, and the low-caste man beyond the pale of merciful regard.

The loving-kindness of which we hear is, in modern

fact and deed, a vague reluctance to take life by a positive sudden act, except for sacrifice,—a large exception,—and a ceremonial reverence for the cow, which does not avail to secure even for her such good treatment as the milch cows of Europe receive. There are some castes who hold it wrong even to accidentally destroy an insect, who keep a cloth before their mouths to prevent swallowing them, and who brush the ground before they seat themselves, so that they may not crush out some minute life. But they teach no gospel of mercy, inheriting only an observance of their peculiar caste, absolutely inert beyond its boundaries. Indeed, it is well for mankind that they are not propagandists, for, clearly a man who refuses to take or to interfere with animal life in any way, and who says that while the cat should be left to kill the mouse, the serpent should not by a truly pious man be prevented from entering the cradle of his sleeping child, is not a teacher of much value. No general temper of pity towards animals in service has been produced by Brahmanical law, and probably not by any merely religious ordinances in any part of the world. Feeling for the sufferings of animals, restraint in their use, and recognition of their rights to consideration, are just as modern in India as elsewhere.

The reluctance to kill, which is the main fact of Hindu animal treatment, is of itself, from a European point of view, a cause of needless suffering. We speak of putting injured or diseased creatures out of their misery. To the mind of the orthodox Hindu there is no such thing as euthanasia, and it is impious to attempt to bring it about. An English correspondent of the *Pioneer*, 30th October 1890, writes:—

"At Chandi, near Kalka, I last week found a

Government dāk horse lying in a public grove, close to the road, a hind leg of which had been broken (according to the people there) three days before, through a kick. This poor beast had been hauled out and thrown down alive to die a lingering death. It was perfectly conscious. I found it surrounded by crows, which had already picked out both of its eyes, and when I arrived were in the act of devouring other tender parts. The horse attracted my attention by throwing its head up repeatedly to drive the crows off. Luckily I had a pistol, and of course shot the animal at once."

There is nothing unusual in this, for it is the fate of all animals that serve the Hindu to be left to die; and though most English people would approve of that pistol-shot, it was wrong according to the Hindu canon.

The cause of the canon is not far to seek. The doctrine of the transmigration of souls is at the root of *ahimsa*, the ancient principle of regard for animals, for it makes all living nature kin with humanity. A bull is more than a bull, he is a potential grandfather. We have all been here before, and the souls of the hosts of men and animals, birds, and fishes have passed in these various disguises through infinite æons of time and change. Believing this, you naturally hold your hand before dismissing a soul to another flight and another change of dwelling.

In this, as in other Indian subjects, a vast and most various population has been labelled with attributes that belong to a few of the upper classes alone. A description of the habits and beliefs of the Bench of Bishops would scarcely be accepted as fairly representative of the masses of Great Britain, but something like this suffices for popular estimates of India. Those who have but little to do with animals are enjoined not to kill, but no command is laid on the low-caste Hindu, while the average Muhammadan, ignorant though devout, knows of none. Even Hindus are not, as is commonly believed, universally vegetarian. Nearly all eat fish, vast and yearly increasing numbers eat mutton and kid, Rajputs and Sikhs eat wild boar, and most low-caste Hindus are only vegetarian when flesh food is not within their reach. All Muhammadans are flesh eaters as a matter of course. A Levitical code is naturally a mother of hypocrisy, so Hindus living among Hindus of higher caste will call mutton *lal sâg*—red vegetable; and fish, water beans; while prawns are ennobled as Shiva biscuits, but they are eaten all the same.

Animal sacrifices, and the peculiar character of the religious ceremonies of certain Hindu Sâkti worshipping castes, at whose meetings the eating of flesh and the drinking of wine and spirits form part of a ritual of orgy, also tend to lower the standard from the ideal Europeans have conceived of the Hindu. There are vast numbers of these "left-hand" worshippers. Here it may be remarked that the "official" books of mythology, etc., are no guide to modern practice, or to a comprehension of modern life. Modern Hinduism, as Sir Monier M. Williams has well said, is "a loose conglomerate," and it is a conglomerate in process of decay and change. The High Gods described in the works one may call "official" may not be quite dead, but they are practically superseded in favour of witchcraft, demonolatry, and fetishism, or by vulgar manifestations, usually of an orgiastic type. Wholesale slaughter and blood are constantly associated with these Gods, Godlings, and demons. Some writers claim for Hinduism a wonderful immutability; and this preposterous contention, which would be scouted if made on behalf of any other race of mankind, has been allowed to pass unchallenged. It has decay inherent in its system, and its history is one long chronicle of protest, dissent, and change.

Persons of the Vegetarian persuasion sometimes claim a moral superiority for the Hindu, in that his delicacy of feeling is not blunted by the horrors of the Western butcher's shop. This is plausible but illusory, for there are plenty of butchers' shops in India, and it should be further remembered that of the thousands who habitually pass such shops in the West, but a very small percentage have seen the act of slaughter, wherein demoralising influence may be supposed to lie. The Hindu, on the other hand, is familiar with slaughter in a most revolting form, performed as an act of sacrifice. When we talk of sacrifice we think of the grave and decent solemnities described in the Bible or in Homer. Such ideas are rudely dispelled by the reality in India. The goat and buffalo sacrifices to Kali at Kali ghât in the highly civilised metropolis of Bengal are not to be mentioned in connection with any slaughtering we know of, for there may be seen thousands of people gloating in delirious excitement over rivers of blood.

There are general injunctions of mercy in the Buddhist religion, but Buddhism has been dead and done with in India proper for centuries, and has left but little behind it. Always vague and abstract, it is doubtful whether its languid prescriptions ever effectively controlled the daily practice of the people. The Singhalese are Buddhists, and yet cruelty to animals is one of the marks of modern Ceylon. The modern Burman is a Buddhist and should not take life. But, like Gautama Buddha himself, he eats flesh, so he contents his conscience by calling the butcher a Muhammadan. We are apt to judge of the results of a creed from the aims of its commandments, which is putting the cart before the horse. Yet we ought to know better, for the main stress of our Christian commandment is to lay up no treasure on earth, to consider the lilies of the field, to sell all and follow the Christ, etc. etc. In the Christian capitals of the Western world one may see how much of this injunction is obeyed.

The ordinary Englishman will not easily be persuaded that the act of killing an animal or bird for food is necessarily a proof of cruelty. I write these lines in an English house in the country, the gracious lady whereof has just returned from a visit to some friends in the village, who had sent word that their pig was killed. Here is a delicate and refined Englishwoman going in cold blood to see a dead pig! Nothing could be more horrible from a Hindu or Muhammadan point of view, but from that of English country life it is natural enough. The lady is a valued friend of a struggling family. Their pig has been kindly treated and carefully fed for months, and its death is a sort of festival; they are proud of its weight and size, and it is one of the triumphs of their provident and thrifty lives. "And the pig?" says the master of the house at lunch. "Well, I had to look at the pig, and it seemed a fine pig enough. They said it weighed 14 score, and I said it must be the largest they had fed since their mother died, and they were all much pleased, and wanted to tell me stories of past pigs, but I managed to escape."

The topsy-turvy morality of the East would give a higher place to the Levitically clean Hindu, who would die sooner than eat flesh, but who would also rather die than touch or help a dying man of a low caste near his door, than to the English lady whose life is spent in active beneficence, but who is defiled by eating beef and approaching the dead body of a pig.

The animal hospitals of India have been frequently quoted, and with some reason, as a proof of the tender mercy of the country. There are three of these interesting institutions on the great continent, at Bombay, Surat, and Ahmedabad, chiefly maintained by Banians of the Jain faith. The Bombay "pinjrapol," however, is said to have been largely endowed by the generous Parsee, Sir Jamsetjee Jejeebhoy, first baronet of the name. They are not hospitals in the true sense, for ailments are not treated, but simply refuges for halt, maimed, diseased, and blind creatures for whom nobody cares. Until the late Mr. J. H. Steel, Principal of the Bombay Veterinary College, took compassion on the inmates and regularly visited the place, no attempt had ever been made to alleviate their sufferings; and the institution is of some antiquity. Ritual reverence for life does not include the performance of acts of mercy. It is enough to save the animal from immediate death, and to place food within its reach. So you see there creatures with unset broken limbs, with hoofs eighteen inches long, and monstrous wens. The dogs, as I remember them twenty years ago, were a heart-breaking sight, confined, with nothing to do but fight, insufficiently fed, and all afflicted with one equal misery of mange. A quaint feature of the place is an apartment supposed to be full of the vermin that feed on mankind. From time to time a man is paid to spend a night in this den in order to give the cherished insects a dinner, but first he is drugged to insensibility, lest in his natural irritation he should be tempted to destroy some of them. I have always doubted this, and certainly never saw it done, but it is one of the proudest traditions of the "pinjrapol," vouched for by Native gentlemen of undoubted authority.

There are admirable points in the ritual respect for life, but it is not true humanity, nor is it practised with sufficient intelligence or feeling to profit the animal. We in the West may at least learn from it the reflection that all living things cling to life, nor need we in the present state of Veterinary science be always so prompt with pistol or poleaxe as is our habit.

But it must be noted that the sect which cares for animal hospitals is comparatively small, with only a local influence, and that its practice in this matter is the subject of a good deal of popular gibe. For it is not easy to respect people who collect caterpillars, and feed fleas and other vermin with human blood, nor is it only to the Occidental that a fantastic glorification of the letter of a law may show the death of its spirit.

Oriental tender mercy has always been liable to this taint of grotesque exaggeration. That renowned model of kindness and generosity, whose name is on every Oriental's lips, and whose deeds are constantly quoted—Hatim Tai—fed his brother the tiger (as St. Francis of Assisi would say) with portions of flesh cut from his own limbs. This may be heroic, but, like many other illustrious examples of Oriental goodness, it is also absurd, and so remote from every possibility of ordinary life and conduct as to exert no practical influence as a lesson.

Yet, while maintaining that no precept of mercy has protected animals in servitude in India, we may gladly admit that a more humane temper prevails with regard to free creatures than in the West. Village boys are not there seen stoning frogs or setting dogs at cats, nor tying kettles to dogs' tails, and it has not been found necessary to forbid bird-nesting by Act of Parliament. The Indian school-boy on his way to school passes numbers of squirrels, much resembling the chipmunk of America, but he never throws a stone at them; and the sparrow, the crow, the maina, and the hoopoe move from his path without a flutter of fear. The india-rubber catapult or tweaker of the West has not yet reached him, while the sling and the *golél* or pellet-bow (the "stone bow" of Shakspeare) seem to be only used when guarding fruit and crops from the hungry parrakeet and the omnivorous crow.

One of the most surprising things in the country is the patience with which depredations on the crops are endured. With far less provocation the English farmer organises sparrow clubs, and freely uses the gun, the trap, and the poisoned bait. And the Indian farmer suffers from creatures that earn no dole of grain by occasional insecticide. The monkey, the nilghai, the black buck, the wild pig, and the parrakeet fatten at his expense, and never kill a caterpillar or a weevil in return. He and his family spend long and dismal hours on a platform of sticks raised a few feet above the crops, whence they lift their voices against legions of thieves. The principle of abstaining from slaughter is pushed to an almost suicidal point in purely Hindu regions, and becomes a serious trouble at times. A large tract of fertile country in the N.-W. Provinces, bordering on the Bhurtpore State, is now lapsing into jungle on account of the inroads of the nilghai and the wild pig. The "blue cow" or nilghai is sacred, and may not be killed even by the villagers whom the creature drives from their homes, and there are not enough sportsmen or tigers to keep down the wild boar.

Gardeners try to scare the birds with elaborate arrangements of string, bamboos, old pans, and stones in their fruit trees; and sometimes a watcher sits like a spider at the centre of an arrangement of cords, radiating all over the field, so that an alarming movement may be produced at any point. Yet their tempers do not give way, and they preserve a monumental patience. Sometimes they say: "The peacock, the monkey, the deer, the partridge, these four are thieves," or include other animals and birds with varying numbers, but always with more resignation than resentment. The wisdom of the village says that public calamities are seven, and are visitations of God, —drought, floods, locusts, rats, parrots, tyranny, and invasion. The professional birdcatcher, however, is never of the farmer race, and owes his victims no revenge; while a scornful proverb on his ragged and disreputable condition shows that he earns no gratitude from the cultivator. Another rustic saying about bird slaughter, expanded into its full meaning, would run: "You kill a paddy-bird, and what do you get?—a handful of feathers!" Yet since Parisian milliners have decreed that civilised women shall wear birds in their head-gear, there is not sufficient respect for animal life to stay the barbarous slaughter of them now going on all over India.

The tolerance or indifference which leaves wild creatures alone is unfortunately an intimate ally of blank ignorance. That townspeople should be ignorant of nature is to be expected, but even in the country a fly-catcher, a sparrow, and a shrike are all spoken of as *chiriyas*, birds merely, and not one in fifty, save outcaste folk, can tell you anything of their habits, food, nests, or eggs. The most vague and incorrect statements are accepted and repeated without thought, a habit common to all populations, but more firmly rooted in India than elsewhere. First-hand observation and accurate statement of fact seem almost impossible to the Oriental, and education has not hitherto availed to help him. In the West public instruction becomes more real and vital year by year, but in the East it is still bound hand and foot to the corpse of a dead literature. Educational authorities in India discern the fault, but they are themselves mainly of the literary caste and direct native Professors whose passion is for words. We talk of science teaching, but forget to count with a national habit of mind that stands carefully aloof from facts and is capable of reducing the splendid suggestions of Darwin and Wallace, Faraday and Edison, to mechanical and inert rote work.

Indifference is intensified by the narrowness of sympathy produced by the caste system, and by the discouragement of attachment to animals among respectable people. Our modern school-books, in which lessons on animal life and humane animal treatment are wisely included, may do something in the course of time to lighten this "blind side" of Oriental character, and in a few generations we may hope for an Indian student of natural history. At present this splendid field is left entirely to European observers, who mostly look at nature along the barrel of a gun. Which is a false perspective.

I conclude that, while admitting the need for a legislative measure for the protection of animals, consonant with the wishes and feelings of the most cultivated classes in India, and of itself a sign of advancing civilisation and morality, it would be a task as difficult as hateful to prove that the people at large have any abnormal and inborn tendency to cruelty. The shadow of evil days of anarchy, disorder, and rapine has but lately cleared away and given place to an era of security, when, as the country proverb says, "the tiger and the goat drink at one ghât." The people are better than their creeds, but it is not easy to defend their practice, though it is often more due to necessity, custom, and ignorance than to downright brutality of intent.

To explain something of this in a familiar manner befitting an everyday, familiar subject is the purpose of this pen and pencil essay. It has seemed to me that an elementary study of Indian animals, their treatment and usage, and the popular estimates and sayings current about them, though involving much that is commonplace and trivial, opens a side door into Indian life, thought, and character, the threshold of which is still unworn.

To Anglo-Indians of long standing a word of apology is due for the apparent confidence with which native beliefs are treated. The truth is, it is hard to state briefly ideas of this nature without a seeming assumption of complete knowledge. But they will recognise the difficulty of translating nebulous Indian notions into stark English print, and make just allowances. We others know that only a fool will pretend to say with absolute confidence what a native thinks. Even in the West, where men think aloud, and the noisy newspaper proclaims the matter on the house-top, it takes a wise man to say how the popular mind is working.

India has a larger inheritance than most other countries in sacred and legendary lore of animals; but much of it has now only a literary interest, and but a remote connection with the actual life of the people. I have neither the scholarship nor the ambition to produce "one of those learned compilations which have no root in actual life, epitomise the past, and have no future." Serious students of Zoolatry and of folk-lore in its scientific sense will therefore find little to interest them in chapters wherein a living dog is frankly preferred to a dead lion.

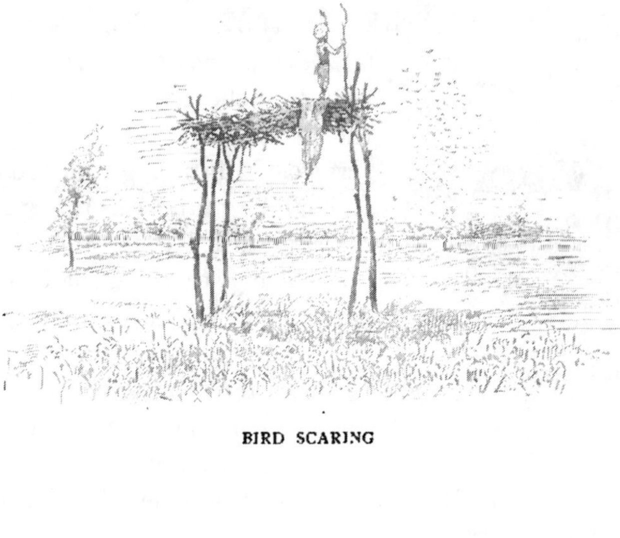

BIRD SCARING

CHAPTER II

OF BIRDS

"Birds, companions more unknown
Live beside us, but alone;
Finding not, do all they can,
Passage from their souls to man.
Kindness we bestow, and praise,
Laud their plumage, greet their lays;
Still, beneath the feather'd breast,
Stirs a history unexpress'd."

MATTHEW ARNOLD.

THE PARROT. — The parrakeet (*Palæornis eupatrius*) is in some regions believed to have earned the gratitude of man by its services in bringing the seeds of fruit and grain from the garden of Paradise after the Flood and sowing them abroad on the earth for his use. Ages of shameless larceny have nearly effaced the memory of that fabled feat, but the creature is still tolerated, and is the familiar bird of the fields and groves as well as the favourite cage bird of India.

The parrot plays a leading part in many folk tales, and has thus come to be regarded as a guardian of domestic honour. In such ballads as "Lord William" and "May Colvine and fause Sir John," the popinjay's share in romance is shown to British readers as a curious survival, but in India we are nearer to the time when creatures spoke and thought, and the literary curiosity of the West is still the belief of the East. The parrot is also reckoned an auspicious or lucky bird to have in the house. An augmentation of honour is its appointment as the vâhan or steed of Kama or Kamdeo, a Hindu god of love.

Unfortunately for its comfort, it has a powerful beak, and quickly destroys a wooden cage. So it is usually confined in a small dome-shaped cage of hoop-iron with an iron floor. During the hot season, when it is painful to touch any metal surface, these cages must be cruel torture-chambers; and when one watches the free birds darting to and fro like live emeralds in the sun, with the wild scream and reckless flinging of themselves on the air peculiar to parrakeets, one cannot but grieve for the captive slowly roasting in his tiny oven-like prison. Leaving the general question that is sure to arise some day as to our right to imprison creatures for our pleasure at all, the confinement we inflict should be at least as little irksome as possible; but it is hard to persuade people that creatures have rights, and a polite smile is the only answer to a plea for these prisoners.

Hindus teach their pet birds the sacred words, Gunga Rām, Rama, and Sri Bhugwān, names of God, grateful to the Hindu ear and easy to parrot speech, while Muhammadans say Miān Mittū, which is only a caressing name from the vast vocabulary of endearing

THE PARROT'S CAGE

nonsense in which Indian domestic life excels. In Northern India a household parrot verse among Hindus is :

Latpat, panchhi, chatur Sujān
Sub-ka dada Sri Bhugwān
Parho Gunga Rām !

or roughly in English: "Pretty bird, clever and knowing, God is the giver of all ; say Gunga Rām !" The word here translated "say" means to read or study, and also to recite aloud, and is constantly used for bird song. "My lark is reading very nicely this morning," a bird-fancier will say. "Little parrot" is a pet name for children, and "parrot talk" is a woman's expression for their conversation when it is pretty and respectful.

"Parrot eyed" is a common phrase for an ungrateful or deceitful person, not, as might be imagined, from the expression of the bird's eyes, but because, after years of cherishing, it will fly away if the cage door is left open. In spite of the opinion of my native friends, I cannot help thinking the phrase was derived originally from the parrot's habit of not looking at the person he is supposed to be talking to ; for when one thinks of it, a parrot's eyes have always a curiously indifferent and "other-where" kind of expression. A certain type of face is well described in "a mouth like a purse, a nose like a parrot's." As a hero of song and story this bird takes part in some domestic observances. A mother will on several consecutive days divide an almond between her parrot and her baby. This will prevent the child from stammering, and make it bold and free of speech. In the Punjab Himálaya there is a whimsical superstition that when a parrot's cage hangs over the door whence a bridegroom issues to be married, it is highly auspicious, but that something dreadful will happen if he passes under it on any other errand. This fancy once caused some trouble to a political officer of Government in charge of a Hill State. The youthful Raja was to be married, and on the eve of the event, while there was still much business to be done, he was inveigled into the zenana, or feminine side of the palace, the inmates of which promptly hung a parrot over the door. It was necessary, for many and urgent reasons, to withdraw the boy from his female relatives; but the little council of the State was sorely puzzled. It would be an awful thing to make the Raja pass under the cage. Could he not be brought out by some other door behind, or even fished up through a hole made in the roof? At last a grave old Wazir came in and asked with an innocent air: "Is it quite certain that the cage is there?" It was quite certain. "Then," said the old gentleman slily, "my eyes are dim, for I did not see it as I passed but now." The Council went to see, were greatly relieved to find the cage gone, and made a great pretence of wondering how it came about. While they were deliberating with characteristic Hindu hesitation and timidity, he had ordered a menial, indifferent to omens, to carry it off. So the young Raja was rescued from his factious women folk and came out.

The parrakeet is often trained as a public performer. In the streets of Delhi I used to see one that went through gymnastic and military exercises, whirling a tiny torch lighted at each end, loading and firing a small cannon, lying dead and coming to life again; all done with a comic air of eagerness and enjoyment which it seemed hard to impute to mere hunger for the morsels that rewarded each trick. It is seldom a bird in native hands speaks really well. Orientals are easily contented, and, though they can take pains in some matters, are inclined to think that parrot speech comes, as Dogberry said of reading and writing, by nature. The Indian bird, moreover, has less natural aptitude for speech than the true parrots of other countries.

A PERFORMING PARROT

The British soldier in India, at a loss how to employ his leisure, is frequently a butterfly-collector or a bird-fancier. Sometimes a stalwart trooper may be seen all alone, leaning over the parapet of a well, apparently in earnest converse with some one who has fallen in. Parrots are believed to learn to talk more readily when taught in a darkened and silent room. There are no such rooms in his barracks, so the soldier lets his cage half-way down a well and spends hours in teaching his pet. The practice is probably an indigenous one, but I have never seen a native engaged in it.

The Baya Bird.—As a performer of tricks, however, the parrakeet is excelled by the little *baya*, the weaver bird (*Ploceus baya*). The plumage of this clever creature is of quaker-like simplicity, but it is a favourite cage-bird and easily acquires tricks, especially of a "fetch and carry" nature. The table servant or waiter of a friend of mine has one that flies to a tree at the word of command, selects a flower or leaf, plucks it, and, returning, places it daintily between its master's lips. Some thread beads with great dexterity, others draw up seed or water, like the European goldfinch; but, judging from the skilful construction of its nest, it is probably more intelligent than the goldfinch. A popular rhyming proverb contrasts the house-building talent of the *baya* bird with the helplessness of the shelterless monkey, which, having human hands and feet, is yet incapable of protecting itself against the weather. This verse is often quoted for the benefit of idle boys and girls who object to learn. The *baya* is believed to light up its nest at night with captured fire-flies, stuck against the fibrous wall over the head of the brooding hen. The bird certainly catches flies, and pellets of clay are occasionally found stuck on the inside of the nest, but further evidence is wanted before one can do more than envy the unquestioning belief of the Oriental in a charming fancy which may be true.

It is true that at nesting time play nests are made with a loop across the opening, on which the birds play and the male sits and sings to solace the female. Some say these are experimental or preliminary studies in the art of nest-weaving.

Caged Song Birds.—Working people in the cities

of Northern India are great bird-fanciers, and find, as they sit for hours over their embroidery, weaving, or shoe-making, that a singing bird is good company. The bulbul (*Molpastes intermedius*), the *chendūl* or tufted lark (*Galerita cristata*), the Shāmā (*Cittocincla macrura*), the hill maina (*Eulabes religiosa*), are most commonly seen, and there are several others. Like the operatives of manufacturing England, Indian

A BIRD-SINGING MATCH (DELHI ARTISANS)

workmen arrange singing matches between their birds, and enjoy sitting in groups in shady places round the cages in which their pets are shrilling their loudest notes. It is a cruel rule among them that a bird to sing well must be kept always in the dark. I have heard a lark-fancier say that the cage holding a good lark should have a fresh cloth cover every year—the old ones being allowed to remain. The hill maina, one of the best talking birds, however, is generally allowed to look about him ; and the tiny lals or male avadavats (*Sporæginthus amandava*), kept mainly for their minute prettiness, a dozen or more in a cage together, are not covered up except at night as a protection against mosquitoes. In Delhi bird-fanciers often take their birds out tied to a small crutch-shaped perch of bright brass carried in the hand. It is curious that precisely the same practice obtains in Pekin, where hundreds of grave Chinamen may be seen, each carrying a small bird. In the English midland counties linnets and bull-finches are occasionally tied to perches and known as "braced birds."

Fighting Birds.—These Arcadian enjoyments are too simple for many tastes, so bulbuls, quails, partridges, and even the small avadavats are encouraged to fight. Twenty-five rupees is by no means an unusual price for a fighting quail, and in Hyderabad (Deccan), the capital of the Nizam, a hundred and fifty rupees is often given for a good bird. Besides the gray partridge (*Ortygornis pondicerianus*), which is the best fighting bird, the chikōre (*Caccabis chukor*) and the black partridge (*Francolinus vulgaris*) are kept as pets. The house-kept artisan goes out in the cool of the morning or evening, carrying his cage with him, and in some garden or open place releases his bird for a run. The creature follows its master with a rapid and pretty gait that suggests a graceful girl tripping along with a full skirt well held up. The Indian lover can pay his sweetheart no higher compliment than to say she runs like a partridge. In poetry the semblance is one of the most hackneyed of Indian metaphors. In poetry, too, the partridge is associated with the moon, and, like the lotus, is supposed to be perpetually longing for it, while the chikōre is said to eat fire.

Indian housewives dislike the quail, and it is by some considered an inauspicious bird to keep; but the partridge, in spite of the taint of blackguardism attached to fighting birds, is thought lucky, for he attracts to himself any ill luck that may be hovering about the house,—a function of most Indian household pets. When treated merely as house pets and allowed to run free at times, partridges develop a good deal of intelligence and become entertaining companions, as they are inquisitive, pugnacious, and perfectly fearless. In cities where there are large populations of artisans and many Muhammadans, as Delhi, Amritsar, Lahore, Hyderabad (Deccan), Agra, Cawnpore, etc., quail and partridge fighting is as popular a diversion as cock-fighting used to be in England, and large sums are betted on their contests. No artificial spurs, however, are worn by Indian birds.

The great London bird market, I am told, now that the "Dials" have disappeared, is St. Martin's Lane on a Sunday morning. In most Indian towns there are bird-dealers, and in some, as at Lucknow, there is a regularly established bird bazár, where all kinds of birds are sold,—quails, cocks, and partridges for fighting, hawks for the chase, fancy pigeons, singing and talking birds, and others for pets. The variety is much greater than in any European bird market, yet there is a family likeness among bird-fanciers everywhere. A Spitalfields weaver or a Staffordshire potter, if he could speak the language, would find himself quite at home with Indian bird folk in all details of handling, feeding, bargaining, and swapping, and in most appreciations of bird points.

What Birds say.—Good Muhammadans think the black partridge pious, since its call fits itself to the words "Sobhăn teri qŭdrăt"—"Thine, O Lord, is the power"; but more worldly ears distinguish the words "Lăssăn, piăz, ădhrăk"—"Garlic, onions, ginger"; or, according to some, "Nūn, tēl, ădhrăk,"—"salt, oil, ginger," the chief condiments of curry. The Indian ring-dove (*Turtur risorius*) is similarly endeared to Muhammadans by its pious persistence in the cry "Yusuf ku"—"Joseph is in the well," which it first raised when the wicked brethren said he was slain and showed the grieving Jacob the blood-stained coat of many colours. Another dove is thought to say "Allah! Allah!" The partridge says "Fakiri Fakiri." A wild pigeon is thought to repeat "Haq sirr hu"—"God knows the secret"; the ordinary rooster exhorts the thoughtless to remember God by crowing—"Zikr' ullah! Zikr' ullah! ya ghafīlin!" while the raven hoarsely cries "Ghâr, Ghâr," as he did when he basely tried to betray Muhammad hidden in the cave of Jebel Thaur to his enemies the Khoreish, when the pious pigeon built her nest and the spider stretched her webs across the entrance. It is quite easy to hear these words in birds' notes—when you know them—and they are at least as much like the original sounds as the renderings of those scientific ornithologists who have tried to express bird music in syllables. In the notes to Mr. Lane's *Arabian Nights* are given versions of bird talk as they strike Arab ears, with wondrous instances of learned parrots, including one which knew the Qurân right through and corrected a misreading!

The Hoopoe.—Other birds are prized for the legends with which they are associated. The hoopoe (*Upupa epops*) has not much to say, but he is a favourite because he was King Solomon's messenger; and he is known as the king of birds from the story of his crest and crown, which, perhaps, is not too hackneyed to be repeated here. One hot day King Solomon, travelling on his angel-borne magic carpet, was oppressed by the heat of the sun, and the hoopoes flew over his head, wing to wing in a close and protecting canopy. Solomon was grateful, and promised to grant whatever boon the hoopoes thought fit to ask. They foolishly asked to be allowed to wear golden crowns like his. The great king granted their request, and presently all the bird-catchers in the country were enriched by the spoil of dead hoopoes. A remnant escaped and ruefully prayed for the removal of the dangerous distinction. So the crest of feathers was given instead, and the bird-catchers ceased from troubling. If you suggest to a native that the hoopoe's crest may serve as "the other end" of the pickaxe-like beak, and point out its balancing action as the bird drives it into the ground, he listens and assents, but his assent informs you he has no great opinion of your sense.

The Crow.—The Indian crow (*Corvus splendens*) acts as a messenger in many folk stories, and is still supposed to announce approaching visitors. In a land where the *pitris* or spirits of the dead are believed to be flitting round continually, seeking rest, and inhabiting the bodies of animals and birds, it is easy to imagine the bold and familiar crow haunting houses, peering into windows and doors, a restless human ghost. They are often fed as a propitiation to spirit land. In this belief it is said that a pair of crows were carried to that imperfectly quenched cinder heap, Aden, forty years ago, by the Hindu labourers engaged on the fortifications there. A Hindu who saw them says: "The poor creatures had no trees on which to perch, and they wandered about from rock to rock cawing piteously." It is firmly believed, and there is more ground for the belief than usual, that crows hold *punchayets*, caste-councils or committees, and inflict summary punishments on offenders. It is at

THE FAMILIAR CROW

least certain that in India, as elsewhere, a maimed or disabled bird, unable to escape or hide himself, is set upon by his kind and killed. I once had for pensioner a lame crow, outcast from his fellows, but strong enough to take care of himself. This habit is reported to have suggested a stratagem by which omnivorous gypsy folk catch crows. A live crow is spread-eagled on his back, with forked pegs holding down his pinions. He flutters and cries, and other crows come to investigate his case and presently attack him. With claws and beak he seizes an assailant and holds him fast. The gypsy steps from hiding, and secures and pinions the second crow. These two catch two more, the four

CALF AND CROWS

catch four more, and so on, until there are enough for dinner, or to take into a town, where the crow-catcher stands before some respectable Hindu's shop and threatens to kill the bird he holds in his hand. The Hindu pays a ransom of a pice or two and the crow is released.

When a child is sick, crows and other birds are bought by its mother and female relatives to be released as a propitiation.

No decent person, of course, would dine on crows, but in Northern India the rook is held to be *halāl* or permitted for Mussulman food, and I have seen them exposed for sale in Peshawar market.

In Bombay, rude street boys call Parsees "crows" —possibly a gibe at the Parsee custom of exposing the dead in the Towers of Silence, where they are eaten by birds.

Of many sayings about the crow it may be noted that for the daw in peacock's feathers, they say in India of a fop, "the crow stuck a pomegranate flower in his tail and thought himself a mighty swell." Also, "the crow swaggered like a swan, forgetting his own gait." A crow fairy or pĕri is a very dark woman. "Krishna's name in a crow's mouth!" and "Though you put a crow in a parrot's cage he will still caw" express his inferiority. Crows and herons are counted wicked birds; the former being considered the more accomplished rascals.

But the main fact about the crow is his note, which is a ceaseless *obligato* accompaniment to all Indian life. A popular cradle song crooned over thousands of children—*Aré koko, ja re koko* = O crow! go crow—might be paraphrased thus—

"Crow, crow! silence keep,
Plums are ripe in jungle deep;
Fetch a bushel fresh and cheap
For a babe who wants to sleep.

"Crow, crow! the peacock cries,
In the wood a thief there lies,
Would steal my baby from my eyes."

Also, they say to a child, "If you make a noise, the crow will fly away with you." The baby-name, or rather women's name, for crow is *koko*.

All over the world women are apt at "stringing pretty words that make no sense, and kissing full sense into empty words," but, while acknowledging the elemental rightness of "woman talk". as a thing apart and a portion of the God-given sweetness of life, it is not too fantastical to perceive in the Indian development of something like a separate language,—*chhoti boli*—literally little talk,—the clipped and childish speech of imprisoned women of starved intellect, an evidence of a great social disability. Affection, common sense, and wit may be and are freely expressed in this talk, and it is passing rich in endearments, but to those who look below the surface, it is one sign more of the disadvantage under which the country is laid by the unnatural treatment, denial of instruction, and seclusion of women. Yet, if the women of India have the faults of an exaggerated domesticity, they have also its qualities, and their estate should be understood before reformers rush to meddle with it.

To most Indian women crows stand as types of knavery, and there is sound reason for this estimate. They are thieves, outcast scavengers, deceitful, and, above all other creatures that hoard and hide, clever in concealing things. "The swan (noble type) has flown away, the tiger (the king) has made the crow (the knave) his minister," is a much-quoted verse from a popular tale. Some intimacy with the bird is needed before one can fairly appreciate this side of his character. I once reared from the nest a pair of hill crows,—ravens in all but size,—who lived with me for three years, till one after the other they were wooed away to mate. They were miracles of naughtiness, delighting in sly destruction and odd turns of malice, ever ready to peck at a servant's hurrying heel, and especially given to torment a little dog who hated them. When he had a bone they came daintily stepping together and concerted measures against him, exactly like the stage villains of melodrama, manœuvring and skirmishing with keen enjoyment. On his part, the dog learned to watch and rifle their hiding-places. Their delight in bright objects was remarkable. The spoon in my early morning tea, taken in the garden or verandah, was of even more interest to them than my buttered toast, and they were never tired of tugging at my watch-chain in order to get out the watch, a deeply coveted plaything. Everything of this shining sort that came within reach was promptly buried, dug up again, reburied with elaborate precautions, and forgotten after a few days. In the hot weather they vastly enjoyed eating and playing with pieces of ice, which they hid for future use. But ice is a treasure fleeting as fairy gold, and the birds showed by the fussy action, sidelong squints, and interrogative turns of the head which make them such diverting comedians, how deeply they were puzzled by its disappearance. "Surely, surely," one would seem to say as he turned up a corner of the matting, "I hid a cold chunk of shining stuff here,—but *where* is it? Never mind, I will get another." So he would hop up to the table and take a fresh piece from the glass finger-bowl, itself a great delight to the glitter-loving birds. To the last the disappearance of the ice was a wonder. But, like that of some other comedians, their conduct was generally low. The way in which they allowed themselves to be sent to bed (an old gate in an out-house), though free to fly at will, pacing meekly as good as gold, after a day of variegated crime, was their only lapse into real virtue.

The Roller.—The Roller (*Coracias Indica*), sometimes called in India the blue jay, is sacred to Vishnu, who once assumed its form, and is caught to be liberated at the Hindu Dasahra festival in Western India and at the Dūrga Pūja in Bengal. "Undreamed-of wings he lifted," is a quotation always brought to mind when this gray and sober-looking bird suddenly rises and displays the turquoise and sapphire-tinted splendour of his wings.

The Maina.—The Maina (*Acridotheres tristis*) is sacred to the Hindu God Ram Deo, and sits on his hand. In stories and talk the *maina* is a popular favourite, which is natural enough, for the bird is one of the handsomest and most vivacious of the starlings; with an elegant tripping gait, like that of a neatly built ballet-girl, alert and brave in bright yellow boots. In flying, a white bar on the maina's wing produces a curious effect of rotation. Like crows and sparrows, these birds go to roost in great companies, and make a prodigious fuss before they settle to rest, as if each bird were recounting the adventures of the day and all were talking at once.

The Kite.—The common Kite (*Milvus govinda*) is often spoken of by Europeans as the Brahminy Kite. Naturalists reserve this name for the smaller chocolate-tinted bird with white head and breast, common near rivers,—*Haliastur indus.* In former times the Kite was held in some esteem by Muhammadans as a presage of victory to the army over which it hovered, and called a blessed or auspicious spirit. Being an eagle in miniature, the Kite perhaps inherited some of the respect born of the ancient and oft-repeated story of an eagle hovering over a future king or leader of men, which is told of Muhammad among many others. In recent times the landing at Boulogne of Napoleon the Last, accompanied by a tame eagle, furnishes a quaint echo of this old world fantasy.

This beautiful creature is almost as common as the crow, and its shrill thin scream, from which the name *chīl* seems to be derived, is, like the crow's note, a constant and characteristic Indian sound, especially at Calcutta in the spring time. Those who delight in the flight of birds, which surely is one of the most fascinating things in life, may find less interesting diversions than throwing fragments of food from a high roof when a fleet of swift pirates soon assembles. Missed by one, rushed at from opposite points by two or three at a time, no morsel is ever allowed to reach the ground. The fierce sweeps and curves are splendid in grace, strength, and skill, for there is deliberation and poise and a marvellous avoidance of collision in this aerial tournament of rushing wings. When the rains break there occurs a great jail delivery of winged white ants. At this stage the termites are fat white little maggots, temporarily furnished with wings which are shaken off when they find a resting-place. The birds assemble in great numbers for this dainty feast, the kite with the rest. One would think this wide-gaping bird would sail round in the insect cloud open-mouthed, whale-fashion. But he uses his claws even for this minute game, and the action of carrying them to his beak as he flies produces a series of most graceful curtseying undulations.

The habits of the kite have suggested one or two sayings, as: "When do you find meat in a kite's nest?"—a Hindu sneer at Mussulman spendthrifts; when do you find money in a Mussulman's house? Of a lover devoted to a gay lady the same expression is used. The *pâras* or philosopher's stone is said in a proverb to be in the kite's nest, a dark saying based on the kite's trick of sometimes carrying off gold ornaments, or on the Muhammadan women's superstition that young kites cannot see until there is gold in the nest. The kite has some of the crow's delight in bright objects, and this belief may be based on observation. A person who loiters round or hangs about a house is said to hover like a kite. The word "hover," by the way, is, or used to be, common for "wait" in North Yorkshire, as,—"If tha'rt titter up t'sprunt, hovver,"—"If you get first up the hill, wait." A Delhi street-cry raised by ragged fowlers is—"Free the kite on Tuesday." The notion that it is auspicious to set captured birds free has been noticed above. The practice in the Delhi region is for a mother to pay a pice to the fowler, who swings the kite round over her child's head and lets it go. This ceremony is thought most lucky when performed on a Tuesday or Saturday. One of the Indian boys' games is called the kites' swoop; a foolish person is styled a kite's chick, which really has a most gawky air; and a child always running out in the street is spoken of as a noonday kite, which still hovers in the heat when all sensible folk are indoors.

The kite is a notorious thief; no other creature is so splendidly equipped for larceny, for no other can snatch so unerringly and escape so securely. The confectioner's tray of sweetmeats, the dishes on their way from kitchen to mess or dining-room, the butcher's shop, and the kitchen itself are all liable to his sudden swoop. A recent case occurred of a registered letter containing money being snatched from a postman's hand. I was once feeding a pair of tame ravens from a plate in my hand when a kite, to their loud and deep indignation, cleared and broke it and nearly knocked me over forbye. This habit is made in a country story to point one of the hundred gibes at the tricks of Indian goldsmiths. Four brethren of the craft were overheard by a Wazir debating their business. Said one: "I always take four annas toll out of every rupee's worth of gold in addition to the labour charge." Said another: "I take eight annas," or half the value; the third said, "I always take twelve annas," or three-quarters; but the fourth cried,—"You are three fools, I always take all." The Wazir reported this to his Raja, who said he should like to see how it could be done. So he sent for that fourth goldsmith and ordered him to sit in the palace verandah and make a necklace for the Queen. Three or four ounces of gold were given to him and he set to work. But first, he drove a nail in the verandah post, and when no one was near, he placed bits of meat on it and a kite promptly learned the way thither. Then, in the evenings when he went home, he made a brass chain exactly like the gold one and put it in his pot of acid water. And one day in the presence of the Raja, who was on the watch for deception, he placed the real chain there and presently took out the false one and hung it on the nail to dry. The kite came and took it as the craftsman was speaking to the Raja, who saw the theft. The goldsmith made a great outcry, and bewailed the loss of so many days' labour, and the Raja made it up to him handsomely and gave him gold to make another. When the Raja's back was turned the goldsmith fished up the real chain from the pickling pot and carried it away. Then the goldsmith repeated the trick; which he finally confessed to the Wazir. And the Raja, being amiable, like most princes in stories, was amused and generously rewarded the goldsmith for his knavery.

Cranes and Herons.—The Sarus Crane (*Grus antigone*) is with some reason regarded as a model of conjugal fidelity, from a belief that, if one of a pair of these handsome birds is killed, the other pines and never mates again. A Spanish proverb says the crane danced with the horse and got a broken leg, but the dancing propensities of cranes and other long-legged birds are seldom noticed in Indian talk, though the birds are common and are often kept in public gardens and by Europeans as pets, and behave in the fantastic fashion well observed and described in the American novel *East Angels.* (The author of that excellent book speaks of the "candid eyes" that taxidermists give to stuffed parrots. Indian observation notices a want of candour in the living parrot's eye.) For grotesque devilry of dancing, the Indian Adjutant beats creation. Don Quixote or Malvolio were not half so solemn or mincing, and yet there is an abandonment and lightness of step, a wild lift in each solemn prance, which are almost demoniacal. If it were possible for the most angular, tall, and demure of elderly maiden ladies to take a great deal too much champagne and then to give a lesson in ballet-dancing, with occasional pauses of acute sobriety, perhaps some faint idea might be conveyed of the peculiar quality of the adjutant's movements. Such a conception is, of course, outrageously impossible to a well-regulated Western mind, for it is only the French who have thought of calling a lady a "*grue.*" It is notable that of late years Calcutta, which used to be regularly visited by adjutants, has been deserted by them. I have heard natives say that they assemble in waste places to hold councils and to dance.

A really fine expression is the ironical Indian phrase: "The saintly heron," or "saintly as a heron." A heron poised on one leg in a remote corner of a pool is the very image of a Hindu Sādhu or Muhammadan faqir, pretending to be absorbed in holy meditation, while all the time he is intent on the next fish or frog that may come within reach, the next piece of fraud or villainy he can compass. The phrase is common, for there is much of the hypocritical "meditation of the heron" in India as elsewhere.

Poultry.—The Brahma fowl of Western poulterers must have been named in Europe, and is counted one of the unclean things in which those unaccountable people, the English, take an unintelligible pleasure. Hindus hear of its name with more surprise than satisfaction. It is amusing, by the way, to note the easy confidence with which French and English writers on India use the word Brahma, and speak of his temples. There are scarcely any temples to Brahma in India, and his name is very seldom heard. Hindus, as a rule, do not care for domestic poultry which are Levitically unclean, nor for eggs which are not eaten by people of high caste. Rajputs are passionately fond of cock-fighting, but do not fit steel spurs on their birds; indeed, they blunt or dub the spurs which nature has given. The fights are thus of interminable length, the poor creatures staggering round each other, blind with blood round after round, long after they are too much exhausted to strike a blow. The ring attendants fancy it restores the creatures to put their heads into their mouths, a sickening detail not unknown in the cock-pits of our English grandfathers. The Goanese (Portuguese) and many Muhammadans, with some Hindus, are also fond of cock-fighting, and daily large sums of money change hands over this sport. Denunciation of a diversion of this kind is of little use, nor is it easy to fix a point at which legislation can effectively intervene. Little by little the barbarity will die out before the changes now taking place in Indian civilisation. Moreover, although we English are apt to denounce and preach, it does not lie in our mouths to say much. There are many Englishmen who would be glad to take up cock-fighting, and it is only a generation since a large number of good husbands and tender fathers were ready to declare it the finest sport in the world. Blake indignantly wrote—

> "A game-cock clipped and armed for fight,
> Doth the rising sun affright."

Yet Professor Wilson (Christopher North), also a Christian poet, wrote of cock-fighting with enthusiasm, and pictures of birds thus hideously disfigured are still shown in London shop windows with other sporting prints. Sir Thomas More is farther off, but it is recorded that he was an expert in the detestable game of tying a cock to a post and throwing sticks at it.

A cock without spurs has the same name as a tuskless elephant,—*makhna*. The old Joe Miller of the roast-fowl with only one leg, of which, when the master remonstrates, the servant said it belonged to a breed of one-legged fowls, is also an Indian story with the same conclusion. The servant shows the master a fowl standing on one leg. The master cries sho! and the fowl runs away with two. "Ah," says the servant, "you did not cry sho! to the fowl in the dish!" Of a man who gives himself airs they say: "Can you have no daylight without cock-crow?" An Afghān proverb quoted by Professor James Darmesteter says: "Though the cock did not crow the dawn would still come." "A hen dreams only of grain" is applied to a sordid person. "A whistling woman and a crowing hen are neither fit for God nor men," is a mild English saying, but the Indian version is infamous, for it says, "A hen's crow and a woman's word no one trusts." If one Hindu wants to insult another (he has of course an infinite variety of ways) he calls him a poulterer. A Bengal proverb says the Bengal landlord treats his farmer tenants as the Muhammadan treats fowls, feeds them only to kill them in the end. A Muhammadan way of expressing that one is dissatisfied with his own havings, is: "A house fowl (one you have bred yourself) is no better than pulse." To one who hesitates to chastise a child they say: "The chick doesn't die from a hen's kick." Domestic duties are regularly taught to the girls of a household, so they say: "When the hen scratches, the chickens learn."

Poultry of all kinds are most cruelly handled by dealers and market people, who never seem to think that a bird can feel. Turkeys are left to bleed to death half a day by native servants with intent to bleach the flesh. A Hindu would be shocked by such treatment of a parrot, but fowls are outside the pale of regard.

The Goose.—A bird that seems to have lost some of its ancient repute is the goose, which, though sacred in Buddhist and early Hindu times, finds only a vague and legendary place in modern degradations of Hinduism.

The popular legend is that the goose was the *Vâhan* of Brahma, on whom fell the curse of Shiva, that henceforth he should not be an object of popular worship. The gait of the goose or the swan (for the two birds seem to be considered the same in the slip-shod talk of the people) is reckoned as next graceful to those of the elephant or the partridge. They say in serious praise of a lady's carriage that she walks like a goose. In Europe we seem to look closer and discriminate the sort of lady with a goose gait, nor do we count it for praise.

The Brahminy Duck.—The note of the ruddy sheldrake or Brahminy duck (*Casarca rutila*) has won for this bird, which is always seen in pairs, a place in Indian classic poetry as the type of longing but divided lovers. Every night across the river the male cries, "Chakvi, may I come?" and the female responds, "No, Chakva." Then the female mourns, "Chakva, may I come?" and the answer is, "No, Chakvi." (The open Indian vowel sounds give the plaintive bird's cry better than the English "May I come?") With a super-subtle elaboration of the idea of nightly separation, the birds in some verses I have heard, but cannot fully recall, are dolorously apart in spirit even when put in the same cage. The simile was originally good in a poetical sense, and is still alive to the Indian mind, which loves familiar and accustomed turns; but its constant recurrence gives it a mechanical creak to English ears.

The Peacock.—The peacock is the *Vâhan* or vehicle, of Karttikeya, a god of war, and also of Saraswati, goddess of learning, and is sacred. Many of the troubles between villagers and English soldiers out shooting have arisen from the ignorance of the latter of the veneration in which peacocks are held.

In Guzerat, throughout Rajputana, and in many parts of the Central and North-West Provinces, peacocks run wild, and are as common as rooks in England. A rhyming proverb says, "The deer, the monkey, the partridge, and the peacock are four thieves," but they are never punished for their thefts. They are, however, sometimes caught alive by out-caste jungle folk and brought to market with their eyes sewn up with filaments of their own quills in order to prevent them fluttering and spoiling their plumage. Solomon rebuked the vanity of the peacock's tail by an ungenerous and not particularly apt reference to the ugliness of its legs, and his gibe is still in men's mouths. They are in reality good legs, strong and capable; but it is said, "The peacock danced gaily, till he saw his legs, when he was ashamed and wept bitterly." In some places this saying is accounted for by a story. The peacock and the partridge, or, as some say, the maina, had a dancing match. In those days the peacock had very pretty feet. So when he had danced, the partridge said, "Lend me your feet and see *me* dance." They changed feet, but instead of dancing, the deceitful partridge ran away and never came back again. The saying is used as an expression of regret for a foolish bargain. Ancient European bestiaries say when the peacock wakes it cries and mourns its lost beauty. In Assam they say with reference to vain people: "If I must die, I must die, but don't touch my top-knot, said the peacock." Women when they dislike a sister woman call her a peacock-legged person, and sometimes after sickness speak of their own limbs in humorous disparagement as like those of the peacock, where an English countrywoman would refer to pipe-stems or bean-sticks. Yet "peacock gaited" is a poetical expression for a graceful carriage, and "a neck like a peacock" is a common compliment to a beautiful woman.

The peacock is credited with a violent antipathy to snakes, and is said to dance them to death, but a vigorous cobra is scarcely likely to be tired out by a bird. In the excitement of a fight the peacock would probably dance round its enemy, and the engagement would be long and doubtful. That the bird is a recognised enemy of snakes in England as well as in India is shown in the interesting volume *On Surrey Hills*, edited by Mrs. J. A. Owen, where gardens and grounds infested by vipers are said to be infallibly cleared by peacocks.

This bird is said to scent the coming rain, and to scream and dance with delight at its approach. "Frogs and peacocks are refreshed by the rain." In Europe the bird's cry is a rain sign, but we do not credit it with a longing for moisture.

In London drawing-rooms peacock feathers are considered unlucky. In India it would seem to be otherwise. I once saw a Hindu servant limping round with a peacock feather tied on his leg. "Yes, sir, I have a bad pain in my leg and this is very good for it." A spell or *mantra* must have accompanied the tying, but this I was not privileged to learn. *Taus*, the Arabic (and Greek) word for a peacock, is current as well as the Hindi *Mor*. A pretty form of guitar, shaped and painted like a peacock, is known as a taus.

The Owl.—There are birds of evil as well as of good omen, and the owl is here, as elsewhere, a byword of ill luck. "Only owls live alone," is a proverb flung at unsociable people, and a man is said to be as drunk as an owl, while a stupid fellow is most unjustly described as "A son of an owl." Of humble folk and their obscure lives it is said, "Only an owl knows the worth of an owl." "What does a phœnix know of an owl?"

It has not occurred to the Oriental jester to speak of a boiled owl in connection with intoxication, but when a husband is abjectly submissive to his wife her friends say she has given him boiled owl's flesh to eat. There are owls of most varieties in India, but a small owl like the cue owl of Italy is the most common and raises a cheerful chuckle at twilight.

In Ceylon the cry of a large owl known as the Devil bird is believed to be a certain herald of death. Nocturnal habits are all that the universal world, including Hindus and Muhammadans, can bring against the owl as a bird of fate. In India, however, though the owl's cry may be dreaded as portending a desolate home, nobody is idiotic enough to kill so valuable a vermin destroyer. That pinnacle of stupidity is the exclusive right of English game preservers.

The Pigeon.—The pigeon, the bird of Mecca, is almost as much a Hindu as a Muhammadan bird, and was chosen by Shiva, the third person of the Hindu Trinity, for Incarnation as Kapoteshwara. I was assured not long ago by a Hindu devotee that in a small temple near the Kashmir frontier, the image of Mahadeo at times takes life as a pair of pigeons which flutter and disappear in the roof. In cities where Hindus preponderate, large flocks of pigeons are regularly fed by Hindu merchants and shopkeepers. The traveller is reminded, by the roar of their wings, of Venice and Constantinople, and if he went farther north he would find them cherished in the villages of Kābul, where they are supposed to pay for their keep by fertilising the soil. Pigeon fanciers are to be found in most towns of Northern India and are generally Muhammadan. They talk of various breeds, and especially prize the Shirāzi and the small strutting white fan-tail, on whose coral-coloured legs they frequently fasten jingling bangles of brass; but they seem to have little of the English skill and care in breeding varieties which Darwin found so full of suggestion. The flight is pretty to watch; it is possible to bet on some incidents of it, and it is also possible to beguile some of a neighbour's to join your own flock. But, like quail fighting, it is not considered a respectable pursuit; and though most boys would like to keep pigeons, respectability is in India as stony and implacable as in the West. A popular proverb says the housewife keeps the parrot, the lover keeps the avadavat, and the thief keeps pigeons. In the English Midlands, thirty years ago, pigeon-flyers were (and are still) called disreputable, and you were supposed to be able to distinguish the scamp from his respectable fellow-workmen by the drake's-tail curl of his hair at the back, the result of continually looking aloft at his birds. It is curious that precisely the same notion obtains here in India.

Although the "homing" propensity of the pigeon is not systematically cultivated and the bird is not regularly employed as a messenger, there are many stories to show that this characteristic trait is recognised. Nor are they always sentimental love tales. A Bengal legend tells the pitiful fate of a Hindu Raja, the last of his race, attacked by Muhammadan invaders. He went bravely out to meet them, carrying with him a pigeon whose return to the palace was to be regarded by his family as an intimation of his defeat, and a signal to put themselves to death and to burn their home. He gained the victory, but while he stooped to drink in the river after the fatigues of the battle, the bird escaped and flew home. The Raja hurried after, but was only in time to throw himself on the still burning pyre.

A common object on the low sky-line of Indian towns of the plain is a light bamboo lattice about six feet square on the top of a tall bamboo pole. This is a pigeon perch, and in the early mornings unkempt pigeon-flyers are seen on the house roofs waving a lure made of rag tied to a stick and whistling through a mouth-call (like that of the English Punch and Judy men) to attract to their roosts the flock of pigeons circling overhead. The evolutions of pigeons in the air, their wheeling and turning on the wing, and the pretty manner of their settling from flight are all so beautiful that it seems stupid to associate a taint of human blackguardism with them.

The Koel.—We English call the cuckoo a blithe newcomer and a vernal harbinger, but we do not, because of the bird's association with the sweet o' the year, consider his song the perfection of all music. A Western ear finds no more in the tune of that cuculine bird, the Koel (*Eudynamys honorata*) than a tiresome iteration of one or two clear, high, and resonant notes. Yet Oriental poetry, algebraic in its persistent use of a limited number of symbols, has officially adopted the Koel as the figure for exquisite sound; so the voice of your beloved, the performances of a musical artiste, and all best worth hearing in life are posted under this heading. A Delhi shoemaker or a Lucknow embroiderer can tell you of other bird music, but they have not read much classic poetry and hear with their ears. The Englishman in India has a grudge against the Koel; listening with modified rapture to notes that warn him to put up his punkah, overhaul his thermantidote, and prepare for the long St. Laurence penance of an Indian summer. And he thinks longingly of an English spring.

"Ah! Koel, little Koel, singing on the *siris* bough,
In my ears the knell of exile your ceaseless bell-like speech is,
Can you tell me aught of England or of spring in England now?"

Natives say crows hate the Koel because it selects their nests for its foundling eggs, which is very probable. I have seen crows mobbing a Koel, but then crows are like London street boys, and will mob anybody of unfamiliar aspect.

The Coppersmith.—The Coppersmith bird is another noisy herald of spring. This is the handsome crimson-breasted barbet (*Xantholæma hæmacephala*), and its cry of tock, tock, fills the air as completely as the sound of a hammer on a brazen vessel. It has the same cadence, and with each loud beat the bird's head is swung to right and left alternately. Sir Edwin Arnold in his *Light of Asia* gives an Indian Spring picture in a few words:—

" . . . In the mango-sprays
The sun-birds flashed; alone at his green forge
Toiled the loud Coppersmith . . . . "

But when you are down with fever and headache you heartily wish the noisy bird would take a holiday or go on strike.

The Sparrow.—To the native of India the sparrow seems to stand as the type of a thing of naught, an intrusive feathered fly to be brushed aside—but on no account to be starved or harmed. Our bird is a size smaller than his Western brother, and is tolerated both by Hindu and Muhammadan. In mosque courts one sometimes sees pretty troughs made of brick with divisions for water and food; and in trees near shrines, or over the places where devotees sit, earthen saucers are slung with food and water, all for the sparrow. A Hindu proverb quoted in Fallon's Dictionary says: "God's birds in God's field! eat, birds, eat your bellies full." This pious and kindly word is easily reconciled in practice with a just appreciation of the essential triviality and impertinence of the bird. A large toll is

TERRA-COTTA SEED AND WATER TROUGH (FROM A PUNJAB VILLAGE MOSQUE)

daily taken all over the country from field and garden, and the equally accessible grain-dealer's basket. The most devout Hindu alive waves them off from his stores, for he also must live.

But though the sparrow is a nuisance, it is seldom you hear the bird reckoned a downright plague, as is undoubtedly the case in America, where it is a type of the worst kind of immigrant from which the country has suffered. The reason may be that the same law of protection which leaves the sparrow free to plunder, is also extended to the hawk, the shrike, the weasel, and the wild cat, who keep the balance fairly even among them. Yet, when you listen closely you may hear, in spite of the vast Oriental tolerance, many an angry word about bird depredations.

London sparrows are said to be familiar, but when compared with their Indian brethren, their manners are marked by dignity and cold reserve. Being much given to marriage, they make a tremendous fuss over their housekeeping, and when in search of a nesting-place nothing is sacred to them. Above all, the nest must be sheltered from the heat, and the coolest places in the land are the interiors of men's houses. An Englishman's house is the coolest of all, so newly-joined couples, conversing loudly, are constantly finding their way indoors, creeping like mice through bath-water channels and under the bamboo blinds that keep out flies, bringing with them straw and other rubbish for their untidy beds. When making a morning call, you may stumble into a darkened drawing-room to find the lady of the house perched on a chair, madly thrashing up to the roof-beams with a carriage-whip, while a servant pulls the long cord of an upper window, crying "sho!" A bird in church is a rare and delightful incident to a bored child in the West, but the Indian sparrow perches on the organ-pipes in full blast, and chatters loudly through the sermon. Its note is a constant part of the out-door orchestra of Indian life, accompanying the caw of the crow, the thin squeal of the squirrel and scream of the kite, the groan of the Persian wheel, the wailing song of the ox-driver at the well, the creak of the ungreased cart axle, and the bark of the village dog.

Falconry.—Falconry, which is still a favourite sport in Sind and Northern India, is too extensive to be more than glanced at. The literature of the subject is just as fantastic as the writings of our forefathers in Europe; as in our old falconry books, hawks are broadly described as light or dark-eyed, round or long-winged, noble or ignoble, and the sport is considered in the highest degree aristocratic. Sir Richard F. Burton is the only English writer who can claim to be an authority on the subject in its literary as well as in its practical aspect. The identity of the Indian apparatus of the sport with that of Europe strikes even the uninstructed. The hawk-hood of soft deerskin, prettily embroidered with silk and gold, the falconer's gloves, jesses, lures, and hawk-bells are still regularly made in the Punjab, with one or two trifling variations. European pictures show the lure fitted with portions of a bird's wing, which are absent from the Indian lure, and the falconer goes afield with his hawks perched on a hoop slung round his body, while here, when more than one are carried, they travel on a horizontal pole. Staying once at the chief town of a native state I wondered at the number of hawks carried about, and concluded that when a man wanted an excuse for a stroll he went to the Raja's mews and got a hawk to take out for an airing on his wrist. ("A man looks so fond without a dog" said the collier in Mr. C. Keene's *Punch* picture.) During a gathering of chiefs at Lahore to meet Lord Dufferin and the Duke of Connaught, falcons and falconers came to swell the retinues of the Rajas, and I observed the constables on duty at the museum in my charge wanted to make the men leave their hawks outside when they came to see that institution. A stuffed bird in a glass case might, of course, tempt a hawk, but when hooded the creature is as well behaved as a sleeping child.

The attendant circumstance of Indian falconry is not without its charm, especially during the clear cold weather of the Punjab winter. I remember riding to a hawking party across a wide sandy plain where cultivation was scanty, a fresh wind blowing, and in the far distance the snowy range of the Himálaya sparkled white against the intense blue. A group of elephants, with howdahs and trappings blazing in colour and gold, furnished the vast wind-swept spaces with a touch of colour, and even the blue and red patterns daubed on their gigantic foreheads looked delicate and pretty. The strange heraldic monsters in beaten silver with glass eyes that supported the howdahs, and the great red cloths splashed with gold embroidery, would have been garish at close quarters; but here they suited perfectly with the cavalcade of horsemen attired in scarlet and gold, the leashed dogs straining

UNHOODED

and snarling, and the motley crowd of beaters, chill in the morning sunshine. The hawks sharply turned their heads in expectation, tugging and straining at their jesses like anchored ships in a gale. But when all was over, the bustards found and flown at had escaped without scathe, and one of the hawks was lost. As a man who has never been able to find pleasure in the chase, and who never possessed a gun, I found no personal fault with this issue, but when people set forth to do a thing they ought to do it well.

Hawks must often be lost ; for a countryside proverb about kangni, the small Italian millet, says that its cultivation is "as risky as keeping a hawk."

I have heard of flights where the hawk does all that is set down for him in the books, and I have watched the careful training of hawks to come back to the lure, where they are rewarded with a bit of newly killed crow, etc., but I strongly suspect the best of the business is the riding and the company. Any one in the habit of looking at birds in India may see free hawking enough,—the shrike, which in a town garden brings down a sparrow nearly as big as himself, the gallant and tigerish sparrow-hawk, and on far hillsides falcons of two or three kinds.

Of a sponging hanger-on they say, "You train your hawk on another man's fist." "Doesn't know cock-fighting and has taken to hawking!" is a good jape at a common kind of fool.

Bird Crumbs.—An odd fancy is current about the sandpiper. It is believed to sleep on its back under the impression that it is supporting the firmament with its slender legs. There are human bipeds who think themselves almost as necessary to the universe. A black-and-white kingfisher is called the dizzy or giddy one from its sudden, vertiginous plunge into the water after its prey. A curious parallel in nomenclature is shown in the water-wagtail, which haunts brook and pond sides,—places where clothes are washed,—and is called the *dhobin* or washer-woman. In France the same bird, from the same habit, is known as the *lavandière.*

The Shia Muhammadans have woven many legends round their martyr heroes, Hussain and Hassan, slain at Kerbela. The handsome King crow or drongo (*Dicrurus ater*) is said to have brought water to the dying Imâm Hussain, while the dove, dipping her beak in his sacred blood, flew to Medina, and thus bore the news of his martyrdom.

In Mr. F. S. Growse's translation of the Rāmāyana of Tūlsi Dass—a book which ought to be studied by those who care to know what the best current Hindu poetry is like, in its sugared fancy, its elaborate metaphors, its real feeling for the heroic and noble, and also its tedious, unaccidented meandering—there occurs a pretty description of the Army of Love, in which some of the birds take parts outside the stereotyped roles occasionally referred to in foregoing paragraphs—"the murmuring cuckoos are his infuriated elephants, and the herons his bulls, camels, and mules; the peacocks, *chukors* (red-legged partridges), and parrots are his war-horses; the pigeons and swans his Arab steeds; the partridges and quails his foot-soldiers; but there is no describing the whole of Love's host." A sentence which might have stood at the beginning closes the long-drawn description—"His (Love's) greatest strength lies in woman: any one who can escape her is a mighty champion indeed."

Bats.—Of bats—the leathern-winged jackals of the

air—there is not much to be said, for although India has an immense number and variety of these wonderful and most useful creatures, the people seem scarcely to notice them. It takes a naturalist to admire and appreciate darkness-loving animals; and among Indian bats there is a fine field, especially those adorned by nature with elaborate leaf-like processes on the nostrils, strange and fantastic beyond telling.

Those, however, who have been received in dull houses will enjoy the fine irony of a saying which runs, "The bat had a guest (and said), 'I'm hanging, you hang too.'" No need to expound this five-word jewel, since most of us know houses whose inmates seem to hang in a torpid row, and where we resign ourselves on entering to be hung up in a similar sleepy fashion. There is also a story about Solomon, the birds, and the bats, but it has no very effective point. I know of no saying in any tongue acknowledging the great utility of the bat in keeping down an excess of insect life.

The large fruit-eating bat or flying-fox is a noble creature, looming largest, perhaps, when in the still breathless evenings he beats his noiseless way high over the wan waters of Bombay harbour or the adjacent creeks, dark against a sky in which there lingers a lurid flush of crimson and orange. The lowest castes eat flying-foxes, which are probably of excellent flavour, seeing they grow fat on the best of the fruit. They are regularly eaten in the Malay Archipelago, and Mr. Wallace says that when properly dressed they have no offensive fumet, and taste like hare. I once kept one, but he could scarcely be called an amusing pet, his strong point being his enormous appetite for bananas. On one occasion he escaped and began to fly away, but promptly came back, for he was mobbed by flights of crows, who had never seen such a creature before. Crows go early to bed, and the appearance of this monster bat in their own daylight seemed to be an outrage on their rights and feelings. So they chivied him—if I may be allowed the expression—much as the street boys are said to have chivied Jonas Hanway when he appeared in London streets with the first umbrella. The flying-fox was in a great fright, knowing that a single stroke of a crow's beak would ruin the membrane of his vans, more delicate than any silk ever stretched on a "paragon" frame.

In pairing time flying-foxes are lively all day, though they do not fly abroad, and the trees in which they hang in great reefs and clusters are so noisy with their quarrelling, screaming, and fighting, as to be a serious nuisance to a quiet village.

CHAPTER III

OF MONKEYS

> "His hide was very mangy, and his face was very red,
> And ever and anon he scratched with energy his head.
> His manners were not always nice, but how my spirit cried
> To be an artless *Bandar* loose upon the mountain side!"
>
> R. K.

MONKEY GOD

SOME of the respect in which these animals are held by Hindus is a reflection of the popularity of Hanumān, or (in Southern India) of Mâruti, the monkey general of the great Hindu epic—the devoted henchman of Ram Chandra, and a marvel of valour and address combined with gentleness. He has now become a god, and is one of the most widely worshipped of Hindu deities. Pictures and rude images are to be seen of him everywhere, but he is not represented in the more ancient Hindu sculptures. A notion exists among Hindus that the English may be his descendants through a female servant of the demon king, who had charge of Sita in captivity, and who treated the prisoner so well that Rama blessed her, prophesying that she should become the mother of a race that would possess the land, and whom Hanumān took to wife. This can scarcely be made out from the poem, but the tradition exists. Others, again, say that the English came from the "monkey army," which unlovely phrase is occasionally used to describe the British nation.

But, while the enthusiastic cult of Hanumān as a divinity is a comparatively modern development of Hinduism, the fondness of Hindus for monkeys is of very ancient date. Ælian describes the offerings of rice which are still customary, and at sacred places, as Benares, Ajodhia, and Muttra, they are regularly fed, and it is regarded as an abominable act of sacrilege to kill one. A large temple at Benares under the invocation of Durga (Devi, Kali, etc.) has swarms of monkeys attached to it, but they do not appear, as might be expected, to be usually attendant on shrines of the Monkey God himself. They naturally cluster round groves frequented by devotees of various kinds for the sake of scraps of food which they are sure to receive there, and because they are safe from molestation. Muhammadan saints as well as Hindu *sâdhus* show kindness to these creatures, and it is quite intelligible that their gambols should serve to amuse the large and languid leisure of professional holiness.

The brown *macacus rhesus* is the commonest type and most frequently seen both in the hills and plains. Ælian in his description mixes up the Macaque with the true Hanumān, the tall, long-tailed, black-faced, white-whiskered *langūr* (*Presbytes illiger*), clad in an overcoat of silver gray. The latter has a face that reminds one of Mr. Joel Harris's "Uncle Remus," and is, in his way, a king of the jungle, nor is he so frequently met with in confinement as his brown brother. In some parts of India troops of langūrs come bounding with a mighty air of interest and curiosity to see the railway trains pass, their long tails uplifted like notes of interrogation ; but frequently, when fairly perched on wall or tree alongside, they

LANGŪRS AT HOME

seem to forget all about it, and avert their heads as you go by with an affectation of languid indifference. This may be a mark of the superiority of the monkey mind, or a sign that some threads were dropped when its fabric was woven. The black gibbon or *hooluck* (*hylobates hooluck*) is better known in Bengal and Assam, and is well adapted for captivity, if a pair can be secured, and the keeper does not object to a gentle, mournful, and timid animal, the spirit of the complaining dove in the form of a black djinn or demon with a voice like a pack of hounds in full cry. The hooluck is monogamous, and seems to have few of the vulgar monkey vices, but is a depressing companion. In Assam, too, is found a dainty little monkey familiarly known as "the shame-faced one"—a gentle, bashful, large-eyed creature, with a quaint trick of hiding its face in its hands and hanging its head like a timid child. It has a peculiarly soft and lustrous pelage of fine colour and texture.

Under a benign rule of protection the monkey increases rapidly, and, being a daring and mischievous pilferer, becomes a serious nuisance. One may hold a creature sacred and yet be thoroughly alive to all the faults of its character, and the monkey in ordinary talk is used pretty much as it is in Europe to point morals against wanton mischief, helplessness, and evil behaviour generally. Nor is it only in field and garden that its depredations are felt. Indian shops have no doors or windows, but are like large cupboards open to the street, in which food grains and other articles are exposed for sale; and in towns where Hindus preponderate and a busy current of trade has not swept the streets, bulls, calves, parrakeets, sparrows, and monkeys take tolls which the dealer would fain prevent, but that he is few and fat, while the depredators are many and active. A stout grocer nodding among his store baskets, while a monkey, intently watching the sleeper's face, rapidly stuffs his cheek pouches with grain, is a common sight, as well as a comical one. Of late years the tradesmen who form the bulk of the members of our municipalities have felt that there are too many Hanumāns abroad, and have ventured on proceedings that would not have been tolerated in the days of complete Brahmanical ascendency. Numbers of the marauders have been caught, caged, and despatched on bullock carts to places many miles distant. There they have been let loose, but, as the empty carts returned, the monkeys, quick to perceive and defeat the plan of their enemies, bounded gaily alongside, and trooped in through the city gates with the air of a holiday party returning from a picnic. From some riverside towns boat-loads have been taken across the Ganges; but they dislike being marooned, and when they have failed to board the returning boats, have found others to carry them back. Railways, which have done much for Indian progress, offer facilities for deportation which monkey-ridden municipalities have been glad to seize. The stationmaster at Saharunpore was recently troubled by a telegram advising him of the despatch of cars laden with monkeys, which he was requested to send out to be freed on the adjacent Sewalik hills. But the cages were broken in unloading the freight and the crowd got loose. Saharunpore is an Indian Crewe or Swindon in a small way, with a railway establishment, a Government Botanical garden and large private fruit gardens. The exiles invaded the busy workshops and lost their tempers, monkey fashion, among the driving bands and machinery, nor were they easily driven out. A large male was seen pulling the point-levers of a siding with the sudden petulance of his kind; and another established himself between the double roofs of one of the inspection carriages used by railway officers on tour as houses, stealing from the pantry such trifles as legs of mutton, corkscrews, lamp glasses and dusters,—articles for which a monkey can have but little use. The bulk of the company trooped into the gardens of the town, where the proprietors, being mainly Muhammadans with no respect for Hanumān, took measures of their own against the invasion.

An amusing case of monkey plunder occurred some years ago at Simla. The chief confectioner of the place had prepared a magnificent bride-cake, which was safely put by in a room that, like most Simla rooms, looked on the steep hillside. It is of little use, however, locking a door when the window is left open. So when they came to fetch the cake, the last piece of it was being handed out of the window by a chain of monkeys who had whitened the hillside with its fragments. A theft of this kind is mainly mischievous, for the wild monkey dislikes food mixed with butter, nor does he greatly care for sugar. A bride-cake, too, looks (and is to my humble taste) about as edible as a plaster cast, and one can scarcely understand how they discovered it was meant to be eaten. The creature has a passion for picking things to pieces. A flower or a fragile toy will amuse a monkey for a long time. If a bird falls into its hands it will not be released till it is plucked of every feather. If the bird resents the process, the monkey with an unconcerned air rubs its head vigorously on the ground. It would not be difficult to train a monkey to pluck fowls for use in the kitchen. It is often said that the monkey kills snakes by grinding the head on a stone, occasionally spitting on it, nor is the feat incredible to one who has observed the constant habit of rubbing things on the ground and holding them up for inspection. Yet in spite of this belief, a popular saying, expressing a dilemma or an opportunity that cannot be turned to profit, is—"Like a snake in a monkey's hand." He is afraid of it, but he will not let go. Natives also say that monkeys rob birds' nests and destroy eggs and young in pure malice. The fastidiousness of the wild monkey's taste is curious, considering the precarious existence it leads. Daily for some months my family and myself were interested in a troop of wild monkeys, which we regularly fed, trying them with very various food. Once we gave them biscuits which, from lying in a dealer's shop, had acquired that peculiarly stale, tinny flavour which Anglo-Indians know too well. They had been accustomed to eat the same kind of biscuit when fresh, and scrambled as usual for the fragments, but after the first bite they made comical mouths of dislike, spat out vigorously, rubbed the biscuit on their sides, on the ground, examined it carefully, and seemed to conclude,—"Yes, it's the same as yesterday," tried again, and then chattered and grinned in wrath and disgust. But they soon learned to discriminate by smell merely.

Like the over-wise crow, which is apt to outwit itself by futile cunning, the monkey is most ingeniously suspicious. Our friends grew bold with encouragement, but their manners were never friendly; with the exception of one which had evidently escaped from confinement. We managed to entrap the creature, and having removed its hateful collar, set it free again. My daughter could coax this experienced person into a room and it would open her hand to take grain, keeping a sharp look-out on the open door. All the rest were keenly suspicious, and irritable. They seemed to circumvent each morsel and, having won it, defied us with angry eyes to take it back again, regarding our free gift as a triumph of their own finesse. This is natural enough when we consider that for generations the monkey folk have been chased from field and garden plot with shouting. They were in no fear for their lives, and had learned the very human satisfaction of defying an enemy from a safe distance.

This shallow cunning has deeply impressed the minds of the people. They say it is absolutely impossible to poison a monkey. For ages this belief has been rooted in the minds of Orientals. Al Masudi, who compiled his Arabic encyclopædia—"meadows of gold and mines of gems"—in the tenth century, wrote that most Chinese and Hindu kings keep wise but dumb monkeys as tasters for their tables, relying implicitly on their judgment of what is poisoned and what is wholesome. A native gentleman told me of a cultivator in the hills whose crops and garden were so seriously injured that he determined to get rid of his enemies. So he daily set out platters of boiled rice which they greedily ate. When they had learned the habit of coming in crowds, he one day set out rice poisoned with a tasteless drug. He heard a great chatter and whining round his treacherous platters, and saw a council sitting round the untasted food in earnest debate. Presently they rose and scampered away, but soon returned, each bearing twigs and leaves of a plant which their instinct taught them was an antidote to the poison. With these they stirred and mixed the rice, which they afterwards ate with their usual relish, returning the next morning for more, absolutely unharmed. This story is also told, *mutatis mutandis*, of an attempt made by a Sikh noble, Sirdar Lehna Singh Majithia, to poison troublesome monkeys at the sacred town of Hurdwar. When you believe that monkeys are capable of speech and only refrain from speaking for fear that they would be made to work, it is easy to credit them with a knowledge of chemistry. Belief in their ability to speak is widely current in India, and the notion is not unknown in the West.

But while native credulity will swallow the impossible with ease, native observation is not without keenness. The inability of the monkey to make for itself a shelter against the heavy rains of the country is noted in proverbs. It is really curious that in the Simla region, where are many built-out roads forming dry refuges of quite natural aspect, they are never resorted to. Troops of monkeys will sit shivering for hours in driving storms within a few yards of covered spaces, which seem as if specially provided for their shelter and comfort.

Their daily life is interesting to watch. The scheme seems to be patriarchal with a touch of military organisation, for they move and plunder in a sort of formation, and the patriarch is at once commander-in-chief and effective fighting force. Its main fact is the tyranny of the leading male of each troop, who grows to a great size, with immensely powerful shoulders. He develops large canine teeth, which some observant Hindu draughtsmen take care to grace their pictures of Hanumān withal. These are used unsparingly on the younger male members of the troop, in fighting for his place of power, and on disobedient females. "The demon" was the familiar name we gave to a leader with whom we were well acquainted. He seemed to be always angry and was easily moved to a paroxysm of rage, when he used worse language than any permitted to man, for there was a savage force and variety in his grunting fury which made one thankful he was untranslatable. He took the lion's share of everything, especially resenting that the rising bachelors of the troop should have a chance. Mothers and babies were merely cuffed aside from a morsel, but there was ruthless war between him and all who might become his rivals. No more perfect picture of headlong, desperate terror can be imagined than a young man-monkey plunging and bounding in reckless flight down the hillside, pursued as he screams by a livid and grunting elder. Natives may well call the monkey sire *Maharaja*, for he is the very type and incarnation of savage and sensual despotism. They are right, too, in making their Hanumān red, for the old male's face is of the dusky red you see in some elderly, over-fed, human faces.

Like human Maharajas, they have their tragedies and mayhap their romances. One morning there came a monkey chieftain, weak and limping, having evidently been worsted in a severe fight with another of his own kind. One hand hung powerless, his face and eyes bore terrible traces of battle, and he hirpled slowly along with a pathetic air of suffering, supporting himself on the shoulder of a female,—a wife, the only member of his clan who had remained faithful to him after his defeat. We threw them bread and raisins, and the wounded warrior carefully stowed the greater part away in his cheek pouch. The faithful wife, seeing her opportunity, sprang on him, holding fast his one sound hand, and opening his mouth she deftly scooped out the store of raisins. Then she sat and ate them very calmly at a safe distance, while he mowed and chattered in impotent rage. He knew that without her help he could not reach home, and was fain to wait with what patience he might till the raisins were finished. It was a sad sight, but, like more sad sights, touched with the light of comedy. This was probably her first chance of disobedience or of self-assertion in her whole life, and I am afraid she thoroughly enjoyed it. Then she led him away,—possibly to teach him more salutary lessons of this modern and "advanced" sort, so that at the last he would go to another life with a meek and chastened soul.

Monkey mothers are tender to their little ones, with a care that endears them to the child-loving Oriental. The babies are quaint little mites with the brown hair that afterwards stands up crest-wise, parted in the middle of their brows; their wistful faces are full of wrinkles, and their mild hazel eyes have a quick glancing timidity, that well suits their pathetic, lost, kitten-like cry. Yet even in the forest there are frisky matrons. I have seen a mother monkey, disturbed in her gambols on the ground by the whining of a tiny baby left half-way up an adjacent tree, suddenly break off, and hastily shinning up the tree, snatch up the baby, hurry to the very topmost branch, where she plumped it down as who should say,—"Tiresome little wretch!" and then come down to resume her play. Thus is a mischievous midshipman mast-headed, and thus is the British baby sent up to the nursery while mamma amuses herself. Natives say that when monkey babies die the mothers often go mad, and that in the excess of their affection they occasionally squeeze their offspring to death. It is at least certain that a mother monkey will carry with her for weeks the dried and dead body of her little one, nursing and petting it as if it were alive. In defence of the little ones the sires will fight savagely, as is their duty. I knew a fat fox terrier, the dream of whose life was to catch a monkey.

Once it came true, and for half a minute, said a man who saw, he held a baby monkey. I was indoors at the time, but as the dog passed me to take refuge under a chair, I knew from his solemn silence that something had happened. The leader monkey had fallen upon him and inflicted three frightful bites—more like deep knife-cuts than the work of teeth—which seemed likely to prove fatal; but first-rate surgical skill was available, and Bob was saved to carefully avoid monkeys in future.

A quaint episode of our acquaintanceship with monkey folk was the arrival during one of our levees of one of the wandering performers who lead about tame monkeys with a goat that serves them as charger. The wild monkeys drew off at first suspiciously, but when the man sat down to his performance and made their tame brethren dance, put on strange raiment, and mount the goat, they crept closer with horrified curiosity and evident disgust. The tame monkeys off duty regarded their free kinsmen with listless indifference, and the artiste at work never seemed to glance at them, though they watched him with jealous and angry eyes, much, I imagine, as labourers on strike watch blacklegs.

There is a belief that during severe winters wild monkeys, instead of furtively hanging about the grocers' shops and watching their chance to steal, come into Simla streets in bands and stand whining like beggars asking for alms. But there is only native authority for this story. It is just possible they may have been so hard pressed as to seek human help, but it is an immense step for such wild and distrustful creatures to take. Some shopkeepers habitually feed them, and they may have whined at a place where they missed their daily dole.

A wistful, watchful melancholy seems to be the

normal mood of the mature monkey, broken by sudden flashes of interest which change as suddenly into indifference or abstraction. Few animals seem to spend so much time in sitting and looking about them, while only the birds can command more lofty posts of observation. Among men, some sailors and many Orientals have a similar faculty of tranquil outlooking. But the sudden flash of interest in a triviality and its abrupt cessation remind one more of lunacy than of sane humanity. Their life is hard and hungry, and as the creatures lope disconsolately along in the rain, or crouch on branches with dripping backs set against the tree trunk as a shelter from the driving storm, they have the air of being very sorry for themselves. Consumption is not unknown among them, and a monkey's cough, heard through the drip of the forest on a wet night, is a dismal sound. But when the sun shines the younger ones play like schoolboys. They have a game like the English boys' cock of the dung-hill or king of the castle, but instead of pushing each other from the top of a knoll or dust-heap, the castle is a pendent branch of a tree. The game is to keep a place on the bough, which swings with their weight as with a cluster of fruit while the players struggle to dislodge one another, each, as he drops, running round and climbing up again to begin anew. This sport is kept up for an hour at a time with keen enjoyment, and when one is nimble as a monkey it must be splendid fun.

The way of a ship on the sea may be strange, but the path of a monkey through tree-land is no less surprising. At one moment a creature is in tranquil meditation on the creation of the world or the origin of evil, at the next it has thrown itself backward apparently into illimitable space, but at the right instant a bough is seized and the animal swings to another and another with infallible certainty. The larger langūr does not

YOUNG MONKEYS AT PLAY
(Copyright 1891, by J. Lockwood Kipling)

seem to play concerted games, and his movements have a bolder sweep and abandonment. He travels on a more lofty story of the tree-terraces, progressing through the pines in a succession of leaping feats, performed with the ease, deliberation, and precision of perfect gymnastic art. The scenery which nature has assigned to this performance gives an impression of freedom which makes the thought of confinement infamous.

On the plains life would appear to be easier, for there is an almost constant succession of fruits and edible leaves in the jungles, and the crops are more accessible. Thievish monkeys sometimes haunt the halting-places of travellers. A friend of mine halted at a *parao* or stage where was a grove of mango-trees affording grateful shade to travellers, and while resting, he watched a little comedy. Apart from the others, a Hindu was preparing his evening meal. In one pot over the fire a stew of pulse was boiling, while he kneaded dough and baked the invariable wheaten flap-jacks. As each cake is taken from the iron griddle plate it is stuck edgewise in the hot embers till all are ready, when they are piled together. This was done, and the Hindu turned to set the ghi pot and drinking vessels in order and to hail his companion to come to dinner. While his back was turned, a big monkey dropped from the boughs overhead, seized the pile of cakes, and was off in a flash. Now the baking of bread is a semi-ritualistic business, involving a good deal of labour, and it was a very angry Hindu who received in his face one of the hot flap-jacks dropped by the monkey clutching his prize with awkward fingers above. Then the other man came and swore too, but the monkey swore the worst, irritated by the heat of his plunder, which, however, he was determined not to let go. The watchman of the stage assured my friend that this trick was a frequent occurrence, for that particular monkey was "as cunning as a *baniya* (or tradesman) and as daring as a *thug* (highway robber)—a very demon of a monkey." Yet it had never occurred to him or to the robbed travellers to take measures against it.

It may be that "advanced India" will in time give up the protection of the monkey, but there are hitherto no signs of a change in popular feeling. In April 1886, in the highly civilised and cosmopolitan city of Bombay, a Hindu of good position was in danger of losing every social privilege of his caste and of undergoing an ostracism more complete than any imagined by Athenian citizen or Irish Land-leaguer, because he was said to have allowed a European officer of police to shoot a troublesome monkey from the window of his house. The officer had been invited by the people to rid them of the creature, and its death was frankly acknowledged as a relief, but the letter of the law forbade the murder. Officers of government are careful not to wound the feelings of the people with reference both to monkeys and peacocks, a delicacy which does not always restrain the hungry low-caste man.

A collector and magistrate of a district in Hindustan proper had been out shooting, and was returning to camp. On a tree on the other side of the Ganges Canal, along which he was walking, sat a monkey. The animal seemed almost out of range, and my friend idly pointed his gun and fired in its direction with intent to startle it, but, to his dismay, the monkey fell and lay dead. Fortunately no one was near, and at night this worshipful magistrate, whose word was law for leagues round, stole out alone with a lantern, taking a long round to the nearest bridge, to look for his victim. It was not easily found, and never, even on the judicial bench, did he so keenly realise the feelings of a murderer trying to hide the evidences of his guilt. He succeeded in disposing of the body, and returned to camp determined never to point a gun at a monkey again. Another friend of mine had for neighbour a Hindu devotee of great repute and sanctity, whose hut, besides being a resort of gamblers and bad characters, had a large retinue of monkeys that were fed by visitors. The animals wrought great havoc in my friend's garden, whereupon in his irritation he threatened to shoot them. The Sâdhu took the will for the deed, and fulminated a curse against the Englishman as terrible as that which the Archbishop of Rheims inflicted on the jackdaw. He was filled with a holy joy when my friend fell ill, and desponded when he recovered.

St. Francis de Sales wrote:—"I am despised and I grow angry;—so does the peacock or the monkey." This is more like an Oriental than a Western word. The irritable monkey is ready to be angry at anything. The Oriental, however, considers the monkey—apart from his sacred affinity with Hanumān, a type, not so much of petulance, as of untrustworthiness. "What is a monkey's friendship worth?" he asks, and he says in scorn of a trivial and foolish person—"a tailless monkey." "A cocoa-nut in a monkey's hand," stands for ill-bestowed gifts or gear and for ineptitude, for the creature cannot get at the kernel, having neither strength nor wit to break the shell. "A flower in a monkey's hand" is a common Malay expression to a similar purpose. "One monkey does not tell another monkey that his buttocks are red" is a homely word with obvious uses. There are ten things, says a proverb, which may not be depended upon—"A courtesan, a monkey, fire, water, a procuress, an army, a distiller, a tailor, a parrot, and a goldsmith." The selection is significant, and—in India—just. In the stables of the wealthy a monkey is often kept to attract to itself stray influences of the evil eye, that ever-present bogy of the East. So there is a saying, —"What goes wrong in the stable falls on the monkey's head." This can be used in daily life by those frequent persons who habitually fancy themselves wrongly accused. It is unlucky to utter the word monkey in the morning, but lucky to see one before breakfast. "Speak of a monkey or an owl in the morning and you'll get no breakfast."

In the Rāmāyana of Tūlsi Dass, (a relatively modern version of the great epic poem in which the Hindus delight) a method of catching monkeys by means of a bait of grain in a narrow-mouthed jar is spoken of as an example of the metaphysical principle of illusion which makes so great a figure in Hindu cobweb philosophy. The monkey is supposed to fill his fist so full that he is unable to withdraw it, and has not the wit to let go his spoil and release himself. This is quite reasonable enough for a metaphysical illustration. A more practical form of illusion is to put some grain in a clear glass bottle and hand it to a monkey. It tries to seize the grain, then, concluding the distance was not properly judged, it takes a careful sight along the bottle, and, with a diverting air of great astuteness, passes a slow hand down and gives a sudden clutch. After one or two attempts it loses temper and interest. Similarly, the illusion of a mirror puzzles a young dog when he is first introduced to it, and, according to his character and temper, interests and excites him, but after a short time he gives it up and waits for more facts, like the philosopher he is. A foolish cock-sparrow, on the other hand, will nearly kill himself in fighting his reflection.

Does the survival of respect for monkeys, amounting at times to a definite acknowledgment of kinship, indicate the early arrival of Hindu philosophers at the latest conclusion of European Evolutionists? Modern Hindu students of the Vedas and other ancient records draw from those vague depths material to support such theories as the Hindu discovery of America and the founding of the ruined cities of its central region; with the use of balloons, railways, and contrivances like the electric telegraph. A slender verbal hint suffices to give a complacent sense of having once at least marched in the foremost files of time. But they would be on more plausible, if not more solid ground in essaying to show that the Hindu respect for life, the admission of the essential unity of the life-spark, whether in man or moss, and the special regard for the ancestral monkey, its deification, and the traditions of its aptitude for speech, labour, and war, were proofs that the philosophy of the East has for ages sat in tranquil occupation of a peak of discovery to which the vanguard of Western science has but now attained.

CHAPTER IV

OF ASSES

"'Twas when the rain fell steady and the ark was pitched and ready,
And Noah got his orders for to take the bastes below:
He haled them all together by the hide and horn and feather,
And all except the donkey were agreeable to go.

"Then Noah spoke him fairly, then rated him sevarely,
And then he cursed him squarely to the glory of the Lord,
'Divil take the ass that bred you and the triple ass that fed you,
Divil go with you, you spalpeen;'—and the donkey went aboard.

"But the wind was always failin' and 'twas most onaisy sailin',
And the ladies in the cabins couldn't stand the stable air,
And the bastes betwixt the hatches, they tuk and died in batches,
And Noah said 'There's one of us that hasn't paid his fare.'

"For he heard a flusteration with the bastes of all creation,
The trumpeting of elephants and the bellowing of whales.
And he saw forninst the windy, when he went to stop the shindy,
The Devil with a pitchfork, bedevilling their tails.

"The Devil cursed outrageous, but Noah said umbrageous,—
'To what am I indebted for this tenant-right invasion?'
And the Devil gave for answer,—'Evict me if you can, sir,
For I came in with the donkey at your honour's invitation.'"

R. K.

PASSING from the free to the fettered, we come to a beast which in India serves at once as an expression of wild liberty, more complete than that of the monkey, and of utter and abject slavery. There is no freedom more unrestrained than that of the wild ass and no bondage more bitter than that of his brother in servitude. For a wholly unmerited obloquy, relic of a dark aboriginal superstition, is added to the burden of toil and hard living. Yet there was once a time when in the nearer East, or ever the horse was known, he was held in high honour, carved in Assyrian sculptures, and reckoned a suitable steed for prophets and kings. Even now in Cairo, Damascus, and Bagdad, although the Bedawi Arab pretends to despise him, he is regularly ridden by respectable people.

The *Arabian Nights* story of a conversation overheard between the ox and the ass shows the estimation in which he was held; and it is written that Muhammad himself had two asses, one of which was called Yafūr, nor did that great man disdain to ride double. But here in India, by formal prescription, only the gypsy, the potter, the washerman, and such like folk, out-caste or of low caste, will mount or own the ass. This prescription, and the ridiculous Hindu association of the donkey with the goddess of smallpox, account for the universal dislike and disdain in which this most useful, sagacious, and estimable animal is held. He is never fed by his owners, and his chronic hunger is mocked by a popular saying that to feed a donkey is neither sin nor sacrifice:—"*na pâp na pŭn.*" A dozen popular Indian versions of "casting pearls before swine" derisively offer cakes, sweetmeats, bread, sugar, saffron, ghi, and curry-combs to the ass, and it has entered into no one's mind to conceive the simple truth that he has deserved them all. Also, with bitter irony, he is said to be always in good case whatever the season—because in the hot, dry weather, when he looks about on the burnt-up plain, he brays with glee—saying:—"This is vastly well! I must be fat since I have eaten up all the grass." While in the rains he brays and says:—"I shall never get through all this fodder." As a joke this popular gibe is beneath contempt, while as an imputation on the donkey's sense it is wholly unwarranted. A purely idiotic and unaccountable fancy is that if one walks over the place where a donkey has rolled he will have pains in his feet or be smitten with paralysis. The Arab superstition recorded by Al Masudi, that ghouls have asses' feet, may have some share in the notion, for in the East ghouls are still alive and have a natural history of their own.

It may not be very painful, but the slitting of the poor creature's nostrils, almost universal in India, and meant to soften the clangour of his voice, has always seemed to me a monstrous affectation of delicacy of ear on the part of people who delight in the tom-tom and the pipe, while it gives a tattered and woe-begone air to a countenance already sufficiently marked with dejection. Nor is it of the least use, for that stormy music, "loud and clear," rings with unabated force in spite of the hideous mutilation. Mr. Villiers Stuart of Dromana mentions an ancient Egyptian wall-picture of a driver trying to stop his donkey when in full bray. The Speaker of the House of Commons in wig and robe may at times succeed in staunching the human,—but nothing short of decapitation would avail to silence the equine ass until that final sound, most like the spasm of a church organ when the wind fails, is reached. And when they slit the nostrils, they proceed in mere wantonness of brutality to split the ears also. For this there can be no reason. It is impossible to write in measured phrase of these cruel tricks, but those who dream of Oriental lovingkindness should be told that they have been practised for centuries, and are still unnoticed and unrebuked.

His very name, *Gădha*—the roarer,—is a reproach. Some Muhammadans have an idea that the donkey sees the devil when he brays, possibly because of the belief that it was he who introduced the Father of Evil into the Ark. When Hăzrăt Nuh (the worshipful Noah) was marshalling the animals into the Ark, the donkey, as is his modest wont, held back. "Nay then, go along!" said Noah; but the ass did not move. Then the Patriarch lost his temper, for the time was short and the clouds were gathering, and he cried, "Go on and may the Devil go with thee!" When the door was shut Noah met the Evil One inside and asked how he came there. "Surely then," replied that Wicked One, "I came by your honour's invitation." If there is a moral in this absurdity, it is that when holy men lose their tempers they open the door to sin; but in some topsy-turvy way, possible only to Oriental thought, the obloquy of the anecdote falls on the innocent ass. If injurious reflections and vile phrases were all he had to bear, there would not be much cause for complaint, but it is hard to write with patience of the constant and cruel beating the poor creature receives.

The race, through centuries of ill-usage, is stunted and weak; and the brutal rule seems to be that to the smallest ass shall go the biggest stick. It is just possible by taking the cudgel from the ass-driver's hand and applying it lustily to his back to convey to his mind some glimmering of an idea that the blows he finds hard to bear may perhaps be painful to the ass. No mere words avail to suggest this new and strange notion. The evangel of kindness to God's creatures can scarcely, however, be spread by missionaries with thick sticks; and for many a year to come the portion of the ass must be starvation and ill-usage. A folk-tale which accounts for the popular saying "As brave as the potter's wife" bears unintentional testimony to the way in which the ass is beaten. One cold dark night a potter and his wife were roused from sleep by sounds in the yard outside and the fall of pipkins. "Get up, man!" said the wife, "and drive the donkey away." But being warm, snug, and sleepy, he replied, "Bother the donkey!" and pulled the blanket over his shoulders. Thereupon, uttering some truisms of world-wide acceptation on the selfishness of husbands, the good wife arose, and seizing the potter's staff sallied out to bestow on the intruder's back all the resentment caused by her husband's laziness. She laid on with a will and the beast was still. So she went to bed again, muttering more truths. But in the morning when they opened the door they found no donkey, but a tiger, which the good woman had unwittingly beaten to death in the dark. The potter and his donkey have

THE POTTER AND HIS DONKEY

originated one of the many ironical gibes of the country. A traveller met two horsemen richly attired, and, a little farther on, a potter jogging along on his ass. He asked the latter who the cavaliers might be. "We three gentlemen are going to Delhi," said the potter, and this speech is murmured when a man brags of the fine company he keeps.

The black mark set against the ass by Hindu superstition from his association with Sitala, the goddess of smallpox, has already been noticed. This awful divinity is one of the ten manifestations of Durga or Kali the Destroyer, and is suspected of having entered the Hindu pantheon from the lower levels of aboriginal superstition. She is dreaded by all, but her worship, which is never performed during an epidemic of smallpox, seems to be confined to women and children, who flock to her shrines in thousands and sometimes throw a few grains of pulse to the ass.[1] But the poor creature draws no real profit from his appointment to be her *vâhan*—vehicle or steed. The bull, on the other hand, as the *vâhan* of Mahadeo or Shiva, often enjoys a full-fed freedom, and those led about by Hindu beggars are known as *nandi*, "the happy one," the name given to the carven stone bull in front of Hindu temples and to the small brass bull which supports the canopy over a domestic *shiv*.

In the days of rough-and-ready Qâzi justice criminals were frequently sentenced to be shaven and blackened and to be paraded, with their clothes

[1] Mr. Ibbetson writes, in his *Outlines of Punjab Ethnography*, "These deities (of disease) are never worshipped by men, but only by women and children, enormous numbers of whom attend the shrines of renown on Sitala's seventh. Every village has its local shrine too, at which the offerings are all impure. Sitala rides on a donkey, and grain is given to the donkey and to his master the potter, after being waved over the head of the child. Fowls, pigs, goats are offered, black dogs are fed, and white cocks are waved and let loose. An adult who has recovered from smallpox should let a pig loose to Sitala or he will be again attacked. During an attack no offerings are made, and if the epidemic has once seized on a village all worship is discontinued till the disease has disappeared; but so long as she keeps her hands off nothing is too good for the goddess, for she is the one great dread of Indian mothers."

rent, through the city, mounted on asses, with their faces tailwards, and a garland of old shoes round their necks. An old Sikh of my acquaintance has seen this punishment inflicted, with the addition, in the case of thieves, of the loss of hands, ears, or noses. In Mussulman countries farther west the penalty is still applied. Even now, in remote Indian villages, a noxious person is occasionally treated to a donkey ride of this kind, with a noisy accompaniment of beaten pans. In the similar "skimmity ride" of the south of England, described in Mr. Thomas Hardy's *Mayor of Casterbridge*, effigies of the offending persons are paraded on the backs of asses. As an example of utter shamelessness they tell of offenders who, after the performance, calmly demand the donkey as their perquisite. In folk-tales unfaithful wives have their noses cut off and are paraded on donkey-back. Nose-cutting, by the way, as in the days of the Hitopadesa, is the punishment still awarded by popular sentiment in India to conjugal infidelity, and not a week passes without a case of this horror, in our police courts; but it is only the woman's nose which suffers, and the greater part of these barbarities never comes to light.

There are evidences of a quaint ritual of obloquy in which the honest donkey was made to take part. When it was decided that a site was infamous for some sacro-sanct Hindu reason, it was formally ploughed up and asses were yoked to the plough. But a re-consecration was possible, and then the lordly elephant dragged the plough. "May your homestead be ploughed by asses" is still a common Hindu curse.

The ass has been made to serve in the conflicts of race and creed which still divide India. Before the establishment of British rule the Hindus on the

North-West frontier, where Muhammadan authority was paramount, were not allowed to wear full-size turbans, and might ride asses only. In the independent state of Cutch Bhūj, on the other hand, where the rulers are Hindus, the Muhammadan Borahs were forbidden to ride on horseback, a disability which has only just been removed (1890). The Borahs, on whom this indignity has for so long been laid, are not, as might be imagined, low-caste folk of no consideration, but include among them some of the most intelligent, public-spirited, and wealthy men in the Bombay Presidency. The Muhammadan is perhaps, in matters of this kind, more tyrannical and intolerant than the Hindu. At this moment the Jews in some parts of Morocco may only ride on asses, with their faces tailwards, and they may not wear shoes.

That caste pride is as strong among people of low estate as in the upper ranks is a commonplace everywhere. Indian grooms of the leather-dresser tribes are supposed to be of low degree; but when a lady of my acquaintance proposed to get a donkey for her little son she learned a lesson in this subject from one of her horse-keepers: "No, madam, my son shall never wait on an ass. You must get a potter's brat for him, and he must not come near our stable."

India follows, or perhaps the East has led, other countries in the use of the donkey's name as a term of reproach. "Ass" is a common word in all contemptuous mouths, and "tailless ass" is an occasional enhancement of scorn. When a fool is praised by a fool they say, "Ass scratches ass," and a similar saying expresses the arts of log-rolling intrigues with homely force. For the sake of ricochet shots at fools the poor beast is insulted by comparisons which would never occur to his humble mind, as "Wash an ass as much as you like, you will never make a calf of him," or "Bray him in a mortar, but he will never be a horse." Muhammadans say, "If even the ass of Jesus went to Mecca he would still come back an ass." The obstinacy born of ill-usage, which is his only fault, points many a gibe. As an illustration of Afghān character a folk-tale tells that at a Punjab river ferry a crowd of passengers and animals were assembled. When the boat came, all went aboard without hesitation, excepting an ass, which refused to move. His driver pushed and the boatmen hauled without effect, until at last an Afghān among the waiting passengers drew his *churra*, the long and heavy Khyber knife, and smote the poor beast's head off at a blow, crying, "Obstinacy like this may be permitted to an Afghān, but to a donkey, never."

Among the Biloch, neighbours of the Afghān, this same obstinacy is honoured. Mr. Ibbetson writes in his *Punjab Ethnography*, "When a male child is born, asses' dung in water, symbolical of pertinacity, is dropped into his mouth from the point of a sword before he is given the breast." Antipathies of race and region, calmly ignored by those who write of "the people of India" as one and indivisible, find expression in sayings wherein the donkey takes part. A Hindustani will say of a Punjabi, "A country donkey with a Punjab bray"; and the Punjabi retaliates with, "A country donkey with an Eastern limp"; while of the Bengali Baboo, who affects English speech and manners, they say, "A hill jackass with an English bray."

Yet while the animal is despised the nutritive value of its milk is recognised. The potter and his family grow strong at the expense of the ass foal, and the high-caste Hindu pretends to be horrified by such an abomination. Vemana, a sage whose sayings take a high rank in Telugu literature, says, "A single spoonful of milk from a good cow is enough—of what use is a pailful of asses' milk?" Most Hindus would say that the use of this fluid is impossible under any circumstances. None the less is it accounted a valuable medicine by Hindu doctors, who on occasion put caste laws aside and compound mixtures, compared with which the most loathsome messes set forth in "Saxon leechdoms" are what our English druggists would call elegant prescriptions. Asses' milk is prescribed for a tendency to phthisis and other diseases, but usually at too late a stage to be of any use.

In some regions the donkey enjoys a moment's honour as the steed of Sitala; for a bridegroom about to start in the marriage procession will mount an ass for an instant, as a propitiation to the dread goddess. In customary talk, however, there are but few sayings which treat him with any touch of consideration. The "donkey's beauty" of Italian and French proverb has an equivalent in "Even a she-ass is pretty when she is young." The creature's sureness of foot is admitted in "A donkey will tumble down hill when you can split a fowl's ear." The poor wretch is turned loose when his work is done to that forlorn freedom of neglect which is the only privilege of the outcast. So they say in varying forms of phrase, "The donkey may be sore with beating, despised of all men and accursed as the *vâhan* of Sitala, but at least he is never plagued with tether or heel-rope." Some alleviation is granted even to the most abject misery.

There is a more complete harmony with the topsy-turvy scheme of Oriental appreciations than can be imagined by untravelled folk in the fact that while the ass is the most despised of creatures he is one of the most useful. There are regions where he is yoked to the plough, but his principal occupation is carrying clothes for the washerman, and earth, burnt and unburnt lime, and stone for the potter, the builder, and the railway contractor. Your great works in the West are built by strong-armed men, but in India railway bank, water-works dam, and Queen's highway are raised by the slender cooly woman and the little donkey. His step is first in the peaceful halls which mark the new civilisation, but his loads are too heavy for his weak limbs, his rude harness seems to be expressly contrived to gall and wound him, his life is one long martyrdom to the stick, and he is shamefully abandoned to starve and die when his strength fails. According to a country tale, similar to one told by Longfellow in his *Tales of a Wayside Inn*, there was once an Indian ruler who took compassion on a donkey. The Emperor Jehanghir caused a bell to be slung over his couch which might be rung by any petitioner with a wrong to redress. One day it was found that a castaway ass, rubbing his sore hide against the bell-rope, had rung a peal. The creature was haled before the throne, and search was made for its master, a washerman, who confessed that he had abandoned it to starve and die. The Emperor gave him a lecture on his cruelty, and ordered him to take back his faithful servant to be fed and cherished and to appear again before him after a season. That one donkey was groomed and fed as never ass before or since and brought sleek and fat into the august presence; but the example has borne no fruit, and the grim "burial of an ass" described by the prophet Jeremiah succeeds a lingering death by starvation.

CHAPTER V

OF GOATS AND SHEEP

"They killed a child to please the Gods
  In earth's young penitence,
And I have bled in that babe's stead
  Because of innocence.

"I bear the sins of sinful men
  That have no sin of my own;
They drive me forth to Heaven's wrath
  Unpastured and alone.

"I am the meat of sacrifice,
  The ransom of man's guilt,
For they give my life to the altar knife,
  Wherever shrine is built."

R. K.

A HINDU SACRIFICIAL KNIFE

HERE is no house possessing a goat but a blessing abideth thereon; and there is no house possessing three goats but the angels pass the night there praying," said Muhammad. And truly, if the animals of India had creeds like the people, goats would be of Islám; for though a vast proportion of the population, including Hindus, possess a goat or two and eat their flesh, it is mostly Moslems who keep them in flocks and trade in them. There is something too in appearances. The Brahminy bull looks every inch a Hindu ; and the goat, to accustomed eyes, has no less decided a Muhammadan air.

Immense numbers of he-goats are sacrificed by Hindus, principally to the goddess Kali, one of the manifestations of Durga ; and the practice is to decapitate them at a blow with a heavy bill-hook-shaped knife. It is supposed, indeed, that only animals slaughtered in this fashion are fit for Hindu food. For many years a goat has been sacrificed daily at a temple within the precincts of the old palace at Ambér, the former capital of the Jeypore state in Rajputana ; and here, as in some other places, the tradition is that the goat is a substitute for a human sacrifice once regularly offered. In some parts of India, Hindus say, "The goat gets its own tail," a saying based on a local sacrificial usage. Each limb of the sacrifice belongs to a deity. The tail is assigned to Vishnu, who only can save. This part is therefore cut off and put into its mouth, so that at least the creature gets salvation, and presumably has less cause of objection to death. The Muhammadan *halál* custom involves a sort of verbal apology to the creature slain, with a prayér ; and, like the Hindu custom, seems to acknowledge that it also has a soul. Some Muhammadans kill a goat by way of sacrifice soon after the birth of a man child, and when a child is sick. The throat is cut with the usual invocation, pronounced by a Moollah.

We say in derision of hasty vows, "When the devil was sick," etc. : in India they mutter, "If I get safe across I'll offer a goat." The story goes that a Meo, one of the crocodile-eating river-side tribesmen, made this promise when starting to cross the Ganges in flood; but when half-way over he found it less

A DOMESTIC SACRIFICE (MUHAMMADAN)
(Copyright 1891, by J. Lockwood Kipling)

dangerous than he had feared, so instead of a goat he vowed to sacrifice a hen. When he had fairly won over, even the fowl seemed too much to give, so he sought for an insect among his clothing. This was easily found, and as he crushed it he said, "A life for a life, and that's enough."

In the hill districts of the Punjab the ancient idea still prevails that the sacrifice is not efficacious unless the animal first shivers. Thus, during the marriage progress of a hill-chief a goat is sacrificed at bridges and dangerous passes, and the long train waits contentedly until the creature shivers. The Brahmans, if so disposed, hasten the tremor by dashing a handful of cold water into the goat's ear, and thus produce a quite satisfactory shiver. In Kulu, a hill province bordering on Tibet, when two men have a difference which would lead elsewhere to a costly law-suit, each leads a goat to a shrine at Nuggur, the chief town, and waits to see which beast shivers first. The owner of that goat wins his case, and the contending parties go home content with a divine judgment for which no lawyer's fees have been paid. But in these cases they do not use the cold douche.

So far as I know, belief in the shivering goat as a favourable omen is confined to the hills, and it is particularly strong in Tibet. It was consulted with disastrous effect to the Tibetans in the recent Sikkim war just before they attacked our forces on the pass above Chumbi on the road into Sikkim.

The goat and the kid are the staple of the flesh food of the Muhammadans all over the East, and also of many Hindu castes, in Northern India especially. It is a fact that while the vegetarian craze is said to be spreading in the West, the use of goats and sheep as food is increasing in India,—popularly supposed to be given up to vegetarianism, even among Brahmanical castes. Throughout Hindustan proper and the Punjab, where contact with Islám has softened the edges of

Hinduism, flesh food has been eaten by Hindus for centuries. By men, that is to say, for Hindu women very rarely taste it. Many more things besides flesh meat are considered too strong and good for mere women. Increasing prosperity is at the bottom of such change as is taking place, and probably the silent force of example counts for something. Hindus have said to me at times, "You English do not suffer so much from fever as we do because you eat flesh meat," and "Your eyesight is strong because you eat plenty of meat." This last might be based on observation of flesh-eating birds, but I doubt it. There is, however, a popular saying which forcibly expresses an estimate of the virtue of meat: "The butcher's daughter bears a son when she is ten years old." The home-keeping brother of the Prodigal Son complained that his father never gave him even a kid to make merry with his friends. Phrases like this which sound strange to town-bred Western ears, occur here in everyday talk. Servants on the march are made happy with a present of kids, and the festal days at the close of the long fast of the Muhammadan Ramazán are red with the slaughter of countless goats. The Englishman in India seldom wittingly eats goat or kid, but often in remote posting houses and in camp his mutton cutlet was originally goat. The native prefers kid before mutton, because the goat is a scrupulously clean feeder, while a hungry sheep will eat anything.

It would seem difficult to be cruel to a goat, but the keepers of the flocks of milch goats regularly driven morning and evening into Indian cities contrive to inflict a good deal of pain. The nipples of the udder are tied up in a torturing fashion, and there is an unnecessary use of the staff. But the worst cruelty is the practice of flaying them alive in the belief that skins thus prepared have a better quality. The Calcutta Society for the Prevention of Cruelty to Animals prosecuted twenty-two criminals for this offence in 1890, and is now inclined to hope the practice is dying out so far as the capital of Bengal is concerned.

ON THE DUSTY HIGHWAY

There are many sayings about goats, but the animal appears to be less suggestive than might be expected. The wilfulness of the creature and his habit of trespass are hinted in "Nothing to bother you, eh?—then go and buy a goat!" A gibe at the greed of saintly people is expressed in verse:—

"My Lord, the goat a saint would be,
His pupil was a cotton tree,
And quickly nibbled up was he."

The bearded Moollah of the mosque also has the goat cast offensively in his teeth. "You were moved by my discourse, I trust it will do you good," says the Moollah. "Yes," replies the countryman, "I could have wept, for when you wagged your beard in the pulpit you were just like our old billy-goat." This is also a European story. For "great cry and little wool" rustics say, "The goat bleated all night and produced only one kid,"—two being the usual number.

In folk-tales holy places are discovered by the milch goats coming home dry. It was found they had let down their milk on some sacred spot on which a temple or shrine is afterwards raised. Many out-of-the-way Hindu shrines are accounted for in this way. In other stories goats lead the way to caves tenanted by mystic immortals of miraculous powers. A quaint belief is that in dry desert places where wells formerly existed goats will group themselves in a circle round the ancient well brink, though not a trace of it is visible to the keenest human eye. Those who sketch animals may have noticed that goats at rest have a way of grouping themselves as if posing for their portraits. It is possible that this unconscious trick is at the bottom of the well-brink belief. So far as I know there are no sayings which notice the fine carriage of the head and the elegant horse-like gait of this beautiful animal. The Indian goat as a rule is much taller and of more slender build than the European animal.

From an administrative and economic point of view there are serious objections to the goat, which is one of the plagues of the Forest Department of the Government. It is the poor man's animal and is supposed to cost nothing to keep. Every green shoot is nibbled off as soon as it peeps above the ground, and young trees are promptly destroyed by creatures which spend half their time on their hind legs and have an effective reach up to the height of a man's head. Thus large tracts which nature is ready to clothe with vegetation are kept barren, and new forests carefully nursed by the provident state are devastated. Many more are kept than the land can carry. The creatures really belong to the purely pastoral

MILCH GOATS

scheme of life, and to the barren hillside, and are out of place in agricultural areas, which are increasing yearly, and may be regarded as at once a sign and a cause of unthrifty poverty and land-leanness.

The goat's trick of picking up stray trifles is sometimes inconvenient. A Bengal saying runs, "What will not a goat eat or a fool say?" Two native merchants in Bombay were concluding a bargain, and while making payment a currency note for a thousand rupees fluttered to the ground and was promptly eaten by a goat.

The receiver contended that the note had never reached

A GUILTY GOAT

him and the loss was not his, while the other insisted

that it was the fault of the receiver's carelessness. A hasty Englishman might have insisted on a sudden autopsy of the goat, but these were high-caste Hindus, who never dreamed of such a thing, so they led the criminal between them to the Government Treasury, where, after due inquiry, I believe the loss was made good.

After death the goat seems to be as much with us as in life, for his skin, carefully withdrawn for this purpose, is borne as a water-vessel by the *bhisti* or water-carrier, and there are few more complete examples of adaptation. The legs, sewn up, form perfect attachments for the strap by which the bag is slung on the water-carrier's back, and the throat, which is a convenient neck to the huge bottle, is ingeniously closed by a thong, and is so supple that the *bhisti* can direct a thin stream into the mouth or hand of a thirsty passenger, or fill a decanter without spilling a drop, or water a road with a far-reaching spray like that of a watering-cart, or empty his burden into a bath-tub or a mortar-heap in a trice. *Bhisti* really means a person from Paradise, a prince, and is one of the half-ironical titles, like khalifa or caliph for a tailor, mehter or prince for a scavenger, thakur or lord for a barber, and raj or royal one for the bricklayer or mason, bestowed may be in time past as an acknowledgment of the dignity of labour; but a little English child will often say, "Here comes the *bhisti* with his beast!" It is a rather pitiful beast, more like a porpoise than a goat; yet at times when lying distended on the well-block, with the leg-stumps in the air, and the man pausing a moment to straighten his back before taking it up, I have thought a Levite at the altars of Israel may have looked like this.

The makers of goat-skin bags have a curious skill in

THE GOAT-SKIN WATERBAG (MASHK)

flaying. One of them once brought me a soft and glossy black kid skin cured with the hair on. "What is this?" "Wait and see, sir," said he with a smile, and producing a reed, he proceeded to inflate the skin in the manner described by Don Miguel de Cervantes. A plump but not too shapely kid, with feet, ears, and even eyes (in glass) complete, resulted, nor could I find a trace of a seam. "Would not this be a fine thing for the 'wonder house'?" (native name for museum). As a museum specimen it was scarcely eligible, but to this moment I have no idea how it was done.

In Europe the goat is associated with the vine. The Bible has familiarised us with the use of its skin as a wine-bag or "bottle," and it is still used for this purpose in Spain and Cyprus. The Athenians during the festival of Dionysus made a pretty game,—Ascoliasmus,—of leaping and dancing barefoot on a wine-filled goat-skin smeared with oil. India is too temperate for such high jinks, and puts no wine into skin bottles, for it makes none. A *dren* is a sort of raft made of goat or deer-skins inflated with air, astride on which is uneasily fixed a cot bedstead. This serves as a ferry-boat, and is used for descending hill-streams, the legs and arms of the men in charge serving as oars and rudder. I have seen a gracious lady of strong nerve, sitting serenely aloft on a contrivance of this kind, attended by splashing bronze mermen, go gaily down a brawling river like a new Amphitrite. When filled with water merely, the goat-skin or "mashk" is a characteristic object. There is a story of an aide-de-camp in Simla who, when walking up hill in full uniform behind a water-carrier on whose kbac a newly filled "mashk" glistened plump in the sunshine, yielded to a temptation that many have felt, and drawing his too-ready sword slashed the thing open.

It had not occurred to him that the "mashk" was full of dirty water for road watering, nor that the whole contents would burst over him in a cataract and utterly

BHISTI, OR WATER-CARRIER

(Copyright 1891, by J. Lockwood Kipling)

ruin his brave attire. One pays dearly sometimes for the gratification of sudden impulses.

In the Himálaya, flour and other food borne on a journey or brought home from the shop are carried in a goat-skin bag which always forms a part of the equipment of the hill peasant. When in accordance with an ancient custom, men are impressed as porters or to work on the roads, as in the French *corvée*—a blanket and a skin full of flour seem to be all they take with them for an absence of three or four days on the hillside. These are Hindus, but down in India proper no Hindu would put his food in a leathern bag. There are many Hindus, indeed, who will not drink water from the water-carrier's bag, and it were well if all shared this prejudice, for, though undeniably handy and useful, it cannot be called a wholesome contrivance. "Pipe-water," *i.e.* the tap-water now being introduced into most large Indian towns, besides lowering the death-rate and increasing the comfort of the inhabitants, has already lessened and will further reduce the number of water-carriers.

It is only in India and Peru that the sheep is used as a beast of burden. Borax, asafetida, and other commodities are brought in bags on the backs of sheep driven in large flocks from Tibet into British territory. One of the sensations of journeying in the hills of "the interior," as the farther recesses of the mountains are called by Anglo-Indians, is to come suddenly on such a drove as it winds, with the multitudinous click of little feet, round the shoulder of some Himálayan spur. The coarse hair bags scrape the cliff side from which the narrow path is out-built or hollowed, and allow but scant room for your pony, startled by the unexpected sight and the quick breathing hurry of the creatures as they crowd and scuffle past. Only the picturesque shepherds return from these journeys, for the carriers of the caravan, feeding as they go, gather flesh in spite of their burdens and provide most excellent mutton.

Sheep are numerous in India, but they are seldom

kept by the cultivator or farmer, for the combination of agricultural with pastoral life, common in other countries, is almost unknown. In the towns of the plains rams are kept as fighting animals, and the sport is a source of gratification to many. A Muhammadan "buck" going out for a stroll with his fighting ram makes a

A SPORTING MAN

picture of point-device foppery not easily surpassed by the sporting fancy of the West. The ram is neatly clipped, with a judicious reservation of salient tufts touched with saffron and mauve dyes, and besides a necklace of large blue beads, it bears a collar of hawk-bells. Its master wears loosely round his neck or on his shoulders a large handkerchief of the brightest colours procurable, his vest is of scarlet or sky-blue satin embroidered with colour and gold, his slender legs are encased in skin-tight drawers, a gold-embroidered cap is poised on one side of his head, his long, black hair, parted in the middle and shining with scented hair-oil, is sleeked behind his ears, where it has a drake's tail curl which throws in relief his gold earrings, and in addition to two or three necklaces, he usually wears a gold chain. Patent leather shoes and a cane complete the costume. As he first affronts the sunshine, he looks undeniably smart, but his return, I have observed, is not always so triumphant. The ram naturally loses interest in a stroll which has not another ram in perspective, and it is not easy to preserve an air of distinction when angrily propelling homeward a heavy and reluctant sheep.

The great God Indra rides on a ram, but, for the bulk of the people, Indra has been dead for many a day.

CHAPTER VI

OF COWS AND OXEN

"By those dumb mouths be ye forgiven
Ere ye are heard pleading with Heaven."

SIR E. ARNOLD.

A BOMBAY MILK WOMAN

IN Europe it is a half-forgotten legend that flocks and herds ranked first among early forms of wealth, and it is only in dissertations on the origin of money we are reminded that the root of pecuniary is *pecus*. But in agricultural and pastoral India, dependent on cattle for milk and labour, and on sheep and goats for flesh-meat, a hundred sayings, echoes of the now forgotten prayers of the Vedic hymns, repeat the ancient estimates of cattle. One of the first sensations of the tourist in India is the ubiquity of the bull, the cow, and the ox. They are, in fact, foremost figures in both the rustic and urban scenery of the country. Yet Lord Macaulay, when painting this scenery for English readers, set down everything but its most essential and familiar features. There is a splendid picture in his essay on Warren Hastings, where the rich oriental detail of palm-trees, idols, elephants, maidens with pitchers, and the rest, is like a profusion of jewels set in florid beaten work of gilded metal, but the cow and ox were not thought fine enough for the place in letters that they own in life.

The people have a passion,—no other word is strong enough,—for the possession of cattle. Indian cities, full of folk, are also vast cow byres or mistals, and hitherto sanitary reform has not ventured to interfere. The cattle come and go at their own pleasure, and rub shoulders with humanity with an ineffable air of security and fellowship. Nearly everybody is, or thinks he is, a judge of a cow; there is no more popular subject of discourse and none with so copious a terminology. Every possible and some apparently impossible varieties of form and colour; of hair, horn, tail, udder, dewlap, hump, eyes, and limbs has its separate name or phrase.

The peculiar sanctity of the animal may be a degradation of a poetical Aryan idea, and the cow,—originally used as a symbol of the clouds attendant on the Sun-God,—may have succeeded by a process of materialisation to honours for which she was not intended, but she is now firmly enthroned in the Hindu pantheon. There is, indeed, a strong tendency among modern Hindus of the reforming order to re-affirm her sanctity as a national shibboleth, and to denounce cow-killing in the strongest terms. The beef-fed Briton who wishes to sympathise with the Hindu does not quite like to be thrust aside as one of the impure (*Malecclia*),—learning with some uneasiness that millions of most estimable people would sooner die than touch the roast-beef of Old England. The damning mark set against the English admits of but faint extenuation. They have done justice and loved mercy, they have protected the lowly and weak, saved the widow from the fire, fed the famine-stricken, taught the ignorant, and made that a nation which was not a nation;—but they kill and eat the cow, and are therefore, in a levitical sense, abominable. The Muhammadan, however, is accounted worse, for he is of the people and among them; his creed is in opposition to theirs, and there are rankling memories of a thousand insults to it wrought on the sacred cow.

The Briton is an outland stranger from beyond the seven seas, he lives apart and knows no better; the Moslem eats beef in pure spite! This is manifestly unjust, but who can reason with a prejudice sanctioned by centuries of usage and tradition? At this moment cow-killing is the dangerous question of the country, always apt to provoke tumult and bloodshed. I have heard the agitation for total abstinence from intoxicating drink in the West mentioned as a parallel to the anti-cow-killing movement in India, but, though touched with a similar unreasonableness, teetotallers have hitherto refrained from breaking the heads of moderate drinkers.

But while surmising that the cow may have come to a place of honour from early and poetical association with myths of sun and cloud, it is possible to regard her dignity from a merely human and reasonable standpoint. Menu or other early law-givers may have proclaimed her sanctity as a means for her protection and preservation among a people careless of the future and prone to live on their capital. And with the same wise intention, the setting free as consecrated gifts of cattle sires (to be noticed hereafter), may have been ordained. At all events, these ordinances, in the absence of any scientific knowledge of breeding, have availed to preserve the cow. Nor is it unlikely that they rescued her from extinction, for it is clear that beef was a popular food when some of the ancient Vedas were written. It would not be hard to show that the same Aryan appreciation of roast beef has served in the West to develop and improve cattle breeding, but you will not easily persuade the modern Hindu of this fact. The establishment of an aristocracy of Brahmans was another stroke of practical wisdom; but the days when a class can be maintained aloft by formal prescription merely, seem to be passing away all the world over.

It is not easy to select instances that shall make clear to foreign readers the Hindu reverence for the cow and the place that her protection from death holds as a sacramental ordinance. In Indian history the slaughter of cows by impious and impure persons has often been the beginning of battle, murder, and sudden death. The chronicles of every State are full of retaliations for cow-murder, and in every local riot Hindu vengeance is first wreaked on the Muhammadan beef-butcher. Respect for the cow and loathing for the pig are the alpha and omega of the faith of thousands of Hindus and Moslems of the lower orders. In purely Hindu States and in Kashmir, where a Muhammadan population is ruled by a few Hindus, the punishment officially awarded for killing a cow is death, and there are cases on record where whole families have suffered death on suspicion of the offence. The fat of the cow was said to be used in making a newly-introduced cartridge, and so became an excuse for the Sepoy mutiny. The cry most frequently raised by the Sikhs against the English in the days before the annexation of the Punjab was that they defiled the country by the slaughter of kine. And it was probably this cry that most availed to raise the armies of the

Punjab against us, for the Sikhs, like other reformed Hindus, have jealously preserved the cow as an object of reverence. One of the customary phrases used when pleading for mercy from a creditor or a person in power is, "You are a Brahman, I am a cow." That is to say, extend to me the same kind treatment that a cow receives.

In ordinary domestic life a Hindu who has accidentally killed a cow voluntarily undergoes a painful penance. He is at once put out of caste and must repair to the Ganges, no matter how long and toilsome the journey may be. He must carry the cow's tail aloft at the end of a long staff, crying aloud when approached so that all may avoid him as pollution incarnate. He may not enter a village, but food is brought out to him when he halts on his march. Arrived at the sacred river, he must pay fees, which he can frequently but ill afford, to Brahmans for purifying rites, and he must eat and drink the five sacrificial products of the cow, which are not milk and butter merely, and do not include beef.

But it is no crime to allow a barren and useless cow to die, nor is it wrong to starve a male calf to death. And cow-murder, in spite of all ordinances, is one of the commonest offences of rustic life. The leather-dressers are a low caste of Hindus whose business is to skin the bodies of dead animals, which skins are their rightful perquisite. Leather is yearly increasing in value, and this low caste seems likely to rise. One speaks of low-caste people in deference to common usage, but Western readers will, I trust, be slow to believe that whole races of mankind are to be condemned to perpetual degradation because of their trade, or the official position it occupied in the once admirable Indian scheme. Among these so-called low castes there is often a complete organisation, a priesthood and in some sort an aristocracy; and their caste disputes are just as intricate and jealous of points of honour as those of the "twice born" folk. Nor is there any need to disguise the fact that the gift of freedom bestowed for the first time on India by the British Government includes the gradual alleviation of the disabilities of low degree, under which so many of the people have lain for ages. The change is coming about without shock to the general system, and is one of the inevitable results of education and life under free institutions. Some of the best artists and craftsmen in India are of low caste, and there are those who resent their rise in life, but it is coming as surely as to-morrow's dawn.

The leather-dressers, then, who take the skins of animals which divide the hoof, consider themselves superior to those who skin horses and camels. They are a most useful and laborious class; and, with education, will make valuable citizens in time, but they have been known to hasten Nature's course by poisoning the cattle of the villagers among whom they live. With curious casuistry they persuaded themselves that it was not cow-murder to insert a skilfully poisoned thorn under the skin of an animal to cause a lingering death, nor to drop poisoned food within its reach, for they also were Hindus and could not kill a cow outright. These are not exceptional practices, for in one prison at one time fifteen hundred leather-dressers have been confined for cattle poisoning. Hindu villagers have been known to make "transactions" with their dangerous neighbours. When the cattle were mysteriously dying (though the cause was no mystery), they summoned a council and asked the leather-dressers for their opinion on the mortality. The leather-dressers gravely replied that the village godlings, especially those of their own peculiar caste, had been neglected, and that it would be well to propitiate them. So a feast was made to the leather-dressers, and their godlings were propitiated by offerings; both sides going through an elaborate semi-religious farce with perfect gravity. Then the deaths would cease for a time. There is a class of English medical officers known as Chemical Examiners to Government, whose researches have largely contributed to the detection and conviction of the cattle poisoners who for centuries have taken a heavy toll on the beast life of the land. Many of the tricks they have exposed must have been well known to the people, but even those who had suffered most were reluctant to tell all they knew. A curious sign of the changing time is the fact that Hindus of good caste, seeing the profit that may be made from leather, are quietly creeping into a business from which they are levitically barred. Money prevails against caste more potently than missionary preaching.

The elaborate damnations ordained by Brahmanical authority for cow-killing will appear monstrous to a future generation of Hindus. Europeans smile no less at their assumption of knowledge of the future than at their grotesque accumulation of horrors and their amazing arrogance, but they are still real and awful to the uneducated Hindu, in spite of his ingrained distrust of Brahmans. One of the characteristic contrasts of native life is the contempt expressed in popular sayings for priestly authority, and the actual respect it receives. Cows are to be given to Brahmans, but they say: "When the cow goes dry or barren she is good enough for the Brahman," or "a one-eyed cow is a Brahman's gift." A black cow is thought to be the most acceptable, but the Brahman of to-day cannot afford to be particular. Of the idle wandering jogi, on the other hand, it is said "even the care of a cow is a bother to him."

The bull receives high honours as the vâhan or steed of Shiva, and as such is known as *Nandi*, the happy one. This name belongs also to the carven stone bull which sits in state before the temples of Mahadeo or Siva, while the small brazen bull forming part of an arrangement for the lustration of a domestic Shiv or phallic emblem is known as *Nandigan*. Hindu devotees who lead about bulls marked with Sivite emblems and supposed to be consecrated to Mahadeo are called Anandis. In ordinary life the respect for the bull finds quaint expression at times. A friend of mine was the owner of a fine sire of a choice breed, which he sent to fairs and cattle shows, where frequently some devout old woman would hang a garland of marigolds round its neck and go through the familiar actions of worship.

The ancient Hindu practice of releasing a bull has been referred to. This is still done on recovery from sickness, or as a propitiation, and is called a *pŭn* or dedicatory offering. The orthodox practice is to present at the same time a heifer to the chief or Maha-Brahman. But it is said that this part of the ceremony is frequently omitted, so that year by year the Brahman's dues fall off. *Pŭn* bulls have been useful as sires, but as the population increases and grazing areas contract, they are a doubtful blessing. In our Law Courts the question has been tried whether an animal set free to stray at will is an article of property. At first sight there would seem to be no great harm in yoking the beast to cart or plough. But while Hindus acknowledge that such bulls may be a public nuisance and rather approve than otherwise of an English District Officer who is reported to have harnessed the dust-carts of a large municipality with semi-sacred strays, it is quite another matter when a Muhammadan or a man of low caste seizes a *pŭn* bull. The decisions of the courts were contradictory. In one it was affirmed that the beast belonged to nobody, and might be appropriated to use, and in another that he was already property and not to be interfered with. Nor is it only as a bone of contention that cattle enter Law Courts, for a very binding form of oath is sworn by pouring Ganges water on a cow's tail.

One of the most popular of the pictures sold at fairs is a composition known as *Dharmrāj*, a name of *Yāma*, the Hindu Pluto, and also used broadly for Justice. The Judge is enthroned and demon executioners bring the dead to receive their doom. The river of death flows on one side of the picture and those go safely across who hold a cow by the tail, while others are torn by terrible fishes. Chitrgupt, the clerk or recording angel of Yāma, considered to be the ancestor of the *Kayasth* or clerkly caste, sits in an office with account books exactly like those of a Hindu tradesman, and according to the record of each soul, punishments or rewards are given. For, as a popular native saying has it,—"God looks out of the window of heaven and keeps account." *Duts* or executioners torture offenders, while the blest sail upwards in air-borne chariots.

The comparatively modern God Krishna is at the bottom of the popular liking for cows. Here it may be again observed that the official mythology of the books known to Europeans gives but a faint idea of the actual estimates of the Hindu Gods in the minds of the people. Krishna is a divinity, but he is much more. He is a man with a history, which is embroidered upon with all that is most congenial to the Hindu

KRISHNA ADORED BY THE GOPIS (FROM AN INDIAN PICTURE)

imagination. The pranks of his youth, when he teased and bewitched the Gopis or celestial milkwomen, stole their butter, entangled them in delirious dances, hid their clothes when they bathed in the river, and the like, are told in stories, acted in plays, and sung everywhere. A small brass figure of the baby Krishna crawling on hands and knees with an uplifted hand holding a pat of butter is known as the "butter-thief," and is to be found in most Hindu houses. Every Hindu mother,—and no mothers are more tender and affectionate,—sees a beautiful and half divine Krishna in her baby boy and worships him with a devotion unbroken by the variety of interests, amusements, and occupations which distract the mind of her Western sister.

It must be confessed that to a fresh occidental mind there is nothing so tiresome as a book of Hindu mythology. So it is unfortunate that books like the *Prem Sāgur* and other mythological stories are given as Hindi lesson books to subalterns and others who wish to pass examinations in the vernacular. An undiluted course of the classic mythology of Europe, shorn of all the allusions, historical elucidations, and modern interpretations which give it life would probably be almost as unattractive. The British schoolboy has harboured some hard thoughts about Apollo and Jupiter, but they are nothing to the distaste which many Anglo-Indians conceive for Krishna and the rest, who appear as merely monstrous creations of a disordered and sensuous fantasy. Seen on the nearer horizon of native life, Krishna is one of the most human of the manifold forms set up by mankind for adoration; being a typical young Hindu, full of the popular conception of life, love, and beauty. It could not well be otherwise, for the God you make must be in some sort the man you are or would like to be.

He leans against a tree, attended by cows, playing the pipe that charmed the frolicsome wives of the cowherds, and drives the cattle home to the gate of Bindraban in a thousand pictures exactly as to-day, save that he now wears a turban instead of a crown. And, as in the pictures, he wields a staff. Sanctity confers no immunity from the stick. One of the first duties a country child learns is to drive and beat cattle. They are docile enough and need no beating, but, from infancy, children are encouraged to shoulder as heavy a stick as they can carry and to use it unmercifully. The zeal of a child in rendering service is usually one of the most

KRISHNA DRIVES THE CATTLE HOME (FROM AN INDIAN PICTURE)

beautiful things in life, but, though the father applauds, it is an ugly sight to see a tiny boy belabouring a cow or ox with all his little strength, while lisping gross terms of abuse learnt from his parents. That he may not be able to inflict much pain is no extenuation of a practice which has hardened the people in a stupid abuse of the stick.

But while it is lawful for a Hindu to take a stick to his cow, it is in the highest degree improper for him to kick it. One of the curses invoked in the Rāmāyana on those who approve of the exile of Rāma is,—"may he touch a cow with his feet!"—and so incur the deepest Brahmanical damnation. To stumble over a sleeping cow is still held unlucky, but not, as formerly, a deadly sin. There is no prohibition against kicking an ox.

The beauty of the cow counts almost as much as her usefulness in popular estimation, and the best breeds are really handsome. It is true that a British amateur, accustomed to the level back of the English beast, at first looks unfavourably on the hump and the falling hind-quarter. The head seems too large and the body too short. But he acknowledges at once the clean, thoroughbred legs, the fine expression of the eye, the air of breeding in the broad convex brow and slender muzzle, the character given by the deep thin dewlap, the smooth mole-like skin, and in the large breeds an undefinable majesty of mien. In addition to their high caste and shapely look, the hind legs are much straighter and less "cow-hocked" than those of the English animal, and are not swung so far out in trotting. On occasion the animal can jump a fence with a carriage of the limbs like that of the horse. So in a very short time the Briton drops his prejudices and is even reconciled to the hump, which, like that of the camel and the fat tail of the *dūmba* sheep, has some mysterious relation to the varying conditions of a precarious food supply. They say vaguely it is a reserve of sustenance, but it would take a physiologist to explain how it acts. Some insist that the sloping quarter is the result of ages of scanty or irregular feeding, but it is now, at all events, a fixed anatomical peculiarity. Indian cattle breed freely with

European stock, but it is not yet settled whether improvement in milking power, which is all it seems worth while to cross for, is really promoted by a strain of European blood. Experiments of this kind have been tried in the hills, where the tiny mountain cattle are absurdly poor milkers. The small Styrian or some of the Swiss or Scandinavian breeds would probably be best suited for this purpose. Some fine English beasts have been imported into the burning plains, where falling into the hands of natives of position, they have been promptly killed by over-feeding, heat, and want of exercise. Moreover the English beast, bred for beef, is only shapely from a butcher's point of view. The British butcher and farmer are more pedantic than Greek grammarians, but happily their lore and standards of beauty are inapplicable to India.

It is with the cattle as with the people of India, the more you learn about them the more you find to interest you. But in regard to the cow and the ox one's admiration is unstinted, nor need it be qualified by hesitation and reserve. To the stranger the great variety of breeds and their adaptation to a wide range of needs and conditions are not at first apparent. He sees an ox and another ox as he sees a native and another native, without noticing that they belong to distinct families. Orientals have a passion for classifying things, and see scores of differences in rice, cotton, wheat, cattle, and horses, which are barely perceptible even to trained English eyes. But among cattle, though there is a bewildering variety of local breeds, some broad differences may be easily learned. The backward slope of the horns of the large and small breeds of Mysore cattle, —perhaps the most popular type in use,—the royal bearing of the splendid white or fawn oxen of Guzerat, and the transport and artillery cattle bred in the Government farms at once strike the eye. These are the aristocrats of the race, but they have appetites proportioned to their size and are too costly for the ordinary cultivator. They trot in bullock coaches or draw the springless and uncomfortable but delightfully picturesque native

PUNJAB BAILI (SPRINGLESS OX-CART)

răth or canopied ox-cart, the wagons of the Government commissariat and of the various Government baggage services. On the wide alluvial plains, where the people are thickly planted, a small, slender, and colourless cow seems to be the usual poor man's animal. The well-to-do keep breeds with foreign names and of stouter build. On the great basin of volcanic trap or basalt, which includes much of Western India, the cattle are more square in shape, large in bone, and varied in colour.

The richer pastures and cold winters of Kashmir and the hill country near develop a sturdy, square-headed, short-legged race with a coarse coat like that of the English cow. In the Himálaya, where the grass is deficient in nourishing power, there are breeds of tiny, neatly formed animals with coats that look like black or brown cotton velvet. These pasture on the mountain-side, climbing almost as cleverly as goats, and their grazing paths, trodden for centuries, have covered leagues

COMPARATIVE SIZES OF THE LARGEST AND SMALLEST BREEDS OF INDIAN OXEN

of steep slope with a scale-work pattern of wonderful regularity when seen from far. Cattle are sent to the uplands to graze in the hot weather and some good sorts are systematically bred in the inter-India hills, but the beast at its best is a true Hindu of the hot plains. The "green country" in the Punjab, the Kistna river in the south, and those gardens of India, Oudh and Guzerat, produce the finest breeds.

I have sketched a diagram which shows roughly the range of size. Still larger beasts than the largest shown occur at times. The smallest represents a miniature race, not much bigger than Newfoundland dogs, but exquisitely finished in every detail of ox form and full of life and spirit. When harnessed to vehicles of a suitable size these tiny creatures trot at a great pace. All Indian oxen can be trained to trot. The sloping quarter and straight hock may possibly count for something in their more horse-like gait. Between these two

THE BOMBAY REKLA

extremes are breeds of every possible size, adapted for many uses. An old Anglo-Indian can scarcely be trusted to recall the freshness of first impressions; but that one of the first things to strike a stranger is the hurrying ox was proved by a distinguished English tourist, who told me of the interest and amusement he found in the traffic of Bombay streets, especially in the *rekla*, a small hack carriage here sketched. The neatness of this vehicle, its sensible canopy to protect the backs of the cattle from the sun, its low fares, its speed, and the continual cry of the driver, impressed my friend so much that he was inclined to describe it as the Hindu hansom. So it is,—in usage; but it is really of Portuguese descent, for the Hindu, left to himself, never dreamed of springs. Nor is it the only good thing that Western India owes to the Portuguese.

The points of cows and oxen, their varieties of horn, breed, shape, and character are expressed in a multitude of sayings whose darkness and esoteric quality seem at times to justify the son of Sirach in asking—how can they be wise whose talk is of oxen? Many of the canons in use are the unimpeachable result of ages of observation and experience, but others seem to be merely fantastic nonsense referring to trivial accidents of hair, horn, or colour. A jumbling of sternest use and wildest fancy is one of the most bewildering of Oriental traits. The cultivator, who, by the necessities of his life, is sordidly practical, will at one and the same moment deliver himself of a grim sweat-and-blood axiom, born of penury and edged with despair, and some blind blundering ineptitude which, though sanctioned by immemorial usage, could be disproved by five minutes' observation of fact. And the language in which these sayings are shaped is strangely and sometimes almost unintelligibly elliptical and idiomatic. They have been turned over in so many mouths that only the bare bones of meaning are left, and are so perplexed by broad, local dialects that an accustomed ear is needed for their comprehension.

There is no shorter cut to the goodwill of the cultivator than an instructed interest in cattle. In the West, too, strangers will fraternise while handling an animal with judicious appreciation of its points. It should be remembered, however, that rustic cattle are not used to Europeans and dislike their odour,—or lack of odour. A saying runs, "Keep seven cubits distance from an elephant, five from a horned beast, twenty from a woman, and thirty from a drunken man," —and, in so far as concerns the beast, the advice is doubly applicable to European amateurs. To be fair, the Indian animal is naturally inoffensive, and always gives warning of irritation by a peculiar hissing snort. I once afforded some amusement to a group of friends by disregarding this sound. We were on a walking trip at the foot of the Western Ghauts, and inquired the way up the Bhau Mullen hill from a boy in charge of a string of empty pack oxen. While talking to him I noticed he was in difficulties with his leading beast, a little black bull with villainously sharp horns, who hissed like a wild cat and presently broke away and came at me with head down. I presented my open white umbrella and dodged aside, but the creature still came on, so I jumped one of the high-banked dykes of the dry rice-fields among which we were walking, but he came over too, jumping as smartly and cleverly as an English hunter; so I took another "lep" and another, while he followed with tail brandished aloft, warming to the chase with each presentation of the umbrella and each dodging turn and leap. At last he became entangled with his empty packs, and his driver secured him, while I breathlessly rejoined my friends, who were doubled up in helpless laughter, vowing that neither circus nor bull-fight was ever half so entertaining. Not being a spectator, I missed the cream of the joke.

With natives both cows and oxen are usually placid enough, and very few cases of goring are reported. Calves are handled freely, the mother scarcely noticing it, except when the intruder is a stranger. But the right of the cow to resent interference with her calf is recognised in popular talk. This indeed is the case in England, among all sensible farmers. I heard of one, the other day, whose son, handling a calf, was severely horned by the mother. A lady calling on the farmer sympathised with his son's misfortune and used very strong expressions as to the abominable behaviour of the cow. The farmer listened and at last said in a judicial tone: "Why, no, marm ;—the cow were in her dooty, for we must all purtect our yong." There is a touch of the Roman father as well as of the natural philosopher in this wise saying, for though the son was sore in bed and the parent was sorry for him, he knew that those who are skilful in cow management seldom suffer from their horns.

Cattle are made to take part in curious rites, and enjoy many holidays of a semi-religious kind, when they are adorned with necklaces of marigolds and jessamine, and printed on flank and shoulder with an open hand dipped in red, so that a modern Moses might be moved to wrath by something very like cow-worship. Nor is this to be wondered at when the value of milk, which takes a high and most important place in the Indian food scale is considered. "Cows' milk is as Mothers' milk" say the women. "Milk and children are from fortune" is another of their sayings. "May you bathe in milk and rear many children" is a benediction among women,[1] and in pure pride a swaggerer will say, "I have drunk more milk than you will ever get of water"—in other words, I have always been well off, while you are a scrub. When a cow is milked into the hollow of the

[1] Mr. B. Malabari mentions having heard this benediction pronounced in Durbar over the present Gaekwar of Baroda.

hand, the milk, drunk at once, is supposed to be peculiarly nourishing in quality. "One can stand a kick from one's cow when she is in milk" has possibilities of application beyond mere cows. Of a hungry country it is said, "One doesn't even get sparrow's milk there." A Bengal saying recalling the French "When the cork is drawn, the wine must be drunk" is, "Milk once drawn from the dug never goes back." A relic of the Vedic times lingers in the name *Kamdhain* applied

COW AND CALF

to cows that are exceptionally good milkers. *Kamdhenu* was the wondrously productive cow of Indra that granted all desires.

There is propriety and sense in the sort of reverence that the poor of most countries pay to God's gifts of food. Milk has a large share of this wholesome elemental respect in India. "When a cow or buffalo is first bought," writes Mr. Denzil Ibbetson, "or when she first gives milk after calving, the first five streams are allowed to fall on the ground in honour of the Earth-mother, or goddess,"—a widely worshipped deity,—" and at every time of milking the first stream is so treated." The last is a custom, however, as much honoured in the breach as in the observance. Hindus of the old school complain of the decay under our educational system of pious household ritual and beliefs. Among these is a rustic observance of bread breaking. The first piece is for the cow, the second for the dog, and the third for the crow. The cow's piece must not be bitten or mangled, but the dog and the crow are expected to take what they can get with gratitude. Regret for the old order as it changes is natural enough, but with the harmless and the good some evil is also passing away; for God fulfils himself in many ways.

Ghi, which is butter boiled to make it keep, is no less esteemed than milk, and stands figuratively as it serves in fact, for richness and well-being. Where we should say that a man lives in clover, they say, "He has five fingers in the ghi." Usually by frugal people one or two fingers only are put into the pot. Another saying is: "A straight finger extracts no ghi," *i.e.* one must go judiciously (or crookedly) to work in order to get anything worth having. A precarious livelihood is expressed by, "Sometimes a handful of ghi and sometimes a mouthful of lentils." The French gibe at England, —"a hundred religions and only one sauce,"—(melted butter) may be warrantable, but it is mere everyday fact in India, where the food would be but sorry and innutritious fare without the mercy of ghi. The prosperity of a man is often gauged by his indulgence in ghi, which has an infallible effect on the figure. Vegetarian Hindus have a natural tendency to eat too much, and a gaunt cultivator will point to a fat and prosperous tradesman as a ghi-fed bullock. It will be observed that the hand is always spoken of, and in fact the hand is always used. A Sikh peasant making you welcome, will bring a bowl of milk, strongly impregnated with the wood smoke with which milk vessels are purified, and, after he has put in some sugar, will stir it with his fingers in the most friendly way. One of the many compromises with the ordinances of caste, that make things pure or impure, is their relaxation with reference to sweetmeats compounded of sugar and ghi, an important part of the food of the people. The confectioner is a man of no very exalted caste, but all may eat from his hand. He abuses this privilege of reputed purity, and is in fact more dirty in his person and more thoroughly saturated with the grease he handles than there is any occasion for. One agent in the vast battery of elements that produces the characteristic Indian odour of Indian cities and crowds is the use of ghi as hair oil and as a lubricant for the skin after bathing. In the south oil is much used for these purposes, but in most regions ghi is popular, nor is it unwholesome except to the alien nose.

Wealth may be no longer expressed in terms of the cow, but the possession of cows is accepted as a sign of being well-to-do. So the freedom from care which is one of the alleviations of poverty, is stated in, "He sleeps well who has neither cow nor calf." Where we should say "The early bird catches the worm," the Indian rustic says "Who sleeps late gets the bull-calf, he who rises early the cow-calf,"—which is more valuable. The saying indicates the division of property among members of a family living together. An early rising brother or cousin could change his bull for the cow-calf of his lazy relative who ought to have been on the spot to look after it, or a knavish neighbour might surreptitiously swap the new births.

Bewitched cattle are not peculiar to benighted India, but may be heard of even in Britain of the Board school. There is a more profound conviction in Eastern superstitions, further intensified by the ever-present notion that once the beast was man. A current story tells how a poor man borrowed a sum of money far beyond his power to repay. Lying anxiously awake at night among his oxen, he heard one say that the master would surely serve the money-lender as an ox in the future life. So he rose and questioned that wise bullock, who said: "Return the money to the usurer, and, since you are in need, take me to the king and back me for that sum to fight his champion elephant." This was done; the amazed king accepted the wager of his fighting elephant against a lean ox, and the beasts were paraded in the arena. The elephant ignominiously fled from the bullock, who snorted and pawed the ground in meagre majesty. So the king paid the wager and the elephant confessed that in a previous existence he had borrowed a large sum and still owed it to the man who was now that starveling bullock. Our English notions on this subject are mainly those of Mrs. Barbauld's tiny but charming classic, *The transmigrations of Indur*, but to the native mind the wandering soul has a more complex and disquieting fate than is there indicated. The old birth stories of Buddhism, also, are milder and less stern in retributive vengeance than many notions actually current. Dire strokes of bereavement or misfortune, and grievous diseases, such as leprosy, inflict a keener anguish, a more hopeless sorrow, when regarded as punishments for sin committed in some past life.

These ideas are not distinctively Hindu in their main issue, which is the vulgar demon belief that sends the souls of those who have died by violence or in childbirth, or who in life showed strong character, to plague or protect the living. In Tibet, under the name of Buddha, there now seems to be no other religion; American Indians know it as well as the Indo-Chinese, and though educated Hindus hint that it is a degradation of Hinduism, it seems to have preceded Hinduism and to have flourished alongside it. At the present moment demonolatry is the real, everyday faith of thousands who profess either Hinduism or Muhammadanism for an official, Sunday creed. Snake demons, animated by the souls of "kenned folk" deceased, are supposed to be charged with the protection of cattle and are regularly worshipped. A cultivator's wife, seeing a snake, will say in effect "O dear! I have forgotten his dues," and will make offerings of milk and curds with quaint formalities. Yet all the eldritch mischiefs attributed to fays and goblins in our old English literature are wrought on cattle by witch and wizard. The evil eye is potent to cripple and kill, nor are Muhammadans a whit more free from fear than Hindus. So you may see an old shoe,—emblem of humiliation,—hung like an amulet round the neck of a Muhammadan's buffalo, or a black thread round that of his cow. Hindus tie amulets and charms round the necks of their cows, or secretly, with invocations, twist strands of human hair round the roots of the horns or on the fetlock and with spells and charms innumerable try to ward off evil. But though devoutly believed in, the people are not readily communicative about these things. Half their force lies in their secrecy. The charm would no longer act if it were blabbed about. So it were presumption to speak too confidently of the details of this phase of Oriental thought, which, like water as described by modern physical science, flows in hidden and undivulged courses as well as in the sun-lighted rivers of the surface. It is also unwise to angrily denounce these notions as some clever and positive young Britons are prone to do. For, after all, they were current but yesterday, and indeed are still alive, among very excellent people in these islands.

When cattle are sick or disabled they are doctored and treated with great, but unintentional barbarity. A European should hesitate before condemning a native practice for its unlikeness to anything within his knowledge, for it has the experience of centuries for a warrant. Yet, while admitting the Indian discovery and use of many valuable medicines, it is not too much to say broadly that native notions on sanitation and the treatment of disease in men and animals amount in practice to a conspiracy against the public health. The cruelty they involve is only an incident. When spells and charms have failed, the branding iron and knife are freely used. Sometimes you see a broad line burnt and cut right round the body of an old ox as a Plimsoll load line is drawn round the hull of a ship, while each deeply sunken eye has a cruel circle seared round its orbit. Curious patterns of gridirons, Solomon stars, and mystic marks of Siva are scored deeply over strained shoulders and muscles whose only disease is the stiffness of age or the weakness of imperfect feeding. Great importance is attached to the form of the brand, which is often a signature of a God. A flower pattern is good for one disease, a palm for another. The ears are sometimes slit as a remedy for colic. Then there is a grotesque nastiness of invention in the medicinal messes the poor beasts are made to swallow, and a perverse ingenuity in running counter to the plain course of nature. I remember being told that our cow which had recently calved was suddenly taken sick and like to die. The cowman had decided that she was suffering from an unusual form of deadly fever. So in the fierce hot weather he had shut her up in a close byre, stuffed the window with rags and straw, carefully closed the door, and happed her in thick clothing. She was very like to die indeed, but recovered promptly on being rescued from heat and suffocation. An amazing ignorance of elementary facts is often shown. A case recently occurred in which a cultivator, familiar with cattle, called in a countryside quack to his sick cow. The practitioner opened the animal's mouth and, drawing forth the tongue, showed the rough papillæ at its root. "This is what is the matter with her,—these rough things must be cut off." And the poor creature's tongue was actually shaved! It would be easy to fill many pages with similar horrors, but I would rather be read than cast aside in disgust, and gladly turn to such hopeful signs as may be discerned.

The veterinary schools and colleges with animal infirmaries attached, established by Government in the great cities, are doing something towards the spread of sounder notions. Improvement must be slow, but it is well on its way. The West can offer no more precious gift to the East than a knowledge of the nature and treatment of disease in men and animals. Yet hope were not, if not dashed by doubt, and no one who knows India can afford to be over-confident. For the worst enemies of medical science are not there, as in Europe, the enthusiast and the quack who pin their loud faith on one imperfectly apprehended idea or one nostrum, but the apathy of the people and their rooted habit of negligence.

It is natural that many things should be likened to

so necessary and sacred a creature as the cow, but some of the similes appear far-fetched to the Western mind. Thus a house with a narrow frontage and wide behind, —an auspicious arrangement,—is spoken of as cow-mouthed. In the Hindu ear the mere word is grateful, for the Ganges itself is said to issue from a "cow's mouth" up in the hills, and there are many sacred wells and stream-pools known as cows' mouths. An upper window is a cow's eye, like the French *œil de bœuf*, an oval loaf of bread like one of the forms of Vienna bread in London shops, is known as ox-eye, and things which taper are "cow-tail fashion." One of the words in use for evening means, when hunted down, "cows' dust," and indicates the return of the cattle to the village. Cow-like means docile and meek, "girls and cows are easily disposed of," says an over-confident proverb which Western mothers can scarcely adopt, and the varying tempers of cows find antitypes in women. "Muttra girls and Gokul cows won't stir if they can help it," says rustic Hindustan. Everywhere, a big stout woman is spoken of as "that buffalo," for all round the world there is a lumbering type of generally admirable womanhood to whom the word is exquisitely suited. One of the drawbacks of polite society is that the use of picturesque and truth-telling similes of this kind is discouraged. We all know excellent ladies who remind us of camels, devoted mothers who suggest cows, charming girls who are as fawns or gazelles, sharp grandames who are like hawks, eagles, or parrots, placid women who bleat timidly over wool-work, fussy, movement-promoting ladies who cluck like hens and throw up their eyes at meetings like fowls when they drink; just as we know men who are pigs, asses, foxes, goats, dogs, etc.—but we may not often say so. The Oriental rustic is under no such restraint, so pepper is added to the natural salt of his talk.

As to the actual treatment of the cow, although some strange and indescribable forms of cruelty are practised by milkmen in large towns with intent to increase the supply of milk, and the animals are often kept in a

AT SUNSET

Between the waving tufts of jungle grass,
Up from the river as the twilight falls,
Across the dust-beclouded plain they pass
On, to the village walls.

Great is the sword and mighty is the pen,
But greater far the labouring ploughman's blade,
For on its oxen and its husbandmen
An Empire's strength is laid.

filthy state; the beast fares on the whole as well as the means of her owners will allow. When, as often happens, a poor family owns one cow, it takes a high place in all the concerns of the household, and is even more cherished than the Irish cottager's pig. The cow-calf too is often petted and made much of. "Six handfuls to the cow-calf and one to the poor labouring ox" is a Kashmiri cry against injustice quoted in the collection of the Rev. J. H. Knowles. But male calves have a hard life and suffer terribly from imperfect nutrition. It is a deed of some temerity to find fault with practices based on centuries of usage and experience, but the treatment of the labourers of the land is a custom of cruelty. Indian cows, owing to the slack-handed management congenial to the people, are difficult milkers, and need at their flank a living calf or a straw-stuffed calf-skin (the latter is not unknown in Europe) before they will let down their milk. The living calf is preferred, and Tantalus himself was not more tormented by baffled longing than are these poor wretches, hungrily watching the stream they may not taste. It is not always profitable to rear a male calf, so the practice, in spite of a theory which allots him a fair share, seems to be to three-quarters starve him on the chance of his surviving to be weaned. Then, in due course, he becomes an ox—the chief pillar of the Indian Empire.

And in no merely rhetorical sense, for the stress of agriculture, the more urgent strain of trade, and the movement of a vast and restless people, are on his strong shoulders. The cultivator is the backbone of the country, and depends on the ox for working the land, while the bullock cart in a great variety of forms is the main factor in Indian traffic. Hence, one of the most pleasant and vivid sensations of the returned Anglo-Indian is the sight of the superb draught horses of Britain, perhaps the most striking impersonations of the dignity of labour that the world can show. Necessity is a hard task-master for the man, but it is on his beast that the worst strokes fall. Loads have to be carried, and even if the carter were so minded, he cannot always contrive that they shall be proportioned to the strength of his animals. A load that travels easily over the hard roads of a town becomes impossible along the deep-mired village tracks. And when the overloaded wain is stuck fast there is dire trouble for the cattle. Even a father chastising his child sometimes forgets how hard he is striking, but in their excitement carters never think of the live sentient animal under their blows. The cattle are but a machine whose motor is the stick. Then, a poor man cannot afford to lay his animals up in idleness when their necks are galled or they go lame. They wince from the yoke at first, but seem to forget it as they grow warm. So does the carter, who is a marvel of apathy and indifference, especially since he is often a hireling. Weak and tired oxen can be made to work better with a free use of whip, stick, or goad, and in judicious and merciful hands such incentives are useful. But there is no precept to protect the ox from abuse of them, save perhaps that enunciated by a Bombay Police Magistrate in deciding a case of cruelty. "There are," said this authority, "fair goads and there are severe goads. The only question is whether in this particular case the goad is a fair one or not." The weapon in court was a sharpened nail three-quarters of an inch long at the end of a stick. "In my opinion," the Magistrate went on, "this is longer and sharper than it ought to have been. A goad of half its length would have done quite as well." So the accused was warned and discharged. But the real question before the Magistrate was whether the carter had used his goad too freely. For needless pain can be inflicted with even three-eighths of an inch of sharpened iron at the end of a heavy male bamboo, if used often enough, and it is certainly sufficient to drive into any of God's creatures. Carters who know their business thoroughly, and are to be trusted with whips and goads three-eighths of an inch long, are everywhere scarce, and most of all in India. But the whip and the goad are not the only means of stimulation at the carter's disposal. He sits low so that he can kick freely, and he kicks hard. And when other means fail he seizes the tails of his team and twists them so that the last four or five vertebræ grind on each other. Immense numbers of Indian oxen, probably the greater part, have their tails permanently dislocated by this practice, and bob-tailed bullocks are often seen who have entirely lost the lower joints of the member, including the necessary fly-whisk with which it was originally furnished. Bullocks are probably less sensitive to pain than human creatures, but their pitiful efforts to keep their tails out of the way, and the prompt effect the brutal trick has upon their pace show that they also can feel.

"Tail-twisting" has found its way into Anglo-Indian slang. Officers of the Transport and Commissariat departments are spoken of as tail-twisters, and there are even members of Her Majesty's Civil Service who are said to need tail-twisting to keep them up to their work.

Yet, while one cannot but grieve for the ox, it is obvious to every fair mind that there must be something to say for the man. He is no more brutal of himself than the rest of mankind of his rank. Generally a thoughtless lout, insensible by habit, he is not always wilfully cruel. The truth is, the bullock, without good training, is not an easy beast to drive. Only by practical experiment can this truth be fully learned, and before wholly condemning the driver it is a wholesome experience to take his place for an hour. Well-trained cattle may be driven even by an amateur, but nine-tenths of Indian teams would scarcely pay him the compliment of stirring unless he resorted to tail-twisting and beating. The strength of the ox is magnificent, and he can plod along steadily with good driving, but he has none of the zeal which animates the horse.

PLOUGHING

The latter may be, as some say, a born fool, but when fairly taught to pull he gives his mind to it and, if of a good sort, goes up into his collar at half a word. The bullock, a cogitative ruminant, seems to be thinking of something else all the time, and has to be perpetually stirred out of his normal indifference. That the main need of the ox is more intelligent training and teaching is shown by the skill which some men attain in bullock steering. A click, a tock, and a hand laid persuasively on the rump is enough for these rare artists, who are as clever in their way as some London drivers. The average cartman has not sense, patience, or skill enough to train his team, and relies on the sudden pain of whiplash, twisted tail, or goad. But to put it plainly, in so far as the well-being of the animal is concerned, it is as bad to be a duffer as a brute. Very many Indian carters are both.

A cultivator, on the other hand, ploughing or harrowing, will often work his cattle for hours together without a blow. His hand will be frequently raised to the level of his brow as if in act to strike, and he is continually talking, coaxing, cursing, or expostulating in very broad language, but he is not very often cruel. He is apt to make pets of one or two of his animals and to cherish a spite against some poor beast, who serves as "whipping boy" for the faults of the rest and as an outlet for injurious language. Yet, though his cattle are his own, he habitually overloads the carts they draw, and in moments of excitement he hammers them unmercifully.

The close association of the ploughman with his cattle, the slow steady tramp at their heels over the field and over again in infinite turns, has given a bovine quality to the minds of those who follow the plough all round the world. Perhaps the Irish potato-digging cottier, the English market gardener, the French vine-dresser and spade cultivators generally, are smarter and more alert. The lagging, measured step may compel the mind to its cadence, and the anodyne of monotony may soothe and still the temper. However this may be, it is certain that the Indian cultivator is very like his ox. He is patient, and bears all that drought, flood, storm, and murrain can do with the same equanimity with which the ox bears blows. When the oxen chew the cud and their masters take their nooning, the jaws of man and beast move in exactly the same manner.

IN TIME OF DROUGHT

The succulent food of the West, rich and full of flavour, is eaten with a closed mouth, while appreciative lips, palate, and tongue relieve the teeth from hard labour. But the Indian peasant's dry thick cake of millet or wheaten meal must be steadily chewed, completely milled and masticated before it can be swallowed, and it is only when it is touched with ghi or dipped in stewed vegetables or pulse that the lips close on a morsel with any semblance of gourmandise. And, as the ox drinks once for all, so the peasant, when he has eaten, drinks; a long draught, poured straight into the depths of him, as one who fills a cistern. Like the peasant, too, the ox is indifferent and devoid of curiosity. The horse is always ready with an apprehensive ear; eager, for all his shallow wit, to know what is going on, but the ox keeps on never minding. So does the peasant. It is not easy to convey a due sense of the serene indifference of the cultivator (and of most Indians) to the mind of readers in England where there are hundreds of fussy societies for minding other people's business. The Oriental would be just as puzzled to understand the English craze for meddling, but he may one day undergo a rueful enlightenment. A current saying shows the queer turns this indifference takes. "The field wasn't yours, the cow wasn't yours,—why did you drive it away?" This is profoundly immoral, of course. A cow is loose in a field of green corn, a philanthropic person comes by and does justice, but the peasant, who also has a cornfield liable to straying cows, resents it and wants to know why the fussy person need interfere! That the trespasser was a cow and not a donkey has something to do with it, but there is more than respect for the cow in the saying.

In a large and historic sense the indifference of the Indian countryman to the wars of Kings and Powers over-head may seem less wonderful to those who have an intimate knowledge of the conduct of European peasantry during continental campaigns than to us who consider Indian history mainly. But while ploughing in one field he has scarcely raised his head to watch a battle in the next. So it has been seen when three great elephants, harnessed to 40-lb. guns of position, refused to risk their precious trunks within the zone of fire, that twenty yoke of oxen tugged the field-piece among the bursting shells and whizzing shot as

IN A GOOD SEASON

impassively as if they were going afield. There is more in this than mere stupidity. The Mogul, the Afghān, the Pindāri, the Briton, and the mutinous Sepoy, with others, have swept to and fro as the dust-storm sweeps the land, but the corn must be grown and the folk and cattle must be fed, and the cultivator waits with inflexible patience till the will of heaven be accomplished and he may turn again to the toil to which he is appointed. A toil, too, in which he feels as much pride as any other of the labouring sons of Adam can boast. This is finely put in a country saying of the Punjab Jat, a farmer who, take him for all in all, is perhaps the noblest Roman of them all, "The Jat stood on his heap of corn and cried to the King's elephant drivers—Will you sell those little donkeys?"

Oxen are careful of their rights and go in due order to the long manger trough of adobe. If one takes the wrong place he is promptly set right by a horn thrust. Here the cultivator surpasses his model, for he loves litigation and enjoys nothing so much as a quarrel.

Quarrels, by the way, between different families and within the family circle, in which the women take a noisy part, are often, I firmly believe, deliberately raised as a variety on the deadly monotony of life. In English low life the virago who stands with arms akimbo and harangues the alley,—"flytes" is the Scotch term,—often says she couldn't rest till she had given forth a piece of her mind, and is notably better after a row. Indian households prepare and conduct a quarrel with more artistic skill, use a more copious and pungent vocabulary, range over a wider field of vituperation, and are less liable to lapse into that personal violence which is the death of true art. Straying calves and goats serve the men as causes of war, and children inflame the women. "Why can't you let my child alone?" is no uncommon war-cry in the slums of Britain, and when emotion is a necessity of your nature, it serves well enough; for a fire may be fed with many things. The man's share when women go on the war-path in India, as elsewhere, is often to stand aside, see fair, and hold the baby. So he pretends to be shocked and in various phrase remarks "When a widow (or a light lady), a wife, or a bull buffalo lose their tempers, who knows what may happen!" The wide currency of this saying proves its aptness to a social situation.

He also says "a drum, a boor, a low-caste man, cattle, and women are all the better for a beating." Our half-forgotten saw of like brutality includes the woman with the dog and the walnut tree. A worse class of sayings refers to the sordid nature of Hindu marriages: "You buy a wife and you buy oxen;" "Wives and oxen are to be had for money," and so forth. It would be idle to pretend to make out a good case for this phase of native life and society. But without much special pleading or any affectation of philosophic breadth of view, it may fairly be said that both men and women are intrinsically better than their talk, their creeds, or their social arrangements would lead one to think. Notwithstanding the marriage abuses justly denounced by reformers, there are thousands of happy households, ruled, as domestic interiors should be, by women, who in spite of superstition and a life whose every duty is a sort of ordered ritual, are virtually as sensible, bright, and good as those of Europe, and very certainly as tender and affectionate. Like most women everywhere, they realise and express the pathos of their lot, but they would strongly resent being told by outsiders that they are downtrodden, unhappy, and degraded. The men, to whom home and family are sacred matters withdrawn from all possibility of intrusion, would resent it still more. This much is certain, that no "movement" or agitation will avail to stir them from their traditional groove. Like all the rest of the world, they are subject to change, but a change in their notions and practice where women are concerned must be the slow work of education. Reforms are supposed to be promoted in the West by associations that career through society as a troop of wild asses sweeps over the desert, but the movement is not yet foaled that shall stir the Hindu to a faster pace than he is minded to take.

In their silence Indian cattle offer an example which the cultivator does not follow. Students in our colleges read Gray's Ode, wherein the lowing herd winds slowly o'er the lea, and say to the Professor, "Sir, what is lowing?" Neither ox nor cow lows in India. Their grunting note is seldom heard and does not carry. An English cow fills the narrow green field spaces with her fine voice as easily as a singer fills a concert room, but the Indian herd, returning to the village, drifts across the wide gray plain silent as the dust-cloud that accompanies them. The herdsman is a vocalist. Not one European in a hundred can follow his song. It begins nowhere in particular and can be broken off short or continued indefinitely *ad lib.*; it is always in a minor key, and has falsetto subtleties in it that baffle our methods of notation. Written down, it seems to want form, but, to be fair, so do most rustic songs.

The talk is easier, for the peasant talks a good deal in a loud heavy voice. When his women folk walk with him, they follow respectfully an ordained number of paces behind, and he flings his conversation over his shoulder. A common gibe of Anglo-Indians is that the talk is always about two things,—money or food, and there is some truth in this. Sometimes women are the topic, but then the speech is not so loud, shoulder inclines to shoulder, and heads roll with chuckling laughter. In the talk of very poor people there is a curious habit of endless repetitions. A company of old women will get through three miles in a discussion whether two or three annas were demanded by the dealer and whether one and a half anna was too much to pay. This, indeed, is rather too coherent and dramatic an example of a talk topic. I have often followed such

THE OILMAN'S OX

a group, wondering when the over-chewed cud would be swallowed down in silence.

In Europe we speak of a monotonous life of labour as a mill-horse round, although the mill-horse has been dead for many years. Even the horse threshing machine, which was so delightful to drive when I was a child, seems to be abolished in favour of one of the steam machines now "huzzin' an' maazin' the blessed feealds wi' the Divil's oan team." But in India a phrase of this kind is quick and lively. The oilman's ox stands as the accepted type of a weary toiler. They say in pity of a man or woman overburdened with labour or domestic cares, "An oilman's ox!" An over-worked servant asks ironically, "What business has an oilman's ox to stand still?" The beast lives at home, and seldom

THE PERSIAN WHEEL

goes abroad, but since he is condemned to a continuous pacing round the oil-mill they say: "The oilman's ox is always fifty miles from home." As an answer to casuistry and super-subtle argument, a popular phrase says, "My ox hasn't read logic," and comes from a conversation held between a learned Hindu logician and an oilman.

"Why," asks the philosopher, "do you hang a bell on your bullock's neck?"

"In order that I may hear that the mill is going."

"So, when the bell tinkles, the mill goes, eh?"

"Yes, of course."

"Then, if your ox stood still and shook his head up and down, making the bell ring, the mill would still be going?"

"Ah, sir," says the oilman, "my ox does not read logic."

The water lift used in the Punjab, known among Europeans as the Persian wheel (apparently because it is the ancient Egyptian Sakieh, and not a Persian invention at all), is also driven by blindfolded oxen walking in a circle, and I have heard the click of a tappet on the cogs spoken of as taking the place of the bell as a tell-tale. It is true this catch is called the *Kūtta* or dog by farmers, but its real function is that of a stop to prevent the wheel laden with water pots from slipping back when the cattle stop. Moreover, its tick-tack is the lightest note in the travail of the uneasy Persian wheel, which fills the air with a groaning, creaking, whining drone of complaint for a quarter of a mile round. The cessation of this sound arrests the ear as surely as the sudden stoppage of the engines of a steamship, so there is no need for the bark of the little wooden dog. There are two or three centuries and thrice as many leagues between this primitive machine and the last triumphs of mechanism in the Western world, but you shall find a "dog stop" even in the latest American type-writer.

I remember, when a child, sitting in a corner of a blacksmith's smithy in a Yorkshire village watching horses being shod. One day, talking to his friends, the smith laid a hand on the horn of his bellows and cried, "Yance I shod a bull." He explained that the animal had to travel to fairs and shows and was liable to become footsore. Much I silently marvelled, after the fashion of children, how the feat was done, for the bull I knew most intimately was a fearsome beast, safe to stroke in his stall, but awful in croft or garth. Since then the shoeing of oxen has grown familiar, for Indian cart bullocks, working on hard roads, are usually shod. Two plates go to each foot, and in some regions a turned-up tip protects the toe. The ox

SHOEING AN OX

is thrown to be shod and held down while the farrier works on the feet tied together in a bunch round a stick stuck in the ground. Plough cattle and cultivators' cattle generally are very seldom shod.

Before macadamised roads made Britain wheelable, the pack-horse had a place of honour now only indicated in a few inn-signs here and there. It will be long, however, before India parts with her pack-oxen in spite of roads and railways, for the continent is vast, and ancient customs are hard to kill. The heavily-laden ox-cart still plods along roads parallel with the rail and underbids it for traffic, and the one-horse ekka or gig plies with passengers between towns connected by the iron road. Yet, though they may be slow to give in, it is plain that on the great high-roads of commerce where formerly the Banjári with their long trains of pack bullocks laden with goods, unladen cattle for sale, big watch dogs for guard, and a host of women, were the organised carriers, the competition of the iron horse will make itself felt. As a matter of fact many of them are already settling down to agriculture and other pursuits. They are a folk apart, with gypsy characteristics, and are credited with strange customs and beliefs. For a long time there will be regions where their trade must be carried on, and there are few more picturesque sights than is presented by one of their trains either in motion, winding slowly through the broken country of Central India, or among the castle-crowned hills of Rajputana, or halted for the night in one of their neatly arranged camps. The men, reputed to be as honest as their oxen, are well set up and have a wild air peculiar to their race, while the sunburnt women, free in gait, and brave in brightly coloured clothing, wear an immense profusion of ornaments, bangles, and anklets in beads, brass, and glass. As much pains are spent on the bedizenment of the oxen as on the adornment of their mistresses. The horns are encased in hempen sheathings woven in zig-zag patterns of brick-red and black and ornamented with shells and tassels. Over the beast's forehead is a shaped frontlet of cotton cloth broidered with patterns in colour with pieces of mirror sewn in, and crowned by a *Kalgi* or aigrette of peacock feather tips. The pack saddle is of hempen stuff woven in patterns of red, and has a high peak in front, something like those seen in France and Spain, with a patch of inwoven pattern and a peacock feather tip. Large necklaces of blue and white beads like birds' eggs, terminating in a pendent heart-shaped brass plate, go round the neck, and lower down is a broad hempen collar with a bell. Over all is sometimes spread a coverlet of stout cotton cloth embroidered in sampler work stitching of coloured thread with circular mirrors let in. The packs themselves are brown, with wide bands of black or darker brown. All this, merely written down, may seem garish, but artists, learned in tones and qualities of colour, might have prescribed the tints, and the effect when seen in the bright lights and wide areas of Indian landscape is simply delightful.

OOPLA (COW-DUNG FUEL)

India is so poorly off for fuel that the droppings of the cow have become one of her most highly prized products, carefully collected and stored. Some observant tourists have recognised in the universal preparation of cow peat or *bois de vache* the characteristic national industry. The collection of the raw material, its mixture with fragments of straw and other combustible refuse, and, after kneading with water, the clapping of each finger-printed pat against a wall, rock, or other sun-visited surface in a bold diaper pattern is the first occupation of the poor girl, the last of the poor old woman. Authorities on Indian agriculture lie awake o' nights weeping over the loss to the soil caused by this industry ;—not unknown in many other countries, but nowhere such a staple as in a land where there is no coal to speak of and wood is scarce and dear. Invaluable for the tiny hearths of domestic life ;—the wheelwright, smith, brass-founder, potter, and other craftsmen to whom a strong heat is a necessity, find dried cow-dung almost as good as charcoal. Before matches came it held a vestal fire everywhere, and still serves, for it smoulders like tinder, and, as the kindling for the dank compost of tobacco, treacle, and spices smoked in the *hŭqqa* or national water-pipe, it is onc of the cherished comforts of the country. There is an extensive trade in it both in city shops and village courtyards. Carts are piled high with it, women bear the light turves on their heads, and men trot along the roads with bundles nearly as high as themselves slung at each end of an elastic shoulder-borne yoke.

The rustic pharmacy of most countries knows the value of the substance as a poultice, but in India the sanctity of the cow lends a semi-sacred sanction to its use, and its application has the prestige of a charm as well as the merely mechanical action of a cataplasm. A respectable clerk or employé will come to work like a Zulu in war paint, with streaks daubed in gridirons over brow and cheeks, or large dabs on each temple, touched with turmeric or sandal paste by way of a high light. Thus fearsomely disguised, he bears himself with

GOING TO WORK (PUNJAB)

(Copyright, 1891, by J. Lockwood Kipling)

the pensive pride of an invalid, firmly persuaded that the dry scales of refuse relieve his headache. Cow-dung ashes are the *blanc de perle*, and the raw substance itself is the ordained cosmetic of Hindu devotees.

As a cement, cow-dung takes a high place as the finishing coat of the floor and mud wall. This coating is renewed at frequent intervals, and periodically applied to earthen floors. During the process of smearing the odour is somewhat strong, but this passes away in an incredibly short time, leaving an undeniable impression of coolness, freshness, and, strange as it may seem, fragrance. Such a floor is soon spoiled by boots, but the Oriental wears no shoes indoors, and is probably right in considering it cool, comfortable, and on the whole cleanly and wholesome. In some regions the women give a finishing touch to the newly smoothed surface by shaking over it coloured powders from a cullender. Farm kitchens in northern England have similar fopperies in red sand on whitened stone.

In an unfenced country straying cattle are frequent causes of trouble and popular talk topics.

"A hand on the horn promise" is a rustic Punjab expression for one that will not be kept and is based on a little story. A cultivator lost a favourite ox and sought it with unavailing tears. In his grief he vowed that if he could find it he would give five rupees to the shrine of Sakhi Sarwar (a great Punjab and frontier saint), nay, he would send seven to the Golden Temple at Amritsar, ay, even ten to his own village temple, and so forth; till his wife cried, "O father of Gopal, but thou hast promised more than the beast is worth!" Quoth the husband, "Hush, wife, only let me get a hand on his horn and I'll soon settle about the promises."

Cattle stealing is an ancient institution, and in the

course of centuries of slack rule has become so thoroughly organised as to be an almost respectable profession to which whole tribes of folk conceive themselves ordained by birth. Year by year the law is gaining on the practice, though bad harvest years often

A RUSTIC KRISHNA

show a notable slip back to the old state. Visitors fresh from Europe occasionally ask in reference to this and other crimes, "What is the Government about, to permit such things?" It is impossible to condense the facts that would answer this kind of petulance within a paragraph, but anybody can perceive that though it may be easy for a police to deal with occasional theft, it is hard to cope with cattle-stealing tribes who have life-long experience, a first-rate organisation of wandering habit, and wide stretches of country in which to disappear.

There are several little jokes concealed in scientific nomenclature. The absurd name Zebu now indelibly branded on the humped cow (*Bos Sacer*) of Africa and Asia is one of these. That noble naturalist M. Buffon once met some showmen going to a fair with a Brahminy bull and was told that its name, when it was at home, was "Zebu." There is a fine foreign touch in this word, as in that other showman's invention, the "Guyascutis," so the great man wrote it down, and scientific Europe, following his lead, has inscribed this fragment of a French showman's *boniment* so deeply on its august records that it cannot now be effaced. No such word is known in India, where "the cow" suffices for all needs. "Brahminy cow" appears to be used by untravelled English folk, and, as distinguishing the true cow from the low-caste buffalo, is the best name possible; if India is to be considered the chief home of humped cattle.

CHAPTER VII

OF BUFFALOES AND PIGS

"Dark children of the mere and marsh,
  Wallow and waste and lea;
Outcast they wait at the village gate
  With folk of low degree.

"Their pasture is in no man's land,
  Their food the cattle's scorn;
Their rest is mire and their desire
  The thicket and the thorn.

"But woe to those who break their sleep
  And woe to those who dare
To rouse the herd-bull from his keep,
  The wild boar from his lair."   R. K.

MANY Europeans speak of the Indian buffalo, which is the familiar buffalo of Egypt and Italy, as the "water buffalo," from its predilection for wallowing in swamps. "Yoke a buffalo and a bullock together and the buffalo will head towards the pool, the ox to the upland," says a proverb, but none the less this unequal yoke is often seen. Hindus of the old rock say a buffalo is unlucky to keep, the black antithesis of the benignant cow,—a demon to an angel. On going out in the morning it is an ill omen if the eye rests on a buffalo, while the sight of a cow is good. The passion of the Hindu for bright colours, and his rooted hatred of black and dingy tones, are the groundwork of this aversion. Its uncouth shape as compared with the smooth outlines of the cow also counts in the buffalo's exclusion from bovine kinship. The vertebræ stand up on its crest like park palings, and the skeleton suggests paleontology as much as actual natural history, though the creature is an unmistakable cow. Not that the Hindu ever thought of generic relationships, for the rhinoceros, which is still more remote in kind, counts as a superior cow, and a vessel used in Shiv worship, representing the female energy, is reckoned of precious sanctity when made of rhinoceros horn. The Nilghai too, which is an antelope, is accounted a cow and equally honoured.

But though the Hindu may affect an academic scorn of the buffalo, he must confess that it is intrinsically a good beast, as gentle as the cow, more courageous and more affectionate, for it bears a better brain. Buffalo milk too is a most valuable food, rich and abundant. Most of the ghi eaten in the great cities is prepared from buffalo butter, and is now made on a large scale in remote districts and distributed by the railways. "The buffalo to the strong man's house, the horse to the Sultan's," is a saying indicating the estimate of the value of the milk of this animal. As a draught animal the buffalo has the fine qualities of willingness and great strength, suited for the strenuous toil of the quarry and the timber-yard, but he bears the sun badly, and to thrive properly should have free access to a pool or mud swamp. "The tradesman to the city, the buffalo to the marsh," says the proverb. The roll of a horse or ass in sand or the pure luxury a tired man enjoys in a warm bath seem poor delights compared with the ineffable satisfaction of a herd of buffaloes in a water wallow. They roll and wriggle till the soft black mud encradles them and they are coated all over with a plaster that defies the mosquito, and for hours they will lie with only eyes and nostril twinkling above the surface in blissful content defying the heat of the sun. English farmers say, "Happy as pigs in muck;"—the beatitude of the buffalo in warm mud beats that homely figure by more than the buffalo beats the pig in size.

It is truly said that herds of buffaloes can defend themselves from the tiger, and they will also defend

BUFFALOES

their herdsman, for they are capable of strong attachments, and have sense enough to combine and form square to repel attack. In remote regions, where a European is seldom seen, they are occasionally inclined to resent his presence. There is something ignominious in a party of stalwart British sportsmen being treed by a herd of angry buffaloes, and obliged to wait for rescue at the hands of a herdsman's child, but this has happened. Buffalo horns offer an example of the wondrous variety in unity of which nature is capable. One blade of variegated ribbon grass, to the incurious eye, looks like another, but if you cut and match a thousand sections you will find no two with identical stripes; so a herd of buffaloes has the same head at the first glance, but the horns offer an immense variety of size and curve. They are always heavy, so they say with pathos and truth of the care of a large family, "The buffalo's horns may be a heavy burden, but she carries them herself."

One of many unpleasing features in the practice of keeping milch buffaloes in great cities is the usage of feeding them on stable refuse. The English housewife in India learns this with disgust, and hastens to buy and keep her own cows. The Oriental does not object to the custom, nor do learned veterinary authorities seem inclined to denounce the practice very severely, and it is undeniable that after the horse has done with his food, the buffalo thrives on the residuum. The filthy state of all native cow byres is one of many causes of the low state of health of the densely over-crowded cities. Through alleys reeking with filth, and an air heavy with the stench of decomposition, native gentlemen of good position are content to pick their way, and over cow byres of unimaginable impurity you may hear young students debating politics and local self-government with that love of wordy abstractions and indifference to practical considerations which have always been marks of the Hindu.

Not only does the Hindu affect to despise buffaloes, but he sacrifices them in great numbers to Kali, especially at the Dasehrah festival. As in the case of goats, only male animals are sacrificed. The head should be smitten off at a blow, a feat in which those who officiate at Hindu sacrifices take great pride. The Moslem cuts the throat with the invariable invocation of God's name.

A buffalo demon, sometimes drawn as a bull-headed man and sometimes like the Greek man-bull, or the Bucentaur, from whom Mysore takes its name, once fought with the awful Goddess, and the sacrifice of buffaloes is supposed by some to be a punishment for this presumption. It is more likely that it is a survival of some barbaric pre-Aryan rite: indeed Kali herself may be suspected of a similar low-born origin. The Todas, an aboriginal tribe of the Neilgherry hills, have been reported to cudgel their buffalo to death, and in

MAHESWAR FIGHTING KALI

some villages in Western India the whole population turns out to the festivity of beating a poor beast till it dies; a long and hideously cruel business, and then they tear it to pieces in a sort of Maenad rage. At the very curious and interesting ceremony of the worship of the sword, as observed by the ancient and illustrious House of Oodeypore, the first of the Rajput Lords, buffaloes are sacrificed, their heads being cut off at one blow. Colonel Tod, in his invaluable *Annals and Antiquities* of *Rajasthān*, describes the ancient practice when the Maha Rana himself pierced the buffalo with an arrow shot from his travelling throne or litter, borne on men's shoulders. Kavi Raja Shyamal Dass, of the State Council of Oodeypore, informs me that this observance was abolished in 1830, and the Maha Rana now only gives the word for the decapitation of the animal. On account of its sanctity the Brahminy cow is never ridden, and the ox but very seldom serves as a steed. The buffalo, on the other hand, is constantly mounted, although its craggy contours do not at first sight seem to offer a comfortable seat. The sacred animal is very rarely used for draught, and only when poverty can be pleaded as an excuse for her degradation, but a barren buffalo cow is set to the plough without scruple. It does not always pay to rear male buffaloes, but it is considered cruel to kill them, so they are allowed to die slowly of starvation. An Englishman would be inclined to say that the Biloch were more merciful, for, not caring to rear colts, they cut their throats soon after birth.

A sacrificial use of this animal, against which there is but little room for complaint, is at a time of unusual sickness. A male buffalo is given or bought, and all the village assists at a ceremony of propitiation. A red caste mark is solemnly put on the beast's brow, and it is adorned with flowers and led round the town by the elders, while Brahmans and the poor are fed. When turned loose if it goes straight away it is a good omen, for the sickness goes with it, and by dint of loud cries and sticks and stones the animal is made to go. When it is out of sight, the village is happy and probably some good Mussulman meets the beast, takes off its garlands, and appropriates it to his own use. Nothing is easier than to laugh at so foolish a performance. But, given the simplicity of faith, there is sound sense in a proceeding which restores confidence and hope to people demoralised by the presence of death, and therefore apt to contract sickness. Who cares may debate whether the prayer of faith can save the sick: it is certain that it soothes the troubled mind.

The Indian village pig is counted tame by a strained courtesy, for he is in nothing like the domestic animal we know in the West. "Without are dogs," says the Scripture, speaking of that extra-mural filthiness, wherein the unclean levitical purity of the East mainly asserts itself. "Without" also are pigs, the outcast property of outcastes, enjoying with the characteristic insouciance of their race a useful and filthy freedom; foul-feeding, slate-tinted, slab-sided, gaunt, and hideous beasts.

Moses, who is always spoken of by Muhammadans as the converser with God (Kalim ulla), never saw a Berkshire or a Yorkshire hog, and his prohibition of pigs' flesh as a food staple was a wise sanitary measure as well as a religious ordinance. In the course of time the pig has become in the estimation of Semitic peoples a boundary pillar of the faith, a black beacon of uncleanness, enhancing the snow-white purity of the chosen people. Never was so lowly and unoffending a Devil, but he is as necessary to the consciences of thousands of ignorant and devout Moslems as our Christian devil is to us. His potentialities of intelligence, humour, usefulness, and surpassing edibility count for nothing in comparison with his religious functions. When strife arises between Hindu and Muhammadan, the pig, dead or alive, goes in the fore-front of the fray, for he is either driven into the precincts of the mosque or portions of his flesh are thrown over its walls or into its courtyard well. And his innocent name, Sūar, is universally considered the vilest word in all the copious abuse vocabulary of the country. We also use the word pig in this sense, but in a merely academic fashion, for we cherish the animal in life and praise it in death.

It is doubtful whether the natives of India have an adequate conception of the influence exerted by Hinduism and Muhammadanism on each other, and very certain that many Anglo-Indians who see the creeds in conflict fail to notice their frequent fusion. When this curious subject is worked out it will probably be seen that Hindus have learned scorn of the pig from their Muhammadan neighbours. Levitical ordinances have always a contagious effect, appealing to the passion for respectability which is a leading note in Hindu character. A high-caste Hindu of to-day might rate the pig as a non-Aryan animal and suggest that the boar avatar or incarnation of Vishnu as a pig was a concession of early Brahmanism to indigenous taste. Something like this I have heard, but it seems too fine-drawn a conclusion. The chase of the wild boar and a taste for his flesh have always been enjoyed by Rajput nobles and Sikh chiefs. At all events the tame pig is now almost as unclean to the Hindu as to the Muhammadan, although there is little that can be quoted against him from sacred lore. Like the donkey, his low caste makes him suitable for association with disease godlings and demons. A pious Hindu who has recovered from smallpox buys a pig and lets it loose to Sitala or he will be again attacked. Mr. Crooke in his *Rural and Agricultural Glossary* mentions a curious licensed robbery of pigs. The people of one village turn out and drive off the pigs of another village by force. The owners resist as well as they can, but never prosecute the offenders. This practice is noted as peculiar to the Azamgarh district, but it seems to indicate a denial of even the right of being owned to the animal, which may once have been general.

As low castes rise, it is just possible that the pigs they cherish may rise with them. Some Europeans have tried to breed and feed pigs in the Western fashion and not without success. Others have imported stock from Europe, but not all the dollars in Chicago will avail to prove the industry respectable in native eyes for many a year to come.

But there is nothing to be ashamed of in the character and conduct of wild pigs. They cut for themselves shelters from the sugar-cane or the tall millet stocks, where they breed and sleep, take the best of the crops and defy mankind. The wild boar has been known to face and defeat the tiger, and though his first impulse is to fly before British sportsmen, he often makes a gallant stand before the unequal odds of horses, razor-sharp spears, and legions of yelling rustics brought against him. No swordsman can cut right and left so swiftly and surely as the wild boar with his tusks when fighting for life. He is sometimes shot by Rajput chiefs, by whom he is as strictly preserved as the fox in England. This protection breeds boldness. My son tells me that he was once shown a lane in a suburb of a Rajput town along which a certain well-known wild boar was accustomed to pass at dawn. The animal was next day shot by the ruler of the State and a side of bacon was despatched by special messenger on a camel as a gift to a brother prince some hundred miles away. The Maharaja took just as much interest in pointing out the course of his bullet as an English sportsman who has brought down a stag, and expressed as cordial an appreciation of the quality of the flesh as if it were venison. And yet we are constantly told that all Hindus are strictly vegetarian!

The story of Buddhism is nowadays so completely forgotten that it is possible to shock a Brahman to the bone by telling him how the Lord Buddha attained Nirvana through the lowly gate of indigestion brought on by eating too heartily of the roast pork prepared for him by a faithful disciple. This is duly recorded by the best authorities, nor is it to any fair mind derogatory. The Master was old and very weary, and the Smith, his host, entertaining him in his garden, naturally pressed him to eat. Here is a pathetic note of nature, of human weakness, too often missing from Eastern stories of the half-Divine.

CHAPTER VIII

OF HORSES AND MULES

"*Johnson.—'Pity is not natural to man. Children are always cruel. Savages are always cruel. Pity is acquired and improved by the cultivation of reason. We may have uneasy sensations from seeing a creature in distress, without pity; for we have not pity unless we wish to relieve them. When I am on my way to dine with a friend, and finding it late have bid the coachman make haste, if I happen to attend when he whips his horses, I may feel unpleasantly that the animals are put to pain, but I do not wish him to desist. No, Sir, I wish him to drive on.'*"—Boswell's *Life of Johnson.*

WAITING FOR THE WAZIR

INDIA has been described by a European as the Paradise of horses, and from his point of view the phrase is not unfitting. The natural affinity between horses and Englishmen becomes a closer bond by residence in India, where everybody rides

—or ought to ride—where horses and horse-keep are cheap, and where large castes of stable servants, contented with a low wage, are capable under careful superintendence of keeping their animals in a state of luxurious comfort. The horses, however, which serve native masters are born to Purgatory rather than to Paradise. Those in the hands of the upper classes suffer from antiquated and barbarous systems of treatment, and are often killed by mistaken kindness or crippled by bad training, while those of low degree are liable to cruel ill-usage, over-work, neglect, and unrelieved bondage.

I have not always thought it worth while in previous notes to dwell on the frequent appearance of notions on animals once current in Europe. But in the matter of the horse, there is no escape from this suggestive subject. The Oriental conception of a horse may be gathered from pictures and current sayings as well as from an inspection of princely stables. In many respects it recalls that of our forefathers before the introduction of Arab blood into Europe and the systematic cultivation of speed. No Eastern horse has anything like the substance of the "grete horse," "the gambaldyne horse," or "the grete doble trottynge hors called a curtal" of old England,—but that kind of animal is plainly the ideal in the Oriental mind. Its artificial paces, air-fighting attitudes, and slow rate of speed are still the model of the high-class Indian trainer when left to himself. This ideal is somewhat contrary to nature, for the climate is not favourable to the pig-like roundness of form shown in all modern Indian pictures as in European representations of a bygone time. For the animals that take their chance with the poor are always light in form and often of spectral slenderness.

But by rigorous confinement and careful stuffing with rich food even this condition is approached. Many horses belonging to persons of rank are fattened like fowls in France, by the grooms thrusting balls of food mixed with ghi, boiled goats' brains, and other rich messes down their throats. And, as might be expected, very many die of diseases of the digestion and liver under the process. The difference between East and West, between old and new, between feudal and free conditions, is shown in few things more clearly than in a comparison of the horse of the Indian Raja with the scientifically treated animal of Europe and America. The latter is carefully fed during the all-important period of its growth, so that its strength and substance are fully developed, while it is made to take regular exercise. Year by year, too, a humane appreciation of its natural timidity leads to a more considerate and merciful training, which is accomplished without cruel constraint, harsh confinement, violence, or nervous shock.

The horse of the Indian noble, on the other hand, is imperfectly nourished in its early youth. Not always in the West will an ordinary farmer understand the requirements of a young horse after weaning, but in India it seems impossible to persuade people that money spent on a growing beast is money invested. All they see is a present loss. Then it is tied up during the greater part of its life, not merely secured by the head but tethered by heel-ropes. No innovation has been more obstinately fought against by native servants of English masters than the loose box, for Orientals have a passion for tying things up. A group of young horses in a pasture, free to exult in their strength, is a sight not seen in India, with a few exceptions to be presently noted. If you watch such a group and note their God-given delight in motion and freedom, the birthright and wild desire of all young things, you must admit that this is a custom of cruelty. But the pedantry of horse-folk, everywhere inclined to stupidity, is inflexible in India.

Some of the foregoing may appear incredible to Western readers. I quote from the *India in 1887* of Mr. R. Wallace, Professor of Agriculture and Rural Economy in the University of Edinburgh,—a witness who writes from first-hand observation, and who, throughout his book, is inclined to the not unreasonable contention that a native custom is *primâ facie* likely to be right:—

"The pampering and overfeeding of favourite animals in the stables of wealthy native princes cannot be too strongly condemned and reprobated, as cruel to the beasts themselves and injurious to the best interests of the country. I spent some hours in one stable where over one hundred of the finest horses—Arabs, Barbs, Marwars, and Kathiawars—that India could produce were tied up and actually fed as fat as pigs. Horses that had cost Rs. 18,000 and Rs. 20,000 were kept in close boxes with most imperfect ventilation, and were taken out only for show at rare intervals, and not at all for regular exercise. In addition to ordinary food, they got mixed with it 2 lbs. of sugar and from 1 to 2 lbs. of ghi daily. The first result of this feeding would be a rapidly thriving condition, accompanied with a sleek and glossy coat and an increase of fat; but the ultimate and most natural consequence proved to be the gradual breaking down of the system in each case at its weakest point through over-pressure. This accounted for the variety of diseases that appeared and developed and were running their course at the time referred to—*e.g.* broken wind, founder (*laminitis*), weed (*lymphangitis*), skin eruptions or diseases, and fatty degenerations of the liver. All these, I noticed, were present, and no doubt there were others besides.

"I was informed that a considerable number died annually of an unknown disease, and I was able to satisfy myself by examining what existed of it at the moment, and from the accounts of the two native veterinary attendants, that this unknown and fatal malady was fatty degeneration of the liver, which seemed to carry off most of those horses that escaped the other more rapid and better-known forms of disease.

"The injury to the community lies in this, that the best horses of the best breeds in the country are picked up—even those bred by government sires—and brought to these stables; and if an animal finds favour in the eyes of the Prince or Sahib, it is supplied with the food of the favourites already described, and whether it is a male or female it soon becomes barren; consequently, the best horses are withdrawn from breeding, and the artificial selection of man is made to act in the wrong direction—the race being reproduced from the poorer specimens.

"I saw a horse suffering from a disease said to be produced by excess of moisture. It took the form of large blotches or swollen raw sores, which may occur on any part of the body, but most abundantly about the legs. . . . There is an extraordinary confusion in the minds of natives of the lower orders, such as grooms, in their ideas of kindness and cruelty to the lower animals. While some were being literally killed by over-feeding and care, I found the one suffering from this loathsome disease tied out in the open, and exposed without shelter to the sun or rain, as the case might be, and to the constant and irritating action of flies which swarmed about and lived on the skinless parts. Although the disease was well developed, no effort had been made to treat it in any way. The animal was suffering severely, but my drawing attention to the fact was received with the greatest astonishment and indifference."

With reference to the last case quoted by Mr. Wallace, a native groom would say that *barsáti*, which seems to be the disease indicated, is incurable and contagious. So the animal must be kept apart from the rest, but it may not be killed—and—"he is only a poor man and what can be done?" But in reality, it has never occurred to him to think that creatures can suffer.

The distinctively native methods of training, which are corruptions of the manège formerly popular in Europe, involve unnecessary cruelty. It is true that even in England, which is, relatively speaking, the true horse paradise, carriage horses are still made to learn certain artificial tricks, relics of unwise old fashions, indefensible because interferences with nature. To teach the outstretched, flying-buttress attitude which is considered good form, the animal is set to stand and the inside of the fore legs is tapped with a whip till he covers the proper extent of ground. The French take more pains to exaggerate this position than the English, but during the season in the Park you may often see an English coachman, on pulling up, fidget with reins and whip till his animals are outstretched like wooden rocking-horses. This is considered quite beautiful, but it is the worst possible attitude for a horse to move forward from, since it may cause strain in back or loins. But it is only done while the animal is at work. In India the poor brute is tied tightly in this posture and left for many hours together without possibility of relief.

When a carriage horse carries his head too low for good form, an English head-groom fits him with a dumb-jockey, on which is an iron standard with a movable hook. To this hook a bridle is fastened at the desired height and left for half an hour at a time,—seldom for longer and not often more than twice a day, usually only once, because the groom knows that nothing is so bad for a horse's temper as this kind of confinement. Sometimes the bridle is fitted with india-rubber pieces, which stretch and allow a little play, but this contrivance seems likely to teach boring. Some grooms tie a wisp of hay round the bit, with intent to keep the mouth occupied, so that the beast does not sulkily hang in his bit all the time and spoil his mouth. At its best, however, there is not much to be said in favour of the plan, for if a horse's head is not meant by nature to be carried handsomely, no amount of training will teach him. But the lesson lasts for a very brief period of time, nor is it physically moie severe than that undergone by recruits in a drill-yard. Moreover, the head is tied up and not down. Another kind of dumb-jockey is used in England as the horse's first lesson in bit and bridle. But its use is intermittent, and when compared with the Indian practice, it allows comparatively free play to the head. The bearing-rein still holds its own and is warmly supported against common sense by the pedants of the English stable, but at its worst it is a tender mercy when compared with the Indian practice of

IN TRAINING

tying the poor brute's head tightly back and down for weeks at a time until a monstrous exaggeration of the natural curve of the neck is produced. A diagram shows how this is done. A poor brute thus treated for the greater part of his life has naturally a heavy grudge against all mankind. So good temper is the last thing to expect from the horse of an Indian person of quality. The physical effects of the practice are no less deplorable. The neck of the horse, a wonderful piece of construction, plays a most important part in all his movements. It is one of the first parts to show fatigue, seeing that like a pendulum it balances every movement. The gait of an animal with a crippled neck becomes mincing and constrained. But it is precisely this rickety, rocking, all-of-a-piece action that most pleases the Oriental, since it is supposed to resemble the dainty stepping and wanton prancing in which young horses indulge at times. A sort of high-stepping caper is taught; the *chābūk sowār* (whip-rider) or breaker, holding, in addition to the bridle, cords tied to the fore fetlocks, with which he gives a jerk, crying Ho! This brings the foot up with a flourish and, one would think, should occasionally bring the horse on his nose.

Some people say high-stepping is taught to horses in England by making them tread on hot iron plates, or among logs of timber, or in soft fallows, or in a very deep layer of straw. But if I wanted to believe in things of this kind, I should prefer the theory of a rustic at a funeral, watching a pair of Flemish blacks throwing their forelegs about. "I *hev* heard tell as they teaches 'osses this by practysin' 'em 'over wheel-barrows.'" Now, a mere man tumbling over a wheel-barrow is in for a most complex catastrophe, but the idea of horses waltzing round a yard full of wheel-barrows is purely fascinating. The truth is that though "dodges" may be practised at times, the really skilful trainer would be almost as much puzzled to describe his practice as a skilful painter to describe the way he painted his picture.

> "It's incommunicable, like the cast
> That drops the tackle with the gut adry,
> Too much, too little,—there's your salmon lost."

Elaborately-ordered curvetings, side movements like those of Western riding-schools, and progress by slow springs or bounds, are also practised. From old pictures it is evident that the last was an admired action of the European manège. A good American or English circus trainer; who, as their phrase runs, can make a horse canter round a cabbage leaf; teaches it in less time and by simpler methods than in the old days, and without the infliction of pain and bondage. The Central Indian idea is that the rider should appear to sit at ease, languidly controlling the movements of a restive steed. In reality every action is as measured as the swing of a wooden rocking-horse, while a touch of the bit suffices to check any tendency to genuine spirit.

The "thorn bits" here engraved are ordinary specimens of those in use; the cut requires careful examination before their murderous character can be made out. Some say the Indian bit is severe because the average horseman, being of slight build, is physically incapable of holding a horse with a fair one. There may be something in this, but the weakness is more moral than physical; nerve is more wanting than muscle, and reason most of all. The whole process of bringing up and handling is faulty, depending on harsh constraint and developing bad form, bad temper, and bad manners. There are of course many fine horsemen in the country, but they have usually been taught by Englishmen, for by means of the turf, the army, and the equestrian civilian, English horse notions have been widely spread. It is no libel to say that the average native horseman is timid, and no timid rider can afford to be merciful. A Bengali saying counselling caution expresses this and gives a picture in a line to those who are familiar with the least equestrian race in the world. "Having taken a firm hold on all sides, then mount the horse." Perhaps it is unfair to see in this sagacious counsel the courage of a Bengali rider desperately screwed up to the sticking place, the convulsive grip, the struggling climb, and the apprehensive face as if the placid pony were some wild hippogriff.

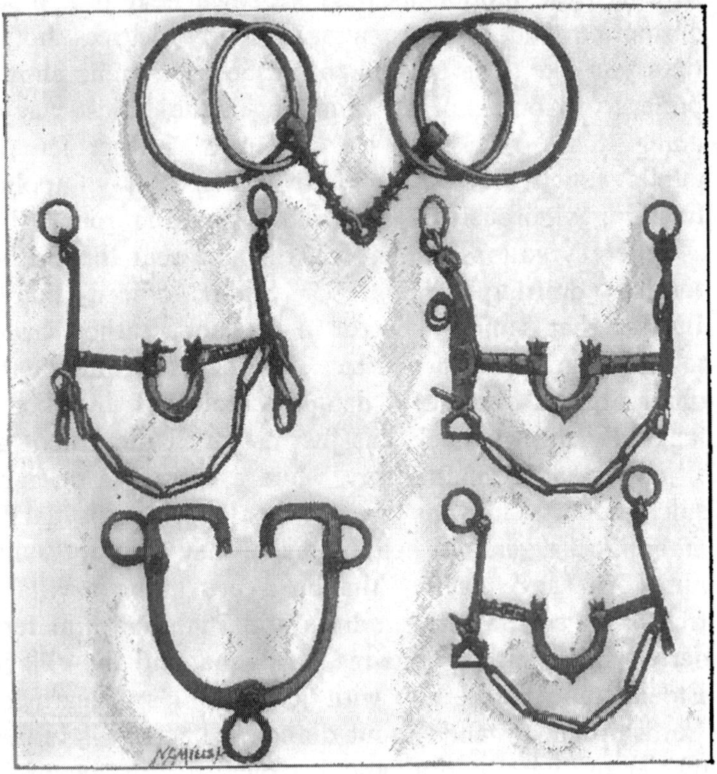

INDIAN "THORN BITS"

Possibly, also, it is unkind to see in the adoption of ambling or pacing another index to the unequestrian character of India. For in America, where they want no teaching about horses, ambling is a regularly ordained gait. It is taught in India, as formerly in

Europe, by tying together the fore and hind legs on each side, but this is not always necessary, for the pace comes naturally to many animals. There are who ride and there are who sit on a horse and are carried. In a hot climate, where for months the aim of life is to exist with as little motion as possible, since heat is a mode of motion, and you are already many degrees hotter than you like, it is natural that equestrian India should prefer to sit on a horse. Ambling is the easiest way of doing this. You shall see at a cold weather fête, or public function, a burly native Inspector of police bumping vigorously in his saddle, charging round like a General's galloper on a field day, so that the British tourist admiringly remarks, "Smart officer, that!" But see that same Inspector in the hot weather, faring to a village away from his District Superintendent's observation. His legs dangle carelessly, his body, languidly thrown back, has just as much movement as a jelly on a footman's tray, while a constable on each side supports him as they run alongside his lazily ambling charger. When he halts, they reverently lift him down, and placing him on a bed under a village tree or in a verandah, undress and shampoo him tenderly while another prepares his hūqqa, and the village Elders stand before him with joined hands to learn his Lordship's commands about dinner. The sun is in fact master of the situation, and his dictates are obeyed in riding as in other matters.

When a native chief goes out, he is accompanied by a *sowāri*, literally a "riding" of ministers, servants, guards, and attendants of all sorts. Formerly all rode, but with good roads good carriages have been introduced, and usually in these days only the horsemen of the guard ride. But on state occasions, led horses, richly caparisoned, always form part of the show, and there are many animals in princely stables kept solely for processional purposes. The animals most liked are the stallions of Marwar or Kathiawar. White horses with pink points, piebalds, and leopard spotted beasts are much admired, especially when they have pink Roman noses and light-coloured eyes with an uncanny

A PROCESSIONAL HORSE.

expression. Their crippled, highly arched necks, curby hocks, rocking gait, and paralytic prancing often proclaim them as triumphs of training.

The passion for bright colour is strikingly evident in these parades, where silk and gold are lavishly spread, and the manes and tails and sometimes the bodies of the animals are dyed magenta, scarlet, or orange. Gold or silver bangles are clasped round the fetlocks or above the knee, where they are hung with silk cloths or streamers. No matter how long the *tamásha* may last, the animal's head is always pulled tightly back and down with bridle and silken martingale, and one longs with such an exceeding great longing to cut them and set the head free that it is hard to be respectful to the bravery of the show. You feel that as a relic of the externals of the brave days of old (which must have been mainly bad old days) it deserves some respect. Yet no writer who has seen the display from near, and writes honestly, can refrain from noting its seamy side. The late Mr. Aberigh Mackay (Ali Baba of *Vanity Fair*), one of the brightest and most original, as well as one of the most generous spirits who ever handled Indian subjects, has drawn a picture in his *Twenty-one Days in India*, of a Raja and his Sowāri which could not be bettered by a hair's breadth.

"In the cool of the evening our king emerges from his palace, and, riding on a prodigiously fat white horse with pink points, proceeds to the place of carousal. A long train of horsemen follow him, and footmen run before with guns in red flannel covers and silver maces, shouting 'Raja Maharaja Salaamat,' etc. The horsemen immediately around him are mounted on well-fed and richly caparisoned steeds, with all the bravery of cloth of gold, yaktails, silver chains, and strings of shells; behind are troopers in a burlesque of English uniform; and altogether in the rear is a mob of caitiffs on skeleton chargers, masquerading in every degree of shabbiness and rags, down to nakedness and a sword. The cavalcade passes through the city. The inhabitants pour out of every door and bend to the ground. Red cloths and white veils flutter at the casements overhead. You would hardly think that the spectacle was one daily enjoyed by the city. There is all the hurrying and eagerness of novelty and curiosity. Here and there a little shy crowd of women gather at a door and salute the Chief with a loud, shrill verse of discordant song. It is some national song of the Chief's ancestors and of the old heroic days. The place of carousal is a bare spot near a large and ancient well out of which grows a vast pipal tree. Hard by is a little temple surmounted by a red flag on a drooping bamboo It is here that the *Gangor* and *Dasehra* Solemnities are celebrated. Arrived on the ground, the Raja slowly circles his horse; then, jerking the

A RAJA'S CHARGER (MARWAR BREED)

thorn-bit, causes him to advance plunging and rearing, but dropping first on the near foot and then on the off foot with admirable precision; and finally, making the white monster, now in a lather of sweat, rise up and walk a few steps on his hind legs, the Raja's performance concludes amid many shouts of wonder and delight from the smooth-tongued courtiers. The thakores (barons) and sardars (squires) now exhibit their skill in the *manège* until the shades of night fall, when torches are brought, amid much salaaming, and the cavalcade defiles through the city, back to the palace."

Is it any wonder that Sir John Malcolm, who had seen so much of this kind of life and could describe it with humour and spirit, was a congenial companion to the good Sir Walter? For it belongs to another world, and another time. Yet, when one knows all about the poor horse and the cruel bit it seems but a dull parody of ancient chivalry.

The ideas current on the qualities, form, and vices of the animal are as antiquated as its treatment. Many are tied up in aphoristic bundles for better preservation. So many parts of the horse should be round, so many square, so many short, and so many long, and everybody speaks of the five vices and of the eight lucky white points of Mangal—Mars. There is an elaborate science of stray hairs with an obstinate twist, of the colour of the markings and the planting of the hair in the skin. The last is a curious, and nowadays but little known subject in England. If you paint a well-groomed, well-conditioned horse in a strong light, you find that the shimmer and reflections of his coat take forms like those in moire antique silk or the "figure" in polished satin-wood and tell in your picture more than the actual form. It is conceivable, indeed, that a sculptor, studying shape only, might find it convenient to dredge his model over with gray powder to kill these reflections. We know that the rich and pictorial effects are partly due to a relatively trivial cause,—the direction in which the hairs are set in the skin, which varies slightly in different individuals. But in Indian horse lore the set of these featherings (they are analogous to the radiating arrangements of birds' feathers), ending sometimes in circles or whorls, are all mapped out like currents on a mariner's chart, and each is named and interpreted for luck, temper, constitution, or quality; but mainly for luck. The "*Ziṇnat ul Khail*" or "Beauties of the horse" is an elaborately illustrated text-book of this absurd science. Absurd enough, but those who have rummaged in old books will feel that in the American phrase, they "have been here before." Three hundred years ago, precisely similar notions were current in Europe and learnedly discoursed upon. Mr. Alfred E. T. Watson, in the *Riding and Polo* volume of the "Badminton Library" quotes from an Elizabethan writer, Maister Thomas Blundevill: "The horse that hath an ostrich feather either on his forehead, or both sides of his maine, or on the one side, or els behind on his buttocks, or in any place where he himself cannot see it, can never be an euill horse."

With reference to colour, we probably have preserved more preferences than we care to admit, though we say "a good horse is never of a bad colour." Such a saying is wildly irreverent from the Oriental point of view, whence colour and colour markings are the first things taken into account. Relics of the old ideas, however, still linger among us in such sayings as the doggerel about white feet,—

> "One, you may buy him;
> Two, you may try him;
> Three, you should doubt him;
> Four, do without him,"—

but there are many similar rules in the East, complicated by moral and fatalistic fancies. Thus, Mūnshi Muhammad, Mehindi writes: "If the two hind and the near fore legs are equally blazed with white, the owner of such a horse will be happy as long as he lives." In another place: "The owner of a horse, which, in the centre of a white blaze on its forehead, has curling dark hairs resembling a scorpion, will be miserly and unreasonable, will lose his intelligence, will be without influence and will lose his senses." Again: "When the near forefoot of a horse is white it is called nosegay and its owner should never know fear." When the off fore of a horse is white, he is to be avoided." Similar ideas are expressed in European books of the old time.

Among horse folk, unfamiliar with books, spoken lore takes such fantastic forms that you would think some fabulous creature was being talked of. A writer is forced to be simple in spite of himself, for the mere process of setting down a fancy reduces it to orderly shape, whereas in long rigmaroles of talk round the dreamy hūqqa, old fancies expand and are distorted. And there is a purpose in elaboration. All craftsmen find it profitable to shroud their art in mystery. Even in the West the esoteric science of the horse expert could give points to the newest mystery of "esoteric Buddhism" and beat it easily. In India it is still more to the interest of horse people to keep up the mystery; for the Raja, the Nawāb, and persons of condition must never be allowed to judge for themselves. "Commission" is one of the High Gods of the country, and always in paying one you pay many. The most eligible animal can be condemned for a curling hair or an inauspicious touch of colour by a master of horse whose palm has not been properly greased. In the West also you hear of commission; but, though few horse buyers exercise as much independent judgment as they think, common-sense and reason have some slight share in their transactions.

There are several varieties of indigenous horses recognisable at once, and you hear of more than you can discriminate. Many grains of salt must be taken with horse talk generally and especially with Oriental brag

A RAJA'S HORSE (WAZIRI BREED)

of purity of breed. The Kathiawar horse is interesting on account of his markings, which include the asinine stripe along the back, and occasionally zebra-like stripes on the legs. Marwari horses are prized especially by native chiefs for their size and form. Among the Biloch, who have strong Arab characteristics, racing is the national pastime, but only mares are ridden, colts being killed as soon as they are born—a practice which may be expected to die out. The Biloch preference for mares is expressed in a saying: "A man with his saddle on a mare has his saddle on a horse; a man with his saddle on a horse has his saddle on his head." Their races are a little wild and irregular if judged by a European standard, but there is no doubt as to their popularity, nor as to certain good qualities of the animals. If a Biloch cannot afford a whole mare, he will own as many legs of one as he can manage; and, as the animal has four legs, will keep her a quarter of a year for each leg of which he is master, after which she passes to the owners of the remaining legs. Akin to the Biloch is the Waziri horse; both remarkable for a lyre-like incurving of the ears, which is a beauty or a defect as the amateur may choose, and both have good qualities of their own. In the Himálaya there is a variety of ponies, sturdy gūnths, and yabus that could carry a church and climb up its steeple, Bhutia ponies, and many other hill sorts from Peshawar to Pegu. The Manipur ponies used for polo or *chaugán* are mostly dun, and are excellent beasts in their way, playing the game with very little help from either knee or bridle.

The characteristic all-pervading horse of the hot plains is the *tattoo* or country pony, a cat-hammed, shadowy animal seldom more than thirteen and a half hands high. In the south they speak of the Deccan *tattoo*, which is a better beast than others, but there seems to be no real difference of breed. Among them you often come across distinctly Arab characteristics, and most are dashed with the noble Arab blood. Though seldom good to look at, lean and unkempt, vicious and ill to handle, he is a beast of immense pluck and endurance. The half-soldier, half-brigand bands of Pindāris who made a desert of the India to which the English power succeeded, used him as their sumpter horse; and indeed few but the leaders rode anything

A MONEY-LENDER ON A DECCAN PONY

(Copyright 1891, by J. Lockwood Kipling)

else. The Duke of Wellington made the acquaintance of the Deccan *tattoo* serving in this capacity, and briefly described him, mentioning twenty-five rupees as the average price. Nowadays he is seldom so cheap; he carries the cultivator, his wife and children, to fair or market, and takes the village banker and money-lender abroad to view the crops and collect debts.

Among Hindus he is often saddled and bridled without a morsel of leather in the whole equipment.

In Bengal and Madras, non-equestrian provinces, the animal often shrinks to a framework caricature of a pony; a heavy head hung on a long weak neck, no chest to speak of, inconceivably slender in girth, with weak hind legs working over each other like the blades of a pair of scissors. A little boy of my acquaintance truthfully described this kind of pony as "a real horse, but very like a bicycle." In the North-West Provinces and the Punjab the creature improves, is useful as a pack pony, and draws the ekka and the *palki gāri*. Cruel over-driving and a heartless disregard of the creature's thirst are the worst features of the immense ekka traffic of Northern India. Probably the pedantic rules about drinking cause more suffering than anything else. The native is always drinking water, for in a land where to live is to sweat, you frequently want drink. But what is good for him is thought bad for the pony, foaming and frothing in thirsty misery.

It is easy to see where the Deccan *tattoo* and the country pony generally get their quality from. Marco Polo wrote of a regular importation of Arab horses from the Persian Gulf ports at the end of the thirteenth century. In those days the vessels went up the Tanna Creek to the King of Callian. The town of Callian is now a high and dry railway junction and ships cannot reach it, but the importation has been going on ever since in vessels of probably identical build with those of the old time. You may see them in Bombay harbour, the horses standing a-row on the bags of dates that form part of the cargo, looking exactly like a Noah's Ark with the lid off. From the countries north of Kábul a constant immigration of the animals we call Northern

BOMBAY TRAM-HORSE WEARING HORSE-CAP

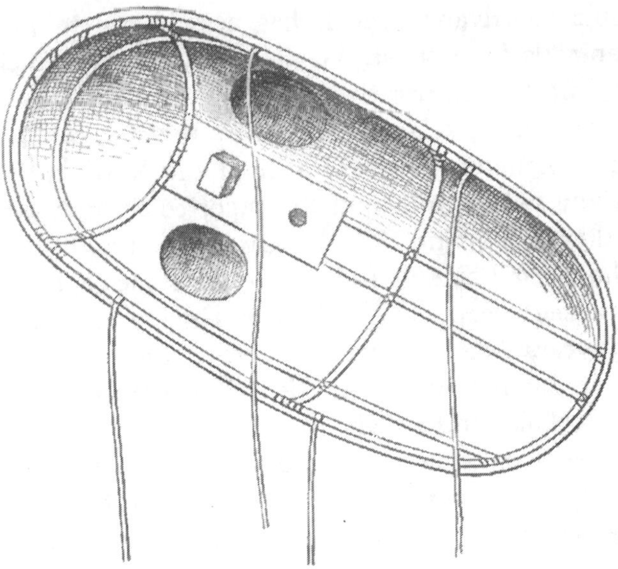

horses, or sometimes Kábulis, has been going on for nearly as long a period, and still continues at the rate of about two thousand annually, according to the calculation of one of the importers most largely concerned. Balkh and the adjacent regions are said to be the main source of the supply of Turkoman horses. The Kafilas or caravans are mostly manned by natives of Ghazni and arrive in the Punjab from Kábul in the cold weather. The Amir of Kábul, through whose country they pass, exacts tolls to the amount of Rs. 32 per horse, mares pay seven rupees less, and His Highness is said to claim the pick of the droves at his own price. Many go to Bombay and Calcutta for the use of the tram companies, and, with the Walers in the same stables, are among the few horses in the world that wear hats as a protection from the sun. Mr. Griffiths of Bombay has been good enough to sketch for me the horse-cap in use, an eminently sensible contrivance, which has been found to protect the animals from sunstroke and headache, to which an animal from a comparatively cold country is liable. The country pony is seldom affected by the sun, but he has not the shoulders and substance of the Northern horse.

Many horses are annually imported from Australia, but they are mainly for the army and wealthy people on the Bengal side of India, and are somewhat outside my present scope. The British Government has for many years been trying to improve the horses of the country by importing English thoroughbreds, Arabs, and Norfolk trotters who stand as sires at the service of farmers under certain conditions, which include the branding of approved mares. So it will be seen that the stock of the country is of a varied nature. The magnificent Shire horse of England is unknown and probably impossible in India.

PUNJAB FARMER ON A BRANDED MARE

A controversy has been going on intermittently for many years as to the merits of the country-bred horse and the question of Indian horse-breeding generally, which it would be impossible to summarise within reasonable limits. But while the dispute has been raging, and Government has been trying experiments and doing as much for horse-rearing as the diverse counsel of experts seemed to justify (and no experts are quite so positive in assertion or so cock-sure in contradiction as horse authorities), a remarkable change has been brought about, and the principle of breeding in India, declared by some to be unworkable, seems to have vindicated itself. At all events, within the last quarter of a century a noticeable improvement has taken place in all sorts and conditions of Indian horseflesh. It is true that the horse-dealer, the Raja, the turf, and the public at large have reaped much of the crop sown by Government for its own army, but, as the Scottish saying has it, "What a neighbour gets is not lost." It is scarcely in the nature of things for a Government to make money in a difficult business like horse-breeding; we can only hope that losing means learning. Nor is it only by the importation of thorough-bred English and Arab sires, or by the establishment of horse-breeding farms, that the influence of Government has been felt. Horse-fairs and horse-shows have been encouraged in the equestrian regions with good effect. Among the prizes given on these occasions are good English saddlery, including bridles with merciful bits, which will one day supersede the cruel thorn bit. But that day is still a long way off.

The Indian turf has played a great part in the improved treatment of horses. One does not look for the nimbus of a saint over the head of the average racing man, but in India he also is a missionary, spreading no ignoble Gospel. For it is impossible to get high speed and quality under the old conditions of starveling upbringing and crippling bondage. The demand for ponies suitable for polo has resulted in an immense improvement in pony breeding. A fair chance for development, good food, and good training are, after all, the most urgent needs of the country pony. Some animals of distinction on the polo ground have been taken from the shafts of the ekka. The high prices given have had their effect, and polo ponies are now to be had which it would be hard to beat for speed, endurance, and handiness, though they may not always be equal to the weight of some players. The prices, in fact, are too high, for the popularity of the game, its increasing fastness, and the importance given to it by inter-regimental tournaments, give the Indian dealer, who is as smart as any other horse-dealer, a great opportunity. Formerly a subaltern of moderate means could afford to buy and keep a string of tolerable animals, but now he must pay fancy prices and often has to abandon the game. Combinations against dealers are frequently discussed, but are scarcely likely to succeed. Though smaller in size and inferior in substance, some of the best modern Indian animals of this sort are not unlike the "cocktail" of England in the early days of English racing, before the final triumph of the thoroughbred; but they have a more elegant contour than the cocktail pictures show, and are probably intrinsically better horses.

That the roads built by the English are a most important factor in Indian progress is one of the notable discoveries of the obvious that I find myself compelled to announce from time to time. In ancient days sculptures and paintings show that horse chariots, recalling the ancient racing chariots of Rome, were largely used, but in more recent times the Prince and his Queens, as well as the peasant and his produce, were drawn by oxen through the deep ruts and mires. There is no evidence of springs until the early Englishman in Calcutta or Madras put a *palki* on springs and four wheels, where it has remained ever since, as the *dāk gāri* or posting carriage. The *ekka*, a single-horse, springless gig, seems to be an indigenous carriage, and has the half-organic air that suggests antiquity. Unknown in the Deccan, Western India, and Sind as far north as Mooltan, it is the people's own "trap" from Peshawar through the Punjab, Hindustan, and parts of Bengal nearly to Calcutta. Nothing could be more characteristic than the primitive, useful, and cheaply-built machine here sketched.

The tea-tray is the top of an inverted three-sided prism resting on the axle, so that every jolt is transmitted straight to the spines of the occupants, who sit doubled up in the "two-foot-rule" fold which the Indian frame seems to take by nature. A long *ekka* drive is sharp discomfort to a European, even when he has the tea-tray to himself; but natives to the manner born pack themselves up like compressed capital N's, occupying but little more floor space when sitting than when standing, and for hours tranquilly maintain a position that would make a European die in an agony of "pins and needles."

It is easy to sketch an *ekka*, but the appearance of the machine is only part of the impression it makes. Noise is a necessity of the Oriental nature; loud, continuous, strident din. So the horse is hung with bells, and the cart has rows of loose plates that clash like cymbals. The maddening din is supposed to cheer the horse as the sheep-bell "keeps a stout heart in the ram

Copyright 1891] [by J. Lockwood Kipling

The ekka, a tea-tray on wheels, dear,
Flies past as its occupants sit,
—For a pony you know never feels, dear—
All five pulling hard at one bit.

with its tinkle." In the dark the jingle may be useful, for lamps do not enter into the *ekka* scheme, as many an Englishman has found to his cost.

The *tonga* is supposed by some to be an indigenous

native of Western India. It is a low, hooded, two-wheeled dog-cart on strong springs, with a centre pole to which a pair of ponies are harnessed by an iron yoke bar, curricle fashion. It is much used in the Deccan, and is now the Himálayan post-cart running to Simla, Murree, and along the new Kashmir road. The vehicle has good points of its own, but its springs proclaim it a modern invention; according to some an importation from the Cape of Good Hope. Travellers by *tonga* often sit behind animals that are simply first-rate of their kind, and perfectly suited to their work.

On the lines under Government control the horses are fairly dealt by, but on routes where the native contractor has his own way sickening examples of barbarity are often seen. A large proportion of *dāk gāri*, or post horses, cannot be started without torture. Some have ears permanently broken and torn by a savage trick of wringing them with the hands and a piece of cord, the twitch is mercilessly applied to the noses of others, the inside of the legs is chafed with a rough rope vigorously pulled with a sawing motion; sometimes fire is applied, while whips and sticks ring like flails on a threshing floor, and all the stable men of the stage yell and swear like demons. The bad temper produced by stupid upbringing is partly to blame, the mysterious nervous affection resulting in jibbing has something to do with it; but dread of the pain of a collar chafing a sore is the usual cause of the trouble.

Many of the *palki gāris* used as hack cabs in Calcutta and other large towns, owned by speculators who know nothing of their business, including liquor-sellers, table-servants, and even priestesses of Venus retired from business, are drawn by scare-crows that recall in a reduced and shadowy form the outlines of

Bewick's grim woodcut,—"Waiting for death." But the mercy of death is denied to them.

Though the North-West *ekka*, the Deccan *tonga*, the Madras *bandy*, the Bombay and Bengal *shigram*, and other variants of the *palki gāri* may be considered characteristically Indian, they by no means exhaust the number of vehicles in use; for, since the days when the craftsmen of Delhi copied the English carriages sent as presents to the Great Mogul, there has been a continuous importation of the best and the worst coach work that Long Acre can produce.

One of the first steps taken in technical progress was the carriage-building trade, now gradually spreading over the country. Oil painting and varnishing, carpentry, smith's work and leather dressing, owe much to this craft. Dog-carts and numerous varieties of one-horse spring carts seem to be supplanting the once universal buggy or hooded gig. The *brum gāri*, brougham; the *fitton gāri*, phaeton or barouche; the *vāgnit*, waggonette, are now built in most large towns by native craftsmen, springs and axle-boxes being of European make. It is of no use to protest against these barbarous words, for, like *bōtel* for bottle, and *kitli* for kettle, with other travesties of our tongue, they are fixed in popular speech. The *vāgnit* seems likely to be the carriage of the future, because of its capacity. The Oriental, like the ant, goes forth in bands, and is capable of piling more people in, on, or about a carriage than would be believed in Europe.

Not only does an improvement in the vehicles in use testify to increased prosperity, but it ought to mean an amelioration in the condition of the horse. One would like to write confidently of the future, but considering all that has been done by our veterinary colleges and hospitals (missionary efforts of the highest value), and all the influence of the British power, it must be confessed that though there is enough for an official triumph, much remains to be done before the horse of the Indian people can be reckoned to have a fair chance. Nor can one who knows the country escape from the reflection that we underrate the apathy and indifference of its various races; alike in this, that they are and must be constitutionally disinclined to take the trouble that merciful and just treatment of animals in servitude involves.

The Indian farrier has some sound notions and is acquainted with a few valuable remedies for disease, but he has a passion for long prescriptions, esteemed according to the number and nastiness of their ingredients. Mixtures of lucky numbers of substances (always odd) must include inert or noxious matter. But the mere number is part of the charm. Like the farriers of Britain, he is given to an abuse of the firing-iron, but cherishes a faith in the pattern of the brand unknown to the Western world. He does his best to make a mystery of his lore and practice, but everybody about an Indian stable seems to have a taste for medicine. Even in England many grooms dabble in quackery and "know of a rare fine thing for a 'oss," which, as a rule, were better let alone. The education of the farrier and of the shoeing-smith is a duty which the Government has undertaken with some success. But the Oriental has a faculty of learning with seeming eagerness and then of laying his lesson aside as one folds a garment and puts it away.

In the West the horse goes to the smith to be shod, in the East the smith comes to the horse; bringing with him a wallet full of tools, a bellows made to work in a hole in the ground, and an apprentice to help him. And the animal's feet are held for him in turn as shown in the accompanying sketch.

Reference has been made at some length to the typical method of dealing with the horses of persons of quality. It is only fair to say that in this field better notions are spreading H.H. The Maharaja of Ulwar, the Maharaja (late Thakore) of Bhaonagar, the Maha-

AN INDIAN FARRIER

raja of Jodhpur, and doubtless other princes, could be cited whose stables and studs, sometimes managed by English experts, show a very different picture from that usually presented. From a series of letters written to the *Pioneer* by my son, describing a tour in Rajputana, I extract a description of a visit he paid to the establishment of a native prince well known on the Indian turf, premising that Colonel Parrott mentioned therein is one of the most successful breeders of horses in India.

"The Maharaja led on from horse-box to horse-box, pointing out each horse of note, and Jodhpur has many. 'There's Raja, twice winner of the Civil Service Cup.' Close to him stood Autocrat, the gray with nutmeg marks on the off shoulder,—a picture of a horse. Next to him was a chestnut Arab, a hopeless cripple, for one of his knees had been smashed and the leg was doubled up under him. It was Turquoise, who six or eight years ago rewarded good feeding by getting away from his groom, falling down, and ruining himself, but who, none the less, has lived an honoured pensioner on the Maharaja's bounty ever since. No horses are shot in Jodhpur stables, and when one dies his funeral is an event. He is wrapped in a white sheet, which is strewn with flowers, and amid the weeping of the grooms is borne away to the burial ground. After doing the honours for half an hour the Maharaja left me, and as I had not seen more than forty horses I felt justified in demanding more. And I got them. Eclipse and Young Revenge were out, down country, but Sherwood, Shere Ali, Conqueror, Tynedale, Sherwood II., a maiden of Abdul Rahman's, and many others of note were in and were brought out. Among the veterans, a wrathful, rampant, red horse still, came Brian Boru, whose name has been written large in the chronicles of the Indian turf, jerking his groom across the road. His near fore is altogether gone, but as a pensioner he condescends to go in harness and is said to be a handful. He certainly looks it. At the two hundred and fifty-seventh horse and perhaps the twentieth block of stables, my brain began to reel, and I demanded rest and information on a certain point. I had gone into some fifty stalls and looked into all the rest, and in the looking had searchingly sniffed. But, as truly as I was then standing far below Brian Boru's bony withers, never the ghost of a stench had polluted the keen morning air. This city of the Houyhnhnms was specklessly clean, cleaner than any stable, racing or private, that I had been into. How was it done? The pure white sand accounted for a good deal, and the rest was explained by one of the Masters of Horse. 'Each horse has one groom at least; Old Ringwood he had four, and we make 'em work. If we didn't we'd be mucked up to the horses' bellies in no time. Everything is cleaned off at once; and whenever the sand's tainted it's renewed. There's quite enough sand, you see, hereabouts. Of course we can't keep their coats so bright as in other stables, by reason of the rolling; but we can keep 'em pretty clean.' This immaculate purity was very striking, and quite as impressive was the condition of the horses, which was English, quite English. Naturally, none of them were in any training beyond daily exercise, but they were fit and in good fettle. Many of them were out on the various tracks, and many were coming in. Roughly, two hundred go out of a morning.

"It was pleasant to sit and watch the rush of the horses through the great opening—gates are not affected—going on to the countryside where they take the air. Here a boisterous unschooled Arab, his flag spun silk in the sunlight, shot out across the road and cried ha! ha! in the scriptural manner, before trying to rid himself of the grinning black imp on his back. Behind him a Kabuli—(surely all Kabulis must have been born with Pelhams in their mouths)—bored sulkily across the road or threw himself across the path of a tall, mild-eyed Kurnál-bred youngster, whose cocked ears and swinging head showed that though he was so sedate, he was thoroughly taking in his surroundings, and would very much like to know if there were anybody better than himself on the course that morning. Impetuous as a schoolboy and irresponsible as a monkey, one of the Prince's polo ponies, not above racing in his own set, would answer the query by rioting past the sedate pupil of Colonel Parrott, his body cloth flapping free in the wind and his head and banged tail in the air. The youngster would swing himself round and polka-mazurka for a few paces, till his attention would be caught by some dainty Child of the Desert, an Arab fresh from the Bombay stables, sweating at every sound, backing and filling like a rudderless ship. Then, thanking his stars that he was wiser than some people, No. 177 would lob on to the track and settle down to his spin like the gentleman he was.

"Elsewhere, the eye fell upon a cloud of nameless ones, whose worth will be proved next hot weather when they are seriously taken in hand—skirmishing over the face of the land and enjoying themselves immensely. High above everything else, like a collier among barges, screaming shrilly, a black, flamboyant Marwári stallion, with a crest like the crest of a barb, barrel-bellied, goose-rumped, and river-maned, pranced through the press, while the slow pacing Waler carriage horses eyed him with deep disfavour, and the young prince's tiny mount capered under his pink Roman nose, kicking up as much dust as the Foxhall colt, dancing a saraband on a lovely patch of sand. In and out of the tangle, going to or coming back from the courses, ran, shuffled, rocketed, plunged, sulked, or stampeded countless horses of all kinds, shapes, and descriptions—so that the eye at last failed to see what they were, and retained only a general impression of a whirl of bays, grays, iron-grays, and chestnuts with white stockings, some as good as could be desired, others average, but not one distinctly bad.

"'We have no downright bad 'uns in this stable. What's the use?' said the English Master of Horse calmly. 'They are al good beasts, and one with another must cost more than a thousan each. This year's new ones brought from Bombay, and the pic of our own studs, are a hundred strong, about. Maybe more. Yes they look all right enough; but you can never know what they ar going to turn out. Live stock is very uncertain.'

"'And how are the stables managed; how do you make roo for the fresh stock?'

"'Something this way. Here are all the new ones an Colonel Parrott's lot and the English colts that Maharaja Pertá Singh brought out with him from home. Winterlake, out o' Quee Consort, that chestnut with the two white stockings you're lookin at now. Well, next hot weather we shall see what they are mad of, and which is who. There's so many that the trainer hard knows 'em one from another till they begin to be a good deal fo ward. Those that haven't got the pace, or that the Mahara don't fancy, they're taken out and sold for what they'll bring. T man who takes the horses out has a good job of it. He com back and says: "I sold such and such for so much and her the money." That's all. Well, our rejections are worth havin They have taken prizes at the Poona horse show. See for yo self. Is there one of those there you wouldn't be glad to take a hack, and look well after, too? Only, they're no use to us, a so out they go by the score. We've got sixty riding boys, perha more, and they've got their work cut out to keep 'em all goi What you've seen are only the stables. We've got one stud Bellara, eighty miles out, and they come in sometimes in droves three or four hundred from the stud. They raise Marwáris th too, but that's entirely under native management. We've got thing to do with that. The natives reckon a Marwári the b country-bred you can lay your hands on, and some of them beauties! Crests on 'em like the top of a wave. Well, the that stud and another stud, and, reckoning one with anothe should say the Maharaja has nearer twelve hundred thar thousand horses of his own. For this place here two wag loads of grass come in every day from Marwar Junction. L knows how many saddles and bridles we've got! I never coun I suppose we've about forty carriages, not counting the o that get shabby and are stacked in places in the city, as I supp you've seen. We take 'em out in the morning, a regular string all together, brakes and all; but the prettiest turn-out we ever turned out was Lady Dufferin's pony four-in-hand. Walers, thirteen two the wheelers and thirteen one the leaders. They took prizes at Poona. That *was* a pretty turn-out. The prettiest in India. Lady Dufferin, she drove it when the Viceroy was down here last year. There are bicycles and tricycles in the carriage department too. I don't know how many, but when the Viceroy's camp was held, there was about one a-piece for the gentlemen with remounts. How do we manage to keep the horses so quiet? You'll find some of the youngsters play the goat a good deal when they come out o' stable, but, as you say, there's no vice generally. It's this way. We don't allow any curry-combs. If we did the men would be wearing out their brushes on the combs. It's all elbow-grease here. They've got to go over the horses with their hands. They must handle 'em, and a native, he's afraid of a horse. Now an English groom, when the horse is playing the fool, clips him over the head with a curry-comb, or punches him in the belly; and that hurts the horse's feelings. A native, he just stands back till the trouble is over. He *must* handle the horse, or he'd get into trouble for not dressing him, so it comes to all handling and no licking, and that's why you won't get hold of a really vicious brute in these stables. Old Ringwood, he had four grooms, and he wanted 'em, every one, but the other horses haven't more than one man a-piece. The Maharaja, he keeps fourteen or fifteen horses for his own riding. Not that he cares to ride now, but he likes to have his horses and no one else can touch 'em. Then, there's the horses he mounts his visitors on when they go out pig-sticking (boar-hunting) and such like, and there's a lot of horses that go to Maharaja Pertáb Singh's new cavalry regiment. So you see a horse can go through all three degrees sometimes before he is sold and be a good horse at the end of it. And I think that's about all.'"

While speaking of the horse as he is, we are forgetting the popular estimate of him. In spite of ill-usage, he stands for honour and state both among Hindus and Muhammadans. Centuries have passed since the Aswamheda or great Hindu horse-sacrifice was celebrated, but the tradition lingers even among unlettered folk. As associated with *Sūrya*, the Sun God, he is held in esteem. Our analytical way of explaining the inner meaning of such associations is not congenial to the blandly receptive Oriental mind, which does not take its stories to pieces as if they were clocks. There may be astronomical facts hidden in the horses harnessed to the chariot of the sun, but so far as the Hindu at large is concerned, they are inventions of European Scholars.

Muhammadans unite to praise him, for the Prophet himself, who at one critical time had but two horses in his whole army, and knew his value, has left a formal benediction: "Thou shalt be to man a source of happiness and wealth, thy back shall be a seat of honour and thy belly of riches, every grain of barley given to thee shall purchase indulgence for the sinner." Also, from the winged horses of Persian invention, akin to Pegasus, and Borak the mystic steed of Muhammad, he stands for fancy and imagination. A dreamer or a poetical person "rides the horse of the winds." Swiftness and despatch have for long been associated with the horse. The rapid transmission of news by the horse post of the first Darius was one of the wonders of the ancient world, so the Persians said that the great King's post-riders flew faster than the cranes. Eastern proverbs and stories never die, but are handed down from age to age, from hero to hero, and in recent times the Emperor Akbar's similar post still further helped to connect the diffusion of news,—literature and intelligence,—with horses in the popular mind. Written words are still said to "gallop on a paper horse," the order of Government goes forth "on a steed of air." The postcards of the Nepal State have a little black horse stamped upon them.

Then, in addition to many esoteric sayings of stable lore, there are homely words in everybody's mouth.

"You can't find out the jokes of a horse, nor the ailments of a baby" hints that spirited horses have more to set them capering and kicking than the human knows of. Of an old woman in gay attire they say, "An old mare in a red rein." Our brutal saw says, "Old ewe, lamb fashion." The Bengalis say, "You tell a horse by his ears and a generous man by his gifts," an inconclusive saying. *Do* you tell a horse by his ears, except perhaps in Bengal? "When the horse's tail grows longer he'll brush his own flies off," is a saying with a reference to the access of influence consequent on official promotion. The Persians say, and the saying is current in India, "It is too late to give barley when you are at the foot of the hill." "The Governor's (or Government officer's) mare eats sixty pounds of corn," is a common and warrantable complaint of the exactions of official underlings in the name of their masters.

Horses take a great part in most Indian weddings, Both Hindu and Muhammadan bridegrooms ride in procession, while the bride is borne in a canopied litter. In Bengal, however, all go on wheels, caparisoned horses being led to swell the show. In some hill regions both bride and bridegroom are carried in litters. The equestrian marriage parade is probably an ancient custom based, it may be, on the marriage by capture of which we hear so much. In Western India the bridegroom rides, covered with tinsel and gay clothing, in the midst of a moving square of artificial flowers and bushes, counterfeiting a garden, borne on long platforms on the heads of coolies. In the case of the trading Hindus of the cities this ride is often the first and last occasion of crossing a horse. The child bridegroom begins his progress with a light heart, but the weight of his finery, the smoke of the torches, the din of the throbbing, screaming music, and the ceaseless clamour soon tell, and you may see the poor little man crying as he is held in the saddle, or lifted off, half dead with sleep, and put into a litter. When the bridegroom is of mature age the effect is often absurdly quaint. Part of the wedding finery is a veil, which has come to be a dropping-well arrangement of tinsel or cut paper fringes through which the most sensible face alive looks foolish. But one of the peculiarities of India is that nothing there is absurd. Disguises that would be grotesque and laughable in the West are accepted in the East without comment.

Some religious mendicants habitually ride, especially on the Punjab frontier. You may also see strings of them entering the towns of the plains in picturesque procession. Mendicancy is an honourable profession, practised by many men of admirable character, and by a host of ruffians who lead vagabond lives, diversified by drunkenness, thieving, and debauchery. Some *Bairágis*, as distinguished from other ascetics, are gathered into monasteries, nor would it be easy for a purist in morals to find fault with their lives and conduct. Other sects that wander and beg have houses and lands ; but there is no escape from the conclusion that the country, notwithstanding its hidden wealth, is too poor to keep vast armies of able-bodied priests and beggars. The wonder is that though the respectable classes complain bitterly of sanctified loaferdom, there is scarcely a house that does not periodically receive and entertain more or less godly loafers.

Concerning the mule there is not much that can be said with propriety, for his mixed descent points salt and perpetual gibes at ill-assorted marriages and bastards, whereon native opinion is very severe. As in Æsop, when the mule boasts of his mother's high family, he is asked for news of his father, whereupon the poor wretch is silent and ashamed. There is a strong pre-

A BEGGAR ON HORSEBACK (HINDU DEVOTEE)

judice in the minds of many Hindus against mule breeding as unnatural and improper. The degradation of the ass, the offscouring of all things, is probably at the root of this. It is wicked to couple a noble creature of good caste with the ignoble, impure, small-pox-defiled donkey. As to mere differences of kind, it is not likely that the Hindu would trouble his incurious mind; for stranger unions than this are recorded with approval. Thus, in a countryside saying current in the Deccan, the beauty of a breed of cows is popularly attributed to the interference of an antelope sire. So one might class the mule as a European introduction (he really is a Government institution); while the Hindu smiles complacently, seeing in the creature a type of the irregularity and inferiority of the mixed lineages of the West.

The mule, however, is bred in increasing numbers, for he is an ideal pack animal, born and made to carry the burdens of armies over difficult countries, and good at draught. Sure of foot, hard of hide, strong in constitution, frugal in diet, a first-rate weight carrier, indifferent to heat and cold, he combines the best, if the most homely characteristics of both the noble houses from which he is descended. He fails in beauty, and his infertility is a reproach, but even ugliness has its advantages. The heavy head of the mule is a mercy to him, for both in practice and the written orders of Government it is ordained that he is not to be bothered with bearing-reins. So that big *chef* serves its natural purposes and is an index, unerring as a steam engine's dial, to how much is left in him. When tired the ears droop back, losing the alert forward tilt of the morning, and the head drops lower and lower. This freedom of the head gives additional play to his heels, for he is a superb kicker. A spirited mule in full fling radiates a rainbow of kicks, an aurora made splendid by the flash and flicker of his iron hoofs. With his fore-feet as a centre he clears for himself a sacred inviolable circle. And there are mules as handy with a swift fore-foot as ever was Tom Sayers with his left. So it is written in

Major Burn's official manual: "Examining a mule's mouth with the view of ascertaining his age is at times a risky operation, and the following method is recommended: Put a halter on the mule's head and blindfold him; stand well in against the near fore-shoulder, pass the hand gently up the neck, patting the animal as it goes, and take a firm grip of the root of the ear with

THE WHEELS OF A MOUNTAIN BATTERY

the right hand. Seize the upper lip and nose quickly and lightly with the left hand. This must be done quickly and resolutely, guarding against a blow from the fore-foot. In this way a glance at the incisors will be obtained, and it will be seen whether the corner tooth is temporary or permanent." It is to no common animal that a careful Government inscribes so respectful a tribute.

Perhaps the finest mules in the service of the Indian

Government are those which carry its mountain artillery, an arm in which equipment, adaptation to work, smartness and efficiency in action seem to have reached their highest point. Some animals carry the guns, others ammunition chests, and others the wheels of the batteries, and all are able to go anywhere. In pictures by amateur artists you may see them represented in action on a mountain summit boldly outlined against the sky. But in practice this most picturesque position is not the best for the health of either gunners or mules, nor for efficient attack. There is a special science of mountain gunnery akin to good deer-stalking or ibex hunting. While watching a mountain battery at work, and studying the hill contours, you may gain some hint of the powers of an arm which delivers its fire from the most unexpected places, and seems to arrive by unseen and sheltered ways at exactly the proper point of attack. It is natural that the officers and men of so highly specialised a service should cherish an *esprit de corps* which is perhaps not exaggerated in a verse from my son's barrack-room ballad, "Screw-Guns"—

"They send us along where the roads are, but mostly we goes
where they ain't;
We'd climb up the side of a sign-board an' trust to the stick
o' the paint;
We've chivied the Naga an' Lushai, we've give the Afreedee
man fits,
For we fancies ourselves at two thousand, we guns that are built
in two bits."

CHAPTER IX

OF ELEPHANTS

"The torn boughs trailing o'er the tusks aslant,
The saplings reeling in the path he trod,
Declare his might,—our lord the elephant,
Chief of the ways of God.

"The black bulk heaving where the oxen pant,
The bowed head toiling where the guns careen,
Declare our might,—our slave the elephant,
The servant of the Queen." R. K.

FROM THE SANCHI TOPE

THE Elephant has always been one of the wonders of the world, amazing in his aspect and full of delightful and surprising qualities. Nor does familiarity lessen his hold upon the imagination of mankind. Next after the cow he seems to be of all the beasts the Hindu favourite. At the present moment the most carefully-kept studs of Elephants are in the hands of Hindu Rajas, and the Muhammadan Nawāb prefers the horse. This is an ancient predilection on the part of the Hindu. While other animals represented in Hindu Art are merely decorative and conventional, or awkward and ill-understood, there is invariably a strong feeling for nature in Hindu elephant sculptures and paintings. The contrast may be noticed in most old temples, but especially in the sculptured gates or tori of the Sanchi tope in Central India, where all kinds of animals are shown, but the elephant alone is carved with complete knowledge, and unvarying truth of action.

The grave beast is as great a favourite of the poet as of the artist. The back view of the elephant as he shuffles along, is like nothing so much as that of the stout and elderly "long-shore" fisherman and sailor of our English watering-places, whose capacious nether garments, alone among human habiliments, have the horizontally creased bagginess peculiar to the elephant. Dickens said long ago that the elephant employs the worst tailor in all the world. But these wrinkled columns suggest feminine grace to the Oriental poet, and "elephant-gaited" is the supreme and also the invariable expression for the voluptuous movements of women: "A voice as sweet as that of the Koil, and a gait as voluptuous as that of the elephant: An eye like the antelope's, a waist like the lion's, and a gait like the elephant's," are specimens of an endless series of descriptions of female beauty. Nor are these expressions confined to ancient poetry, for they are as current to-day as ever they were. Walking behind elephants and women, I have occasionally seen a hint f the poet's meaning, but only a hint; and one is riven to the conclusion that the simile, like many nore in Oriental verse, is mainly conventional. The east gets along so quietly he might almost be said to lide, but his movements have little of the fine rhythmic wing and poise one ees in the noble gait of a well-formed Hindu woman.

GANÉSHA (FROM AN ANCIENT HINDU SCULPTURE)

As furnishing a head to Ganésa, Ganésh, or Ganpati, the wise and humorous god who is invoked at the beginning of all enterprises, whose auspicious image is placed over most Hindu doorways, and whose mystic sign (familiarly spoken of as a Ganésh) stands on the first page of Hindu ledgers and day-books, the elephant has an immense hold on the affections of the people. His sign 卐 is the *svastika*, the cross fylfot of our Western heraldry and the hermetic cross of Freemasonry, traceable from Troy town to China. The traveller and the pilgrim look to Ganésha for protection, the merchant for fortune, the student for advancement, and the housewife for luck.

The popular version of the origin of Ganésha is

that during one of the absences of the great Lor Shiva, Parbati his wife, taking a bath, rubbed some tin pellets off her skin and amused herself by mouldin them into the form of a child, till at last she breathe life into it. Shiva returned and was outraged to fin a baby where no baby should be, so he promptly cu off its head with his sharp war-quoit. Then Parbat explained and Shiva said in effect: "Dear me! this i

SHIV OR MAHADEO, WITH THE INFANT GANÉSH
(FROM AN INDIAN LITHOGRAPH)

very sad, why did not you speak sooner?" Then catching sight of an elephant standing near, he cut of its head and clapped it on the decapitated baby "Now, it's all right!" said he, "I was always rathe hasty." And, to make amends, he ordained that in every enterprise Ganésa's name should be the firs called upon. So the elephant's head grew on the God-like body, that is to say, on the corpulent body of a well-fed Baniya, who in his four hands bears suitable emblems,—a disc or war-quoit, sometimes interpreted as a cake, an elephant goad, a sacrificial shell, and a lotus. His seat is a lotus, and his steed or vâhan a rat. In this state he sits over thousands of Hindu doors. His effigy is modelled in clay and gaily painted for most Hindu households in Western India, and on his great feast-day, after four days' worship, thousands of such effigies are borne with shouting and rejoicing to be thrown into the sea or the nearest water. If Ganésha stood he would be the very image of many fat, rupee-worshipping Baniyas, to be seen all over India,—even as—with some irreverence—I have ventured to draw him. But he never stands, though a fat man is often spoken of as a "cow-dung Ganésh."

Although at first sight merely monstrous to Western eyes, this quaint personage grows in interest as one learns his attributes and becomes familiar with his character and person. He seems, as he sits meditatively poising his heavy head, to be the Nick Bottom of the Hindu Pantheon, with a touch of the jovial humour immemorially associated with fat men. Like Falstaff, he appears to chuckle over his bulk and to say, "I cannot tell whether it is the weight of my head or of my belly (in Southern India he is familiarly known as the belly God) that prevents my rising, but here I sit and survey mankind with cheery geniality." Campbell in his "Pleasures of Hope" speaks of "Ganesá sublime," which to those who know him for what he is,—the sagacious and respectable "God of getting on"—is a deliciously incongruous epithet and a false quantity besides.

He is mixed up in country-side stories with mere human creatures in a friendly fashion which shows that he is a popular favourite. Thus, once upon a time Shiva and Parbati were strolling about on the earth, and they visited a temple of Shiva, in the precincts of which sat a poor beggar-man asking for alms. Parbati said to her awful husband, "It is really too bad that this man, who has been begging here for years in your name, should not be better provided for. I call it discreditable." They passed, wrangling, into the court of the temple till Shiva impatiently cried: "Ho! Ganésha." The voice of Ganésha came from the inside — "Ho!" "Let something be done for the tiresome beggar-man your mother has been bothering me about!" "Very good; I will see that he has a lakh of rupees within the next three days." "That will do," said the great Mahadeo, and he passed away with his quarrelsome wife. Now, while they were talking, a Hindu Baniya (dealer and money-lender) was standing hidden behind the pillars, and though nearly frightened to death, he cast about in his greedy mind how to secure that lakh of rupees. So he went to the unconscious beggar, sitting in the outer court, and asked about his earnings.

IF GANÉSHA STOOD

"My earnings are nothing," said the beggar, "sometimes a copper or two, sometimes only cowries, sometimes a handful of rice or pulse;—nothing." Pretending to be interested in the matter from mere curiosity, the usurer offered five rupees for all the beggar earned during the next three days. Startled by this large sum, the beggar held back, protesting the Baniya would be a loser, whereupon more were offered. The talk went on in the dawdling inconclusive way that only those who have tried to strike a bargain in India can understand, till finally the beggar insisted on consulting his wife. As frequently happens in Indian stories, as in Indian life, she was a very clever woman: "Depend upon it that usurer is after no good; offered you fifty rupees, did he? Then it's worth more than fifty times as much. God knows how, but that's not our affair. Go back and don't give over bargaining even if you go as high as half a lakh of rupees."

The beggar went back and the bargain began again, and was finally closed at half a lakh of rupees, which were duly brought to the wondering mendicant.

The usurer hung round the temple, anxious to see how Ganésha would bestow the lakh of rupees on the beggar-man. At last he heard the approach of the Gods, and as they passed the beggar, the mother of Death and Life asked Shiva if anything had been done for him. Again Ganésha was summoned, and as Shiva spoke, the great stone threshold of the temple rose from its place and jammed the trembling usurer's leg against the wall. Said Ganésha—"It is all right! the beggar has received half of the promised lakh of rupees, and I've got the man who owes him the other half fast by the leg here, and he will not be released till he has paid the uttermost farthing."

Then that covetous one's liver was turned to water, for he knew that he who owes to the Gods must pay.

When a native storyteller repeats a triviality of this kind, one seems to see the belly-god asleep in the dusk of the temple and to hear the rustle of his dry trunk uncoiling as he awakes, the jovial carelessness of his voice echoing in the carved vaults and roof, and his chuckle of satisfaction as the usurer is caught.

There is no trace of the humorous and friendly vulgarity by which Ganésha the elephant-headed and Hanumān, the monkey god, are distinguished among the Gods of the Vedas, where the clouds sail high; while the comparative rarity of their sculptures in the older temples shows that they had at first but a small share in official mythology.

Here it may be worth while to say of the popular impression that the Vedas are text-books of Hinduism, that it is incorrect. Most educated Hindus talk of the Vedas, and modern Hindu reformers, like Rammohun Roy, Keshub Chandra Sen, and Dayanand Saraswati, insisted that the Vedas contain the elements of all the religion the world can want; but to whip a dead horse with deep emotion and lively faith does not necessarily bring it to life again, and the Vedas have been dead for centuries. Their literary resurrection is part of the revival of Oriental Scholarship brought about by European Scholars such as Colebrooke and his many successors. It has been said by a competent authority that nine hundred and ninety-nine of every thousand Hindus know nothing about them, and that they are not Hindu in any real sense.

In the earliest myths the elephant is said to take the place of thunder and lightning, and is one of the steeds f Indra, but while horses and cows are perpetually eferred to, mentions of the elephant are comparatively are. The Solar Garuda still survives—(the Brahminy ite is called a garuda in Southern India),—and he arries an elephant in his beak as in the Hindu epics. The ancient fantasy that four elephants support the four orners of the earth is still alive, and they are thus epresented in mystic diagrams printed and painted on alico for Hindu Jogis. Pictures and sculptures of the oddess Lakshmi show her seated while elephants pour vater over her head from vases upheld in their trunks. t seems fair to conclude that though the elephant was a avourite of the earlier poets, he came late to his present igh place in the celestial company through the side loor of popular liking. It is also possible that he was dmitted late because he was unknown to the earliest vriters.

Buddhism, now dead and done with as far as India proper is concerned,—and so overgrown with fungous growth of idolatry and demonolatry in other lands as to be almost unrecognisable,—has its elephant legends. The elephant takes the place of the dove in the Annunciation to Maya Devi of the coming of the Bodisát. She lies asleep and the creature appears to her in many sculptures at Amravati and Southern India, but, hitherto, only once in the extensive series from the North-West frontier where the Buddhist legend is told with more than a mere touch of the classic Art of Europe. Another incident of the legend is the miracle of the subjugation of the elephant, made *mast* or frenzied by Devaditta, the envious schismatic, and sent to meet and murder the Lord Buddha. They met as the conspirator hoped, but instead of trampling the master underfoot, the creature stood still and worshipped as Buddha touched its forehead. Later storie tell of an elephant's body hurled an immense distanc by the Lord Buddha, but they belong to a cycle of ir crustations of dead matter.

An ancient use of the elephant has come to light i the copperplate and other inscriptions which are all th: is left to record early Hindu dynasties. Grants of lan wells, and buildings made for religious purposes we set forth in poetical terms in inscriptions which are ofte of great length. Frequently, in fixing a boundary a elephant was turned loose and the course the wise bea took was accepted as the limit of the grant. How l went north by such and such a stream, then turne north-east towards a clump of mango trees and so fort is elaborately described; the notion evidently being th: the elephant was heaven-directed. But one can see tl astute attendant Brahmans from here, skilled in direc ing the heavenly intuitions of both men and beasts their own profit. The praises of kings as rehearsed c these documents are monuments of hyperbole. Ruttin elephants, fighting elephants, thousands of elephant millions of elephants, billions of elephants frenzied wit blood and irresistible in strength, are as naught to thes monarchs of the prime, who also are represented miracles of benevolence and virtue. No superlative too strong for these absurd rigmaroles, among whic antiquarians grope in search of a fact, a name, or a dat There are many lies in history, but Hindu writers a remarkable for having deliberately and of set princip ignored all the facts of life. All is done, however, wit such an air of conviction and pious purpose that w must use Dr. Johnson's kindly discrimination and sa they are not inexcusable, but consecrated liars.

I know a Jemadar of Mahouts, *i.e.* a head elepha

keeper, who says there is a tradition among men of his craft that elephants first came to India from the farthest East,—"from China and beyond." This notion was supported by quotations from elephant words of command, some of which "are not Indian talk and must be Chinese" (or Burmese). An elephant driver's philology may not command much respect, but the notion is worth mentioning. The Sanscrit word *hāthi*, the "handed" one (Lord Tennyson, following Lucretius, says, "serpent handed"), in popular use is less used by mahouts than the Pali, *gaj*, frequently compounded with weapons, flowers, etc., to make a name, as *Katár-gaj*—dagger elephant; *Moti-gaj*—pearl elephant. The Persian word *pil* is also used,—the chess bishop is a *pilah* or elephant, and an elephant stable is a *pil-khana*. No beast has so many pretty names; Pearl, Diamond, Necklace of Beauty, Lightning, Lily, Rose, Jasmine, Lotus, Silver Star, Garland of Flowers, Golden One, Black Snake, are a few, and the heroes and heroines of poetry also lend their names to my lord the elephant, and testify to the esteem in which he is held. For female elephants the word *piyāri*, love or darling, is frequently added to some pretty female name, as *Radha piyāri*; (Radha is Krishna's wife). Mahouts also claim that he is the only animal in man's service who is told in so many words to eat and sleep. As a matter of fact, although there may be a word of command for sleep, it can be of little use, for no creature sleeps so little or so lightly,—seldom for more than four hours out of the twenty-four.

A popular and ancient name for a king is *Gajpati*, Elephant Lord. The beast is a pageant in himself, and when arrayed as only the Oriental knows how, he is splendid in colour and majestic in mass. The finest part of the ceremonial at the Delhi Imperial assemblage, was the great fleet of elephants riding at anchor, so to speak, among the serried waves of troops and people. When the tremendous *feu-de-joie* that followed the proclamation was fired, there was a movement of alarm among these mighty creatures. "That startled them," we said, but did not guess the truth, that several people were killed in the crush that followed the slight stir we saw in the distant host as when a breeze stirs the growing corn. Kings are not now the only lords of elephants, for a significant sign of the prosperity of the country is the possession of elephants by men whose fathers never owned them, and whose rank would be better represented by the word Squire than Lord. Many merchants and traders can now better afford the glory of elephants than real kings. There is a Raja in the hills,—a very small Raja,—with a very small income, exactly four-fifths of which are spent in maintaining an elephant, the awe and admiration of his little handful of subjects. They all spend much of their large staple of leisure over the elephant, and rightly too, for he is a more imposing symbol than a crown and sceptre or a diamond plume, and when their Raja rides forth, they follow him with pride and shouting.

Though essentially amiable, the elephant was often made to serve as public executioner by native princes in the ante-British days. Sometimes the victim was bound hand and foot, then the living log was chained with a fathom long chain to the hind foot of an elephant which was swiftly hurried through the city for all to see the battering out of his life. It is only a year or two since the executioner elephant of a Hill State, which was known to have killed a large number of persons in his official capacity, died from cold while crossing a mountain pass. The Raja to whom he belonged towards the close of his career was more than half mad and led his little court a terrible life. He used to appear in durbar saying: "I have been dreaming of such an one, let him be slain." A respectable old gentleman whose forehead was disfigured by a scar, told a friend of mine how it was once his fate to be dreamed of and ordered for execution, and how he was only saved at the last moment by a friendly Wăzir or Minister suggesting to the Raja that if the poor man paid a fine of a thousand rupees and was branded on the brow, he would probably take care in the future not to interfere with His Highness's dreams, whereas if he were killed out-right his ghost would surely reappear. This argument prevailed for once. It was the Raja's pleasure to officiate as mahout on these occasions. The bound victim was handed to the elephant, who at the word of command seized him with his trunk and whirled him right and left against his fore-legs with the familiar action, peculiar to elephants, of swishing the dust from each wisp of provender before putting it into the mouth. Then he was thrown on the ground and kicked from fore to hind feet to and fro, then his arms were wrenched from his body. Then the great feet came down upon him in turn, and at a final word he was knelt upon; the now lifeless body being crushed to a shapeless mass. And all was done with a slow deliberation of ordered movement that must have been terrible to see. Dr. Wolff describes another hill Raja as a most stupid and ignorant man, and "the most horrid brute that ever lived. His great delight was to ride upon an elephant, which was made to tread upon a little child, so as to crush it to death."

Yet cruelty ought not to be a tradition of the Himálaya, for the only Oriental I have seen shed a tear for an animal was a Wăzir or Minister of that same Hill

State, which need not be named here. Once at a halting-place far in the hills, leaning on a rail with a friend, we watched the sunset. At a little distance a pony was grazing on a tiny green meadow terrace above the road. As we looked we saw with amazement that the pony was disappearing, hind-quarters first, until it sank completely out of sight ; nor, from our point of view, was there any apparent solution of continuity in the green carpet on which but now it stood. One of those absurd occurrences that incline you to pinch yourself to feel if you are awake,—it was in reality quite simple. The meadow was the roof of some long disused huts, and the rotten timbers supporting the soil had given way, letting the surprised pony down into a sort of cellar. The beast was the property of a Wăzir returning with his retinue from a visit to Simla, and his grief was quaintly demonstrative. Weeping hard, he laid alongside the chasm trying to embrace his steed, nearly tumbling in himself, and while we were busy with ropes and timbers hauling the creature up and contriving that he should emerge on the side towards the hill, the good Wăzir distractedly hovered round, wringing his hands, and doing less than nothing in the work of rescue. The pony was never in danger, was no whit the worse, but its master's tears were real and his words of sympathy were sincere.

The real character of the elephant has been studied exhaustively and described once for all by Mr. G. P. Sanderson in his admirable book, *Thirteen years among the wild beasts of India.* Mr. Sanderson is not only a master of Indian woodcraft and a Nimrod of varied experiences, but a most sympathetic observer of animal life and character, and yet as acute and discriminating as a Judge on the Bench. He has disposed of the wonderful stories of cunning and devotion attributed to the elephant, such as the douche of dirty water thrown over the spiteful ninth-part man who pricked the creature's trunk with his needle, and the artilleryman snatched from under the wheel of a gun. Mr. Sanderson also says that "the natives of India never speak of the elephant as a peculiarly intelligent animal, and it does not figure in their ancient literature for its wisdom, as do the fox, the crow, and the monkey." My experience is that the popular estimate of the elephant's character and intelligence is a high one ; and with regard to the neglect of the animal by ancient writers as a type of wisdom we should remember that Oriental poetry and legend have adopted from the earliest times a series of similitudes to which they adhere with mechanical fidelity. There is a polity of animals, so to speak. The jackal is cunning and clever ; the tiger is fierce and deadly, but may be most ignominiously deceived and played with by clever jackals and old women ; the crow is sly and ready ; the parrot is wise, a tale-bearer, and full of resource ; the monkey is intelligent and kin to man ; the serpent, when he is not a prince bewitched, is secret, malignant, and powerful ; the dove is gentle ; the deer and the antelope are tender and affectionate, pious Brahmans of the jungle—and so forth and so following ; but the elephant invariably appears as the image of power and might in war. Kings are elephants and so are great warriors. Ticketed, as it were, with this lordly label, the poet and the storyteller of the prime, whose means were simple and whose discriminations were broad, would hesitate to notice in the elephant homely qualities already assigned to the jackal, the crow, and the monkey.

The permanent retention of the elephant as the type of martial prowess is another illustration of the merely literary and unobservant quality of much of the work for which our admiration is challenged by scholars. The real fact of the animal's nature is gentleness. His trunk might be packed full of the jewels of which he is said to carry a priceless sample in his head, so careful is he to guard it from danger. Nor is he cautious without a cause. He cannot live without his trunk, and though guarded by a pair of ivory bayonets, it is as vulnerable as a garden slug. It is admitted in a saying still current that "the mad elephant destroys its own army." If, for mad, we say frightened, we reach the main truth of elephant warfare from the time of Porus to that Mohurrum fête day when Raja Sahib drove his elephants with iron-clad brows against the gates of Arcot, and Clive's bullets sent them raging back to trample on their own masters.

Mr. Sanderson speaks of mahouts as "rascals more often than not," and as "invariably superstitious and ignorant." They tell and believe of the beasts in their charge more wonderful stories of intelligence than any in our children's books. These stories have spread and are so firmly credited that I venture to question his assertion that natives of India never speak of the animal as peculiarly intelligent. A mahout told me and a group of native friends, of an elephant that cherished a grudge against his driver, who, being aware of this, kept carefully out of the animal's reach, and on the march spread his sleeping-blanket at what he thought a safe distance. But one night the elephant chewed the end of a long bamboo till the fibres were loose and brush-like, and, pushing it "gently, gently, slowly, slowly," towards his sleeping enemy, whose long hair was loose, twisted the bamboo so that its fibres were firmly entangled, and before he could awake pulled the poor wretch within reach of the quick kicking feet, which promptly made an end of him.

All my friends believed this terrible tale, and so did I,—for the moment; and that is quite enough for all artistic and Oriental purposes.

They also gave credit to a calculating elephant who was allowed a ration of twelve flap-jacks of wheaten meal for his supper. But the mahout had a large family and appropriated one of the cakes. The wise elephant turned the pile over and laid out the eleven cakes in a row, trumpeting loudly when the master came by; so that mahout was beaten with shoes.

Another tale, for which I do not claim implicit belief, tells of an elephant who with his mahout was engaged to root up bushes in a tea garden. The mahout, like more of his class, was in the habit of going on periodical drinking bouts. Once he asked for ten days' leave to attend a funeral, assuring the Planter that he could instruct his beast to work faithfully under the goad of a substitute who was there and then introduced, while the elephant was formally charged to behave well and work hard during his master's ten days of absence. But the funeral was a very thirsty one, and on the eleventh day the mahout had not returned. The substitute came rushing up to the Planter's bungalow, crying that the elephant refused to work. The British Planter said he would see about that, took his whip, and went to reason with him, but presently came back at his highest speed, followed by the angry beast with uplifted trunk. The coolies ran away in fright, and for two days my lord the elephant roamed round the deserted gardens at his leisure. On the thirteenth day the mahout returned and was received with gladness by the animal, who forthwith set about his work with a will; but they say the Planter, being a bloated capitalist, refused to retain a creature which could go on strike to such purpose as to shut up the whole concern.

Mahouts also believe that when a wild elephant is coming downhill and cannot reach forward with his trunk to sound a dangerous foot-hold, he breaks a sapling and, holding it like an alpen-stock, probes and feels his way. Colonel Lewin tells me of a belief in the Chittagong Hill tracts, that wild elephants assemble together to dance! Further, that once he came with his men on a large cleared place in the forest, the floor beaten hard and smooth, like that of a native hut. "This," said the men, in perfect good faith, "is an elephant nautch-khana"—ballroom. It is a common remark that stout people are often light dancers, and sometimes most eligible partners. The elephant, in spite of his bulk, is both on land and water a very buoyant person, quick on his feet and, in his deliberate way, as clever a kicker as a mule, which is saying a great deal. There is therefore no reason why he should not dance, and I confess to a deep envy of the Assam coolie, who said he had been a hidden unbidden guest at an elephant ball. Elephants are easily taught to dance by American and European circus trainers; and it is recorded by an American trainer that elephants off duty, left entirely to themselves, have been seen to rehearse the lessons they have learned. Let us believe, then, until some dismal authority forbids us, that the elephant *beau monde* meets by the bright Indian moonlight in the ballrooms they clear in the depths of the forest, and dance mammoth quadrilles and reels to the sighing of the wind through the trees and their own trumpeting, shrill and sudden as the Highlander's hoch!

It is firmly believed that dead elephants are buried by their kind. Mr. Sanderson admits that he is unable to account for the total absence of their remains in the jungle, and so gives us leave to share for once in an Orient mystery, dim and inscrutable. The free-thinking native who solves it by boldly claiming that the great beasts, left to themselves, do not die at all, does not diminish the marvel, which still remains to delight all those who love to wonder.

It is natural that a creature so highly esteemed should be made to reflect the popular conception of Hindu character in its weaknesses and failings as well as in its placid and gentle strength. He is believed with little cause to be keenly sensitive; they say he breaks his heart like a proud Rajput, and dies at will of resentment or grief. So do some Orientals. He is said to have a memory for insult or injury as tenacious as that of a usurer for a debt, and soon or late he will be even with his oppressor. He can be taught to master his natural timidity, and when properly led he will face the tiger in his lair, but he is not ashamed to fly before a little dog. In sickness he comes very close to the human, for the mahouts say he resigns himself like a native when stricken with fever; when he lies down they give him up, for he gives up all hope of himself, and against a despair of that bulk there is no argument. He is liable to sudden bursts of rage, and can sulk in ill-temper for days at a time. When downright mad nothing can stand before him. Death in Hindu poetry and talk is a mad elephant, for who shall stay him? Love and lust are also mad elephants, blind, unreasoning, and cruel.

"There are many footsteps in the footprint of the elephant," for elephant lords have many followers. In most native forts and palaces there are elephant paths and high-arched elephant gates, slopes or stairways of wide tread, down which the State elephants march, taking the women of the Zenana or their lords for an airing. The milky way in the heavens is sometimes called the elephant's path. Silver ingots of a certain shape are "elephant's feet" and among silversmiths the name is used to discriminate a quality of silver.

In Assam, where they are familiar with elephants, they say, "The elephant brings forth one at a birth, the pig ten." "A small elephant is still larger than a big buffalo," and "Bamboos are tied with bamboos and elephants are caught by elephants," are also sayings from that region. Where the Englishman would say the back of a job was broken, or "All is over but the shouting," an Oriental often says, "The elephant is out, only the tail remains." "Teeth for use and teeth for show," carries an understood allusion to the elephant, who has tremendous molars hidden in his head as well as handsome external tusks. Sometimes for state occasions an animal with poor or elementary tusks is fitted with a jury pair, a feat of dentistry of which mahouts are proud. To the over-bold who would meddle with the great it is said: "Would you snatch sugar-cane from an elephant?" "The dog may bark but the elephant moves on" is sometimes said to indicate the superiority of the great to popular clamour, but the best form of the phrase is, "Though the dog may bark the caravan (*kafila*) moves on." For the elephant hates and fears dogs as much as some great men of to-day hate noisy newspapers, and with better reason. Nature, in furnishing the beast with a soft and tender trunk, has bound him down to keep the peace with all creation. That in spite of this disability he can be brought to face the tiger shows convincingly the docility and superiority of his nature. Yet though the beast is counted lordly, he still has a master, so they say again, "The elephant's god is his goad." Big things and men are naturally called elephantine. Maharaja Ranjit Singh used to speak of the fine English cart-horses sent out to him as a gift from the English Government as his "elephant horses," and he tied them up and fed them to death in the native fashion with great pride and satisfaction. "When the handed one puts forth his handiness, a man is but a fly before him," is a clumsy paraphrase of a saying that plays with the word *hāthi.* "The poor have no friends, but elephants wait at the rich man's door," is one of the rare complaints of Indian lowliness. It is doubtful whether any other races in the world are more free from envy. The beggar cries, "God will give you an elephant to ride on, I'll take a farthing to-day." When English girls marry, their parents say they are sorely grieved to lose them; but Indian fathers are frank, and acknowledge at once the trouble and cost of daughters and elephants

AN ELEPHANT GOAD (ANKUS)

in "The daughter is best at her father-in-law's house, as the elephant is best at the Raja's."

A man's saying is "A man at sixty is a young elephant, a woman at twenty is growing old." There is a fine braggadocio in this, but the honest truth is that the Indian woman has not a fair chance, being deliberately sacrificed by the custom of too early marriage. English poets write prettily of Hindu maidens, but there are no Hindu maidens in any true sense. A brutal saying like this drives home the fact that millions of girls, bright and charming as any in the world, are deprived of that period of springtime freedom and lightness of heart which is their birthright. Nor is there any excuse for this deprivation, for it has been demonstrated that the Indian woman comes no earlier to maturity than her sister in the West. And the Hindu man at sixty is like a young elephant in nothing save bulk.

The docility of the elephant is never more evident than when he is dressed for parade on an occasion of state. It is a long and tiresome business to clothe the creature in the ornaments and housings with which luxuriant Oriental taste loves to bedizen him. You may make a four-post bedstead very splendid in a cinque-cento or a Louis Quatorze manner; a horse can carry a great load of finery; even men and women, duchesses, actresses, kings and queens, stagger proudly under fine trappings, but the elephant is made for display as a mountain range for sunset effect. Sir Henry Cole, in years gone by, used to contemplate the vast brick walls built by Captain Fowke for the 1862 Exhibition, and say, "That is a surface which invites decoration." The façade of the nude elephant is no

UNDRESS

less noble and no less urgent in its appeal to the eye. But the great beast, shifting uneasily on his feet, does not always take kindly to his trappings, and is much less steady than a brick wall.

Yet at the worst there is little more difficulty in decking the elephant than in dressing a fidgety child for church. First he must be washed, sometimes at a well-brink, where, if properly taught, he draws his own water, but an irrigation cut or tank is generally preferred, where the great baby is made to lie down, to raise his head or leg at a word, while the mahout, often assisted by his son, who assumes tremendous airs of authority if he is very young, climbs about his huge bulk and scrubs him with brick-bats. A brick flesh-rubber is in common use for men's feet, and seems to suit the elephant perfectly. But the creature is generally inattentive during the process, he "plays with the soap" so to speak, blows clouds of vapour from his trunk, lifts up the wrong leg, rolls over at the wrong minute, and is scolded like a child, with now and then, from a hasty mahout as from an irritable nursemaid, a blow. When the washing is finished he slings his nurses up to his neck with his trunk, or gives them a "leg up" behind in the friendly fashion peculiar to him, and shuffles back to the serai or yard to be dressed. If the occasion be a very grand one, a day or two will be consumed in preparations. First the forehead, trunk, and ears are painted in bold patterns in colour. This is a work of art, for the designs are often good, and the whole serai, excepting always the elephant himself, is deeply interested. His mind and trunk wander; he trifles with the colour pots; so with each stroke comes an order to stand still. Some mahouts are quite skilful in this pattern work. Then the howdah pad is girthed on with cotton ropes riding over flaps of leather to prevent the

A PAINTED ELEPHANT

chafing to which the sensitive skin is liable. The howdah itself, a cumbrous frame of wood covered with beaten silver plates, is slung and tied with a purchase on the tail-root, and heavy cloths broidered in raised work of gold and silver thread are attached, hanging like altar cloths down the sides. A frontlet of gold and silver diaper with fringes of fish-shaped ornaments in thin beaten silver, necklaces of large silver hawk-bells and chain work, with embossed heart-shaped pendants as big as the open hand, and hanging ornaments of chains of silver cartouches, are adjusted. A cresting of silver ornaments like small vases or fluted soup tureens, exaggerations of the knobs along a horse's crest, descend from the rear of the howdah to the tail, anklets of silver are sometimes fitted round the huge legs, and a bell is always slung at his side. The pillars of the howdah canopies, and then the canopies themselves with their finials, are fitted as the beast kneels. A long business, because in India things are apt to be missing when they are wanted, and though much of this brave upholstery fits at the first attempt, there are always, even in the best-regulated elephant stables, little deficiencies to be supplied: and many odd bits of string are used. From the right distance, however, they do not show, and if they should catch the eye, why, "the screw was lost or worn out," or, "it was always so," or, "the smith or the tailor has been told a dozen times about it"—and a deprecating smile ends the matter.

At last my lord the elephant is ready, but even now is apt to get into trouble. His natural habit is to fling dust, leaves, and fodder stalks on his back, just as it is the natural inclination of the smartly-dressed little boy to go straightway and make a mud pie. So he must be looked after while the mahout puts on a coat and turban, and, armed with his *ankus* or goad hook of gilded steel, and a fly flap of yak tail in a silver handle, is ready to mount. "*Mâil, Mâil Barchhi gaj Bahadur!*" "Go on, go on, my Lord the Spear!" and they join the retinue of spearmen, mace and staff bearers, and other attendants waiting for the Raja. And frequently you will see in the midst of the blaze of colour and silver and gold one of the mahout's little boys leaning with folded arms and legs crossed at ease against the fore-leg of the foremost elephant. He is as near nude as may be, but from the complacent grin on the unkempt little monkey's face you might fancy he considered himself the most important figure in the show. Nor would he be ignominiously sent away, save by some officious underling. Urbane old Wazirs would glance at him with an amiable smile, though they did not confess aloud that his was an auspicious intrusion: as of the black spot in the splendour of the poppy:—a "*năzăr wăttu*" or averter of the evil eye, the Nemesis always waiting for those who do not acknowledge by some lowly touch of imperfectness that "the glories of our birth and state are shadows, not substantial things."

It is not now thought a great feat to send elephants down to the sea in ships. They are engirdled with slings as they stand, little dreaming that presently they will be snatched up, swung aloft, and lowered deep into a dark hold.

Some of the earlier cargoes were not so easily managed. A distinguished officer told me of his troubles with a batch of elephants he took from Calcutta to Chittagong, and how they very nearly wrecked a ship. The first to be shipped was awkwardly handled, caught the hatchway with his tusks and trunk, slung himself askew, and struggled

WAITING FOR THE RAJA
(Copyright 1891, by J. Lockwood Kipling)

and fought hard. But at last all the forty were stowed, and the steamer went down the Hooghly, anchoring for the night in an oil-still sea off Saugor Point. Now the elephant is the most restless creature alive, always in motion; a fact which native observation has noted in the saying, "An elephant's shoulder is never still." At first they said it was a ground swell that made the ship roll so much, but soon the Captain came in dire alarm to the officer in charge of the freight. The elephants had found that by swaying to and fro all together, a rocking motion was produced which seemed to please them immensely. So the great heads and bodies rolled and swung in unison, till the ship, which had no other cargo and rode light, was in imminent danger of rolling clean over. The mahouts were hurried down into the hold, and each, seated on his beast, made him "break step" so to speak. There they had to stay for a long time. An unforeseen difficulty was found in carrying fodder along the central avenue. The elephants would allow a laden coolie to proceed a little way, and then, with the quiet mischief of their kind, one would lay him by the heels with his trunk while the others snatched his bundles of grass. So they made a gangway over their backs along which the coolies crawled. The worst was when the elephant first shipped died in his place, of vexation, mahouts would say, who believe the creatures only die when they are so inclined. He was the farthest from the hatchway, and in the awful heat of the Bay of Bengal he had to be taken to pieces and passed through the line of his brethren, up and over the side in ships' buckets! Arrived in port there was no wharf, and the animals had to swim and wade a mile of water from the anchorage to the shore. The first was slung

IN ROYAL STATE

(Copyright 1891, by J. Lockwood Kipling)

down, his mahout on his neck, to the water, as it seemed from the deck, a lascar clinging to the chain to let go the swivel. He let go too soon, the elephant fell with a mighty splash, losing his mahout, while the suddenly released chain shot the astonished lascar like a bolt from a catapult some fifty yards away.

It is not, however, trials of this kind that make the English transport officer, struggling across creation with mules, oxen, and elephants, gray before his time, but the number of reports and dockets he has to write. That dead elephant's tusks were a congenial subject to Commissariat clerks, and they "had the honour to inquire" in many letters.

We have turned from the elephant as he appears to the Oriental, to the creature as he really is, and it may be interesting to hear the account of him that the paternal Government of India has to give. For that Government is itself elephantine in its nature, capable of supporting great weights, but prone also to busy itself in infinite details with restless and inquisitive trunk. The proper treatment of the animal in health and disease is set forth in a manual by the late Mr. Steel, a high veterinary authority, while the Commissariat and other departments concerned with the large property of the State in elephants are carefully instructed in their management. It is officially stated that—"all who have had to deal with elephants agree that their good qualities cannot be exaggerated; that their vices are few and only occur in exceptional animals; that they are neither treacherous nor retentive of injury; and that they are obedient, gentle, and patient beyond measure." This is higher and more sympathetic praise than is usually tied up in the pink tape of Secretariats, and it is all true. The next sentence, however, of the official characterisation declares that in many things the elephant is "a decidedly stupid animal!" It was ever hard to find wit and virtue combined, but it may be doubted whether the sentence is quite just. Intelligence among animals is a matter of delicate and difficult comparison. Simplicity of character were a better word than stupidity. A stupid creature refuses to learn and to obey. The elephant under sympathetic treatment always tries to obey, and can be taught to perform acts foreign to all we know of its nature. This entitles it to a higher place on the strictly limited scale of animal intelligence than the word "stupid" indicates. Its inquisitiveness is confined to objects within elephant range, and its sympathies, like those of all purely vegetarian animals which have to spend a large proportion of their time in eating, are narrow. Of a dog, on the other hand, it was once delightfully remarked in the American tongue, "Don't say that before Snap. Snap don't know he's only a dog; he thinks he's folks!" No mahout would begin to think of his placid self-contained charge along this line. They all seem to regard elephant character as a thing apart, and with a respect which a stupid animal could not command, —even from mahouts.

As to the strength of the beast and the best way of turning it to account, there is less room for controversy. On a march, weight-carrying is the work an elephant can best perform, for though he can pull strenuously and well, his frame is not suited for long spells of draught work. His chest is relatively small and weak; so sometimes he is made to pull with ropes tied to the tusks, and sometimes from his waist, if an elephant can be said to have a waist—but the mighty forehead would, to an amateur, appear to be the best hitching point.

The normal load for continuous travel of a fair-sized elephant is 800 pounds, so the animal is equal to eight ponies, small mules, or asses; to five stout pack-mules or bullocks, and to three and one-third of a camel. Under such a load the elephant travels at a fair speed, keeping well up with an ordinary army or baggage train, requiring no made road, few guards, and occupying less depth in column than other animals. He is invaluable in jungle country and all roadless regions where heavy loads are to be moved. In Burmah and on the east and south-east frontier elephants are absolutely necessary for military supply. When once a good road is made, the beast is, of course, easily beaten by wheeled carriage.

He shines most as a special Providence when the cattle of a baggage train or the horses of a battery are stalled in a bog or struggling helplessly at a steep place. An elephant's tusks and trunk serve at once as lever, screw-jack, dog-hooks, and crane, quickly setting overturned carts and gun-carriages right, lifting them by main force or dragging them in narrow winding defiles where a long team cannot act; while his head, protected by a pad, is a ram of immense force and superior handiness.

I write "he" mechanically, but it ought to be said that in consequence of the liability of the male to occasional fits of ill-temper from functional causes, it has been decreed that only females are to enter Government service, and they should not be less than twenty or more than thirty years of age, capable of carrying 1200 pounds for a first-class elephant (eight feet high and over) and 960 pounds for a second-class animal (under eight feet in height), exclusive of gear. No recruit under seven feet should be admitted. Male animals are preferred by Native Princes on account of their larger size and prouder bearing, and among about two thousand elephants owned by the British Government a few males are kept for State and parade purposes. An elephant at twenty-five years of age may be compared to a human being of eighteen. He

ELEPHANT PILING TIMBER (BURMAH)

attains his full strength and vigour at about thirty-five, and has been known to live a hundred and twenty years.

A born forester, it is in jungle-work that the labouring elephant outside Government service is seen at his best. The tea-planters of Assam and Ceylon find him useful in forest clearing and as a pack animal. They even yoke him to the plough. He is the leading hand in the teak trade of Burmah,—unrivalled in the heavy toil of the timber-yard, where he piles logs with wonderful neatness and quickness. Small timbers are carried on the tusks, clipped over and held fast by the trunk. A log with a thick butt is seized with judicious apprecia-

ELEPHANT LIFTING TEAK LOGS (BURMAH)

tion of balance, while long and heavy baulks are levered and pushed into place.

As to its keep, the elephant is a chargeable beast; costing from £4 to £8 a month when rations of rice or wheaten flour cakes are given, as they should be, with fodder-stalks and leaves of various kinds. Rum, brandy, or arrack, mixed with ginger, cloves, pepper, and treacle, and made into a paste with flour, provide the elephant with a sort of tipsy-cake that cheers and comforts him when suffering from fatigue or cold. In the matter of food and stimulants, however, mahouts have no conscience, and steal without a qualm. Ages of slack-handed usage have settled that the servant of the elephant and three generations of his family shall live on the beast he is paid to cherish. Allowances are given for flour, fire-wood, oil, and spices, but the elephant only gets a share in them, and not always that. So the worst ailment he has to face is semi-starvation, the lot of most elephants in captivity. The beast is in truth a noble anachronism, belonging to a young world time of denser foliage than this dried-up age which packs hay in trusses and treasures ensilage in pits. But the thievish mahout is responsible for the worst of his belly-pinch. Yet elephant men are usually spoken of as models of devotion to their beasts. "They love 'em, sir," said an English officer to me once. But that does not prevent their showing an indifference to their comfort, characteristic of all Orientals, whose talk often drips with sentiment, while their practice is of dry brutality. The acknowledged authorities on the subject, Mr. Sanderson and the late Mr. J. H. Steel, agree that mahouts invariably make the animals' comfort subservient to their own. Even the best of them will seldom take the trouble to put their beasts under the shadow of a tree at mid-day. They also have the cruel Indian trick of securing the animals fore and aft in the most irksome manner possible. A rope or chain fastened to one foot and to a peg in the ground is sufficient restraint for most elephants, and allows them to turn to and from the sun and wind as they find agreeable. Mahouts think nothing of securing an animal so that one side is exposed day and night to wind or rain.

The practice of tight tying up is particularly repugnant to those who have a sympathetic knowledge of the restless, swaying, Johnsonian habit rooted in the beast's nature. The native servant himself keenly appreciates his liberty and is the most elusive creature alive, perpetually slinking from his duty into the jungles of the bazar. But when he ruleth he is a terrible despot.

Outside India it is believed that elephants are dying out of the land. The example of America, where the men and creatures natural to the soil have been exterminated to make room for a too triumphant civilisation, has taught the world a lesson of anxiety. But animal lovers may rest content, for the elephants of India, like the people, are increasing in numbers. They are carefully protected in their natural haunts, whence English officers of experience draw supplies for use with as much system and regularity as sheep are drafted from the hillside flock. The details of the Government kheddah or capturing arrangements are full of interest,—sport in its finest sense; nor is it easy to say whether the skill in woodcraft of the English directors, or the courage, endurance, and patience of the natives employed, are most admirable. Like a strong ass between two burdens, the British Government has been beaten with many staves, and also with fools' truncheons of pantomime paper, but, at least, it has tried to husband the resources of the country.

The thoughtful Germans are said to meditate the re-capture and domestication in their new Equatorial realm of the African elephant, free since the days of Hannibal. It is to be hoped this is true, for there is naught sillier under the sun than the slaughter which has hitherto been all that civilisation had to bestow on these blameless Ethiopians.

CHAPTER X

OF CAMELS

"When spring-time flushes the desert grass,
Our Kafilas wind through the Khyber pass.
Lean are the camels but fat the frails,
Light are the purses but heavy the bales,
As the snow-bound trade of the North comes down
To the market-square of Peshawar town.

"In a turquoise twilight crisp and chill,
A Kafila camped at the foot of the hill.
Then blue smoke haze of the cooking rose,
And tent-peg answered to hammer nose;
And the picketed ponies, shag and wild,
Strained at their ropes as the feed was piled;
And the bubbling camels beside the load
Sprawled for a furlong adown the road;
And the Persian pussy-cats, brought for sale,
Spat at the dogs from the camel-bale."

The ballad of the King's jest.—R. K.

HILE some mahouts hint vaguely that the elephant came to India from the farther East, it is an accepted belief that the camel came from the West, *i.e.* from Arabia. No account is taken of the herds of wild camels seen on the high table-lands of Central Asia. So the saying has it, "The camel let loose, goes westward," or "The camel is a good Mussulman, for when free, he runs towards Mecca." In default of proof that the beast really follows the setting sun, it may be suspected that Oriental fancy, always strong, has more play than Oriental observation, which is often weak. For the camel is a peculiarly Muhammadan creature both in his life of to-day and in his wonderful origin. It was on his back that the body of Shah Ali Shah was laid after death, and he was sent into the wilderness till the Angel Gabriel met him and, taking the rope, led him no man knows whither. Before that ghostly funeral the camel resembled a horse, but the Angel gave him a hump like the mountain into which he disappeared, and feet to spread on the yielding sand, with other anatomical peculiarities, all duly enumerated by good Mussulmans. This story is also told of Moses, the friend of God, or the converser with God, the place of whose sepulchre no man knoweth unto this day. Probably the saying has its origin in the propensity of the stupid camel to stray and lose itself, for it has none of the "homing" faculty so strongly developed in the horse. People who religiously face westward several times a day to pray naturally get an occidental twist in their minds. Nay, there are those who maintain that all the world has this trick, and that, like Wordsworth's friends, we still go "stepping westward." South Australia has not yet discovered a Mecca twist in the thousands of camels it now owns.

The Prophet himself was a camel driver or *Serwán*, and always cherished the liking of a true Arab for the beast of which he said, "Speak ill neither of the camel nor of the wind; the camel is a benefit to man and the wind is an emanation of the Spirit of God." When he was married to Kadijah, two young camels were slain for the wedding feast.

But Indian popular observation lacks the Arab keenness, nor is the beast so important and highly thought of as in Arabia. There is no strong insight in calling the long shafts of the camel's limbs crooked, as in the angry saying to a shifty ne'er-do-well, "O camel, hast thou *one* straight bone in thy body?" The pride of a big man is rebuked by the saying, "The camel thought he was the biggest thing in the world till he came under the mountain." Of a very tall man who, in India, is often a simpleton, they say, "Tall as a camel, but silly as an ass," and of an unwilling, grumbling servant, "He snarls like a camel when you load him." The bite of a camel is very severe and sometimes poisonous, so the saying goes, "God preserve us from the nip of a camel and the snap of a dog." Of a notoriously unlucky man they say, "Even if he were perched on a camel a dog would jump up and bite him." The Kirgiz have a pious expansion of this saying: "Whom the fates bless with a good son may light a bonfire; but the father cursed with a bad son will be devoured by dogs, though he be mounted on the back of a camel." We express the completeness of ill-luck by saying, "The bread never falls but on its buttered side." The Kirgiz say, "One never falls but from a *nár*"—the large-sized Bokhariot camel. A common saying similar to our "waiting to see which way the cat jumps" is based on a trivial story. A potter and a greengrocer hired a camel between them. The camel reached round with his long neck and ate some of the cabbages on the greengrocer's side, whereupon the potter jeered. "Wait and see which side he sits down upon," said the greengrocer. The camel sat down on the potter's side and smashed his wares. Æsop's frog tried to swell himself as big as the ox, but in India they say of pretentious little people, "When the camels were branded, the frog also held up his leg," as who should say, "brand me too." "The goat-keeper went to buy a camel and wanted to feel its ears" (a point of handling which no judicious goat-buyer omits) is a saying which has several applications in India; but in Britain also we may see critics a-tiptoe, reaching up with tiny and inapt canons of judgment to things they do not understand.

The decorative value of the camel cannot be appreciated by those who have only seen one or two at a time. He was made for a sequence, as beads are made for stringing. On an Indian horizon a long drove of camels, tied head to tail, adorns the landscape with a festooned frieze of wonderful symmetry and picturesqueness. Five hundred camels go to a mile.[1] If I had a very long and lofty hall to decorate I should pray the architect to let me loop it round with camels, with here and there a Biloch driver, as the frieze turned a corner or was interrupted by a bracket or girder. For a quaint and almost comic spectacle, a bivouac of a camel Kafila or caravan on the march is not easily surpassed. The beasts are seated four or five on each side of a sheet or table-cloth on which their fodder is placed. Camels are as symmetrically constructed as gun-carriages, and their hind-legs fold up like two-foot-rules. They rest in great part on a pedestal behind the chest with which Nature has furnished them, and sit close together in high-elbowed state with an indescribable air of primness and pro-

[1] This is the present official estimate, allowing a little over 10 feet 6 inches per camel. Sir Charles Napier, however, writing of his first day's march from Rori to Imaín Ghur in the Sindh desert, allows 15 feet to each animal: "Oh! the baggage! the baggage! it is enough to drive one mad. We have 1500 camels with their confounded long necks, each occupying 15 feet! Fancy these long devils in a defile; four miles and a quarter of them!"

priety. With, as often happens, a driver supping at each end of this table in the wilderness, the whole arrangement has an absurdly formal and well-regulated air, suggesting a tea-party of elderly maiden ladies, as the long necks curve and bridle and the mincing mouths move busily.

The deliberate movement of the beasts under their burdens is impressive and not without a touch of scornful majesty. Only an Oriental, one would think, could

IN A SERAI (REST-HOUSE)

accommodate himself to that unhasting cadence of step. Perhaps the reported existence of wild camels in Arizona territory is a fabulous or jocular illustration of American character. It is said they were imported into the United States to serve as pack animals, but nobody foresaw that the nervous, electric American was the last man alive to pace placidly at the end of a camel's nose-rope. He naturally dropped it in disgust ;—and now there are wild camels in Arizona. If this story is not true, it ought to be.

The truth about the camel's character has often been debated. He is wonderful, and, in his own way, beautiful to look at, and his patience, strength, speed, and endurance are beyond all praise. The camel-riders of Rajputana and Central India, mounted on animals of a swift breed, cover almost incredible distances at high speed, finding it necessary to protect themselves against the racking motion by broad leathern belts tightly buckled, which are often covered with velvet and prettily broidered in silk. Even they, who know the beast at his best, never pretend to like their mounts, as one likes a horse. So useful a beast is estimable, but the most indulgent observation fails to find a ground for affection.

RAJPUT CAMEL-RIDER'S BELT

Europeans, at all events, who have to do with camels seem to think it were as easy to lavish one's love on a luggage van. He is a morose, discontented, grumbling brute, a servant of man, it is true, as is the water that turns a mill-wheel, the fire that boils a kettle, or the steam that stirs the piston of a cylinder. He does not come to a call like other beasts, but has to be fetched and driven from browsing. There are but few words made for his private ear such as belong to horses, dogs, and oxen. An elephant has a separate word of command for sitting down with front legs, with hind legs, or with all together, and he moves at a word. A camel has but one, and that must be underlined with a tug at his nose-rope ere he will stoop. But he has a large share in that great public property of curses whose loss would enrich the world.

The camel has so little sense, one wonders he is credited with malevolence, but so it is, and there is sound appreciation of his vindictiveness in a phrase in use for bearing malice, equivalent to "camel-tempered," and of his aimless wandering in another addressed to an idle man, "Why are you loafing round like a loose camel?"

"Camel colour" is a common word among weavers, embroiderers, and the like; but it is not a good colour name, because camels vary much in tint. Other names of this end of the colour scale are better, as "*badámi*" or almond; "mouse colour"; *khâki*, or *khara*, catechu tinted. An ostrich is a camel-bird, and so says Western science,—*struthio camelus*,—and a giraffe a camel-cow; no notice apparently being taken of the creature's spots.

The camel's grumble has led the British soldier to christen him "a humming-bird." "Commissariat scent-bottle" has also been heard, and when in camp with camels, you see more in these schoolboy absurdities than would strike a stranger. The relations of the British soldier with the camel, however, have been so vividly and truly put in my son's barrack-room ballad, "Oonts!" (camels), that I make no apology for quoting it at length,—premising that Mr. Thomas Atkins, who takes his own way with Oriental languages, invariably shortens long vowels, and makes *oont* rhyme with grunt.

OONTS!

(NORTHERN INDIA TRANSPORT TRAIN)

What makes the soldier's 'eart to penk, what makes 'im to perspire?
It isn't standin' up to charge or lyin' down to fire;

But it's everlastin' waitin' on a everlastin' road
For the commissariat camel and 'is commissariat load.
O the oont, O the oont, O the commissariat oont!
With 'is silly neck a bobbin' like a basket full o' snakes,
We packs 'im like a idol, an' you ought to hear 'im grunt,
An' when we gets 'im loaded up, 'is blessé d girth-rope breaks.

What makes the rearguard swear so 'ard when night is drorin' in,
An' every native follower is shiverin' for 'is skin?
It ain't the chance o' bein' rushed by Paythans from the 'ills,
It's the commissariat camel puttin' on 'is blesséd frills.
O the oont, O the oont, O the hairy, scary oont!
A trippin' over tent-ropes when we've got the night alarm,
We socks 'im with a stretcher-pole an' 'eads 'im off in front,
And when we've saved 'is bloomin' life, he chaws our bloomin' arm.

The 'orse 'e knows above a bit, the bullock's but a fool,
The elephant's a gentleman, the baggage mule's a mule;
But the commissariat cam-u-el, when all is said and done,
'E's a devil an' a ostrich an' a orphan child in one.
O the oont, O the oont, O the Gawd forsaken oont!
The 'umpy lumpy 'ummin'-bird a singin' where 'e lies,
'E's blocked the 'ole division from the rearguard to the front,
An' when we gets 'im up again—the beggar goes an' dies!

'E'll gall an' chafe an' lame an' fight—'e smells most awful vile,
'E'll lose 'isself for ever if you let 'im stray a mile;
'E's game to graze the 'ole day long an' 'owl the 'ole night through,
And when 'e comes to greasy ground 'e splits 'isself in two.
O the oont, O the oont, O the floppin' droppin' oont!
When 'is long legs gives from under, an' 'is meltin' eye is dim,
The tribes is up be'ind us an' the tribes is out in front,
It ain't no jam for Tommy, but it's kites and crows for 'im.

So when the cruel march is done, an' when the roads is blind,
An' when we sees the camp in front an' 'ears the shots be'ind,
O then we strips 'is saddle off, an' all 'is woes is past:
'E thinks on us that used 'im so, an' gets revenge at last!
O the oont, O the oont, O the floatin' bloatin' oont!
The late lamented camel in the water-cut he lies.
We keeps a mile be'ind 'im an' we keeps a mile in front,
But 'e gets into the drinkin' casks, an' then, of course, we dies.

Through the humorous lilt of these lines you may perceive many facts, especially the mortality among camels in our Afghan campaigns. In that of 1878-1879, about 50,000 camels were paid for by the British Government. But this was in no wise the fault of the brutal Briton, for the beasts were deliberately sacrificed by their native owners, who were guaranteed compensation for their loss. It was easier to allow the camel to die than to toil after him over a difficult country. It is now laid down as an axiom of the Transport service that animals required to proceed beyond the bases, and to act with troops in the field, should be the property of the Government, while the transport of supplies within the bases should be mainly hired. But on the next pinch the chances are that the axiom will be disregarded. A history of the military services of the camel would be the history of Eastern wars. He has served and served well both as baggage cart and troop-horse, and whether from stupidity or courage is as stolid and unmoved under attack as were the British infantry squares at Waterloo. Herodotus, Pliny, Livy, Diodorus, and Xenophon are quoted by Major Burn of the Intelligence Branch in his excellent official manual on Transport and Camel Corps. In modern campaigns camel corps were organised by Napoleon in Egypt, Sir Charles Napier in Sindh, by Carbuccia in Algeria, and during the Indian Mutiny the "Ninety-twa" Highlanders had a camel corps of 150 native drivers, and 155 well-bred camels on which sat 150 kilted Highlanders. Sir Charles Napier's Sindh camel corps seems to have been the most complete in design and equipment, and in every way worthy of that great soldier's genius. The principle on which it was based is the plainest of all the plain truths ignored by our system—that the transport is the most vital part of military matters, and should be organised with just as much care as a regiment. In an expedition for the capture of a robber chief in Sindh, Sir Charles Napier's camel corps travelled 70 miles during the night, captured the thief, and returned, thus accomplishing 140 miles in twenty-four hours. Feats of this kind, of course, were not continuous, and their bringing-off was due to the care with which the rest and upkeep of the animals were maintained. This splendid property organised in 1845 was allowed to die down, and no such efficient organisation existed in subsequent campaigns, where money, hastily spilled like water, purchased discomfort and sickness for the troops, and that tardy and confused movement of his masses which breaks the heart of an anxious general.

As a rule, the management of camels should be left to Orientals, though the French say their men learned to imitate the Arab camel cries. Our Thomas Atkins is a poor ventriloquist, ill at outland tongues. Like his officers, too, he cherishes the ancient illusion, filtered down from book to book, about the extra water-tank stomach of the camel, and his power of going without water. As a plain physiological fact, the camel has no such chamber, his digestive arrangements are like those of the ox, but simpler, approaching the horse character; and, if he goes without water, it is only because he cannot get it. There are pouches in his stomach, which frequently after death are found to contain fluid; but that they are reservoirs pure and simple is doubtful, says Mr. J. H. Steel in his *Manual of the Camel.* "It is very certain that the parched traveller who cuts open his dying camel to obtain its water store will thus procure only a very little fluid of a temperature of about 90° Fahr., of a mawkish, sub-acid flavour and an unpleasant odour." He should be watered twice a day in the hot weather, and once in the cool season. It is true, of course, that he has been known to go dry for seven or eight days, but it was labour and sorrow to him. Also, although he can travel twenty miles a day, carrying 360 lbs. weight, he is capable of fatigue as other beasts are, and once out of condition does not regain his strength in less than six months. And in spite of his unfriendly and unsympathetic disposition, it is a fact that, like the rest of God's creatures, he is more tractable under kind treatment that when bullied and roughly handled. Of a man we sometimes say "he has an unfortunate manner," nor do we always mean it, for such a manner often shows the aggressive selfishness and ill-temper that command fortune and respect. The supercilious expression framed in the camel's lips, which disclose with savage threat the long upper teeth, denied by nature to other ruminants, and his curiously indifferent air, are real misfortunes to him. We bow respectfully to the camel-tempered man of private life, but it is hard to be civil to a beast whose face is a sculptured sneer.

The long-shanked, cushion-footed creature is especially good at fording rivers where the bottom is sandy. A drove going across will sometimes make a ford practicable for horses, acting like a roller on a loose road, but a few yards of greasy clay will throw many a camel. A fair slope is not much of an obstacle, but a steep hill of slippery wet clay, up which a mule goes gaily, is a sad business for the camel. Nature has made his shoulder, chest, and fore-legs strong, but the attachments of the hind limbs are weak and ill-considered. So the beast is liable to dislocations of the hip in climbing, or, as the British soldier says, "he splits 'isself up." Some Afghan short-legged breeds are good climbers, but of most the Arab saying holds good: "Which is best for you, O camel, to go up hill or down? May God's curse rest on both wherever met, quoth the camel." None the less, at this moment long strings are pacing with heavy burdens

RAJPUT CAMEL GUNS

up and down the hill roads to Kashmir, Simla, and Kabul.

Camels, like mules, can be used to carry field-pieces, the equipment of a gun being divided among three animals. The indigenous practice was to make the beast himself a gun-carriage, bearing a Zambūrah (wasp), a piece like our old falconet or like the heavy swivel muskets sometimes seen in English armouries, intended for the tops of a ship or the stern sheets of a boat. The saddle also carries a rider who holds the heavy wooden stock and fires the gun with a slow match. The lingering nature of this arrangement must in action have lent a lively interest to the evolutions of a gun camel, for there is always the chance that just at the critical moment the beast may sling round and point the gun at its friends. Another camel gun is a sort of *mitrailleuse*, carrying twenty-one barrels in a framework of iron-clamped wood. Both these contrivances are still in as much use as the brooding pax Britannica allows in Rajputana, especially at Oodeypore and Jeypore, and make a great figure in State processions when salutes are fired. The Sikhs had a great number of camel guns of the Zambūrah type, and at the battle of Sobraon it is said that over 2000 were captured. Some of these still survive in the armoury at Fort Lahore.

Besides his services as a slow-pacing pack animal and as a steed capable of covering long distances at a high speed, the camel has many uses unnoticed by Europeans. He is blindfolded in Sindh and made to go a mill-round, grinding flour or oil seeds; working sometimes in such a confined space, one wonders how they got the huge beast in, or how they will get him out again. He takes the place of the ox at the plough and the well, and acts as water-carrier in parts of Rajputana, on the edges of the Indian desert and in the camel districts of the Punjab. On the Grand Trunk road to Delhi are wonderful double-storied wagons drawn by camels. These old-world contrivances go at the rate of about three miles per hour, and are like nothing so much as the cage wagons of travelling menageries. They are in effect iron cages intended originally as a protection against robbery. The passengers are huddled together and seem to sleep most of the time, and, to do him justice, so does the driver. The most picturesque "property" of the Punjab Government house is a huge *char à banc*, to which is harnessed a team of four or six fine camels with leopard skin housings and gaily attired riders. The camel van will probably be run off the road by the railway, but modified versions of it must for long survive in the desert regions off the line of rail.

It ought to be unnecessary to say that while one camel is like another to an untrained European eye, there are in India, as in Arabia, carefully classified breeds, though they are not distinctively branded with caste marks, as is the case in the West. One listens to this lore with respect, but it is not easily remembered, nor is it of much importance, save to the camel owner or the Government officer sent forth at tuck of drum to buy or hire all the good camels he can lay hands on. By common consent the very best of the animals of the plain are considered to be those of Bikanir and Jessulmir, Rajput States on the edge of the great Indian desert, where the hot dry air suits the austere Arab constitution of the beast. But it has a wider range of variety than is generally thought, each suited to its *habitat*, until in the hills the slender, high-caste form becomes square, sturdy, and thickly covered with a coarse, cold-resisting pelage. The two-humped Bactrian camel is prepared by nature to withstand a cold almost as keen and piercing as that the reindeer feels, and yet will breed with the one-humped camel of the burning plain. Signor Lombardini, an authority on cameline anatomy, finds a rudimentary second hump in the ordinary one-humped camel.

After the he-goat, a whole camel seems a large offering for the most pious person to make, but he still occasionally serves as a sacrifice. Colonel Tod wrote that the Great Mogul used to slay a camel with his own hand on the new year festival, and the flesh was eaten by the court favourites. He is certainly eaten, and they say camel in good condition much resembles beef. After his death his bones are valuable, being whiter and more dense than most other bones, and a fair substitute for ivory. But they are neglected except by the lac-turners of Dera Ismail Khan, who use them for the studs and ornaments with which they adorn their ware. Possibly some camel bones are picked by English turners and button-makers out of the Indian bones now imported. It may not be generally known that the attention of traders has been recently drawn to the cattle remains that lie near Indian villages. Each hamlet has its Golgotha, where worn-out animals are left to die. Hitherto, only the vulture, the crow, and the jackal have visited these spots, after the leather-dresser has taken the skin of the last comer. But though it never occurred to the Oriental that they could be of any use, Western science, like the giant in the child's tale, grinds bones to make bread. So the village bone-heaps are swept up and shipped to Europe. Perhaps a day may come when the people, awaking to their value, will cry out that they have been robbed. The bone heaps will certainly be missed by the scientific Indian agriculturists of the future, but there is no way of keeping them in the country. Learned authorities on economic questions say it is a mistake to use customs duties with any beneficent intention, just as literary critics say it is bad art to write a story with a purpose, and both have some right on their side. Otherwise, in the interests of India, one would like to impose a heavy export duty on wild bird skins, feathers, and bones, and a crushing import duty on aniline dyes and Members of Parliament.

THE LEADING CAMEL OF A KAFILA (AFGHANISTAN)

Camel trappings are not so gaudy in India as in Egypt or Morocco, where riding animals are bedizened in scarlet and yellow. They are in a different key of colour, belonging to a school of pastoral ornament in soberly-coloured wools, beads, and small white shells, which appears to begin (or end) in the Balkans and stretches eastward through Central Asia into India, especially among the Biloch and other camel folk on our North-West frontier. Camel housings may be the beginning of the nomad industry of carpet weaving. It is perhaps not too fanciful to trace on the worsted neckband the original unit or starting-point of the carpets and "saddle-bags" which have given lessons to English upholsterers. There is not much room for variety in a narrow fillet with only black, brown, and dingy white as a colour scheme, but you may watch a long Kafila go curtseying past and find no two neck-bands quite alike in the arrangement of zig-zags, diamonds, bars, and squares. These bands, with more richly coloured rugs and saddle-bags, and the homely russet splendours of worsted cords, tassels, shells, and beads, with which the leading camel is adorned, are wrought by women. Like more women's work, it is done at intervals. The English lady complains that her Turkoman or Biloch rug lies unevenly on her par-quet floor, and does not reflect that the perverse "buckling" marks the times when camp was shifted to follow the pasturing flocks, and the loom with its unfinished carpet was rolled up to be staked anew with Oriental carelessness as to straightness. "Saddle-bags," said a London tradesman to me, "have had their day, they've got common." This sounded sadly, but they will not cease to be for all that.

CHAPTER XI

OF DOGS, FOXES, AND JACKALS

"Hev a dog, Miss!—they're better friends nor any Christian."
GEORGE ELIOT, *The Mill on the Floss.*

A SUBALTERN'S DOG-BOY

THAT the dog has served for ages throughout the East as a byword of loathing and contempt is of itself no hanging matter so far as the real character of the animal is concerned, and need not surprise or shock the English dog-lover. For, like the sacred writings of the Hindus and Muhammadans, our own Holy Bible, from which we profess to take our rules of life, contains the same low estimate, and has no hint of appreciation of canine character, no recognition of his services to man, no word of compassion for his fate. Yet Christians have learned and perfected the lore known to the Assyrian and the Greek of the varieties and qualities of dogs, and, following them rather than the ancient Hebrew, have come to love and cherish the unclean animal. The wonder is that the Oriental has stuck so servilely to the skirts of his Scripture and taken so much to heart the belated nonsense that Moslem and Hindu authorities have uttered in disparagement of one of the best of God's creatures. He ought to have found out for himself that the figurative expressions of orators, poets, and law-givers have but a local and temporary significance; but if you look closely you will find that for centuries he has most faithfully tried to take all that he has been officially taught *au pied de la lettre*, and has crystallised the metaphors of poetry and the rhetorical flights of law-givers into canons of conduct. The enormous difficulty of this task has, of course, driven both Hindu and Moslem to much hypocrisy and compromise, but on the whole their faith is greater than anything we know of in the West.

The official condemnation of the dog by Muhammadans, and the formal terms in which he is outcasted by Hindus, are too monstrous and sweeping to hold good, when one considers the friendly nature of the beast and the real claim he has on the gratitude of mankind. But there are not many examples of human sympathy passing the narrow bounds of a cruel law. The ingenious Mr. Pope has a much-quoted passage about the poor Indian whose untutored mind leads him to hope that when admitted to the equal sky of heaven his faithful dog may bear him company. But ages before Mr. Pope lisped in numbers, and indeed before America was discovered, Asiatic poetry had created the hero Yudhishtira, who refused to enter heaven at all unless his dog might accompany him. Modern India, however, has for the most part forgotten Yudhishtira, and in these days the only dog admitted to the company of the Gods is a cur that serves as the vehicle or *vâhan* of Bhairon, now one of the most popular of Hindu divinities. This deity bears a bottle of strong drink, in defiance of those shallow folk who claim all Hindus as total abstainers and Bands of Hope, and a staff which is vulgarly reckoned to be the *Kotwāl* or town magistrate of Benares. His semblance is that of a black or dark blue man, whose raiment is a cloth round his loins and a serpent round his neck; his dog is a black tyke of low degree, nor does the canine race appear to gain in popular esteem from his association with the God, unless the very vulgar saying: "If all the dogs go on pilgrimage to Benares, who will be left to lick the dishes clean?" is an obscure reference to his sacred character.

Muhammadans have granted in popular lore a place in Paradise to Khetmir, the dog of the seven sleepers, who has been suspected of being the same animal as Yudhishtira's hound by some scholars. But they follow the Bible in speaking of him in injurious terms as an expression for disgust and loathing, unclean by immemorial prescription. It is written that the angels of God will not cross the threshold of a house whereon there is even a hair of a dog. If a dog is known to have drunk out of a vessel, it must be washed in seven waters. (A Muhammadan cure for hydrophobia is to look down seven wells.) Neither by Hindu nor Muhammadan writer is ever a kindly word said in appreciation of the admirable sides of canine character. When he has a fair chance he is as faithful and zealous in service in India as elsewhere, but no one notices him. "A dog's death" is an Indian as well as a European phrase for a miserable ending, and it has a peculiar force in India; an idle babbler is said to have eaten a dog's brains, a hasty movement is a dog's jump, the hungry stomach is spoken of as a dog that must be quieted, and it is an ancient saying that though you imprisoned a dog's tail for a dozen years in a bamboo tube, it would still be crooked. That it would probably be perfectly straight after such a process is an irrelevant physiological detail unworthy the attention of a poet or a proverbial philosopher. "What business has a dog in a mosque?" is a scornful snub to an intrusive person of low degree. The sons-in-law and other relatives of wealthy, high-caste Hindus who, under the patriarchal scheme of domestic life, live with their wives' families, are familiarly described in quite a long series of enumeration as household dogs. A sponger or parasite is a *tabáqi kūtta*, a dish (licking) dog. And the Persian monosyllable for dog, "*Săg*," is often in a native mouth a more savage term of contempt than "*Sūar*," pig.

A saying goes, "do not travel in the evening, the Raja and the dog are asleep in the morning"—and in the lawless days but lately past there was sense in the counsel. Of oppressive native subordinates they say: "Why should not a dog bite a defenceless poor man?" To an abusive underling: "Cur! it is not your mouth but your master's that barks." The messenger wears a scarf and brass badge, and is often a jack-in-office, so he is familiarly spoken of as a dog with a collar on. Another saying is based on an incident: "You ate the dawn meal, so you must fast." A Muhammadan during the Ramazān fast found that a dog had eaten the meal which may be lawfully taken before sunrise, and with these words he locked the creature up, and, conceiving himself released from obligation, he breakfasted and dined as usual. We say "Love me, love my dog"; the Oriental admits that if you are devoted heart and soul to a person, you may even take her dog into favour: "Even Leila's dog is dear to Majnūn." This languishing hero is the accepted type of a devoted lover. The dog plays no great part in the story, and I suspect it is in respect of the proverb that a dog is generally introduced by native draughtsmen into the popular bazaar pictures representing these personages. The ordinance in the Code of Menu that certain out-

OUTCASTES (A BEGGING LEPER AND PARIAH DOGS)

caste tribes should possess no animals but dogs and asses has been a millstone round the necks of these admirable and most useful animals.

We say that one may as well hang a dog as give him a bad name, thereby admitting the possibility of a good one. But no such allowance seems to have been made for the Indian pariah dog. He has always been on the downhill slope of popular contempt, and it will be long before he can hope to rise. The noble potentialities of his character are ignored, he is discouraged by the distance at which he is kept, for he is never allowed to enter a house, nor to consort on intimate terms with man, the inventor of morals. Perhaps it is not too fantastical to say that when compared with the English dog the poor Indian outcast is a pagan, a creature without faith, or at least without that soul-saving reverence for authority which ennobles character. Lord Bacon says that the master of a properly trained dog is the divinity of the animal who waits upon his will. The Indian pariah does not know the joy of adoration; he has no master, and is an atheist in spite of himself. Tainted with the worst of the philosophy to which he gave his name some centuries ago in Greece, he reveals more of the currish side of canine character than English dogs and dog lovers are aware of. He uncovers more of his teeth when he snarls—and he often snarls—than the civilised dog; he slinks off with inverted tail at the mere hint of a blow or a caress, and his shrill bark echoes the long note of the great dog-father, the wolf, and the poor cousin the jackal. In a fight he does not abandon himself to the delight of battle with the stern joy of the English dog, but calculates odds and backs down with an ignoble care for his skin. In short, he is a *lendi*, a cur, a coward. We English call him a pariah, but this word, belonging to a low, yet by no means degraded class of people in Madras, is never heard on native lips as applied to a dog, any more than our other word "*pie*." Like other words, both will be learned from us and incorporated in that wonderful pudding-stone conglomerate of language known as Urdu.

The pie-dog, pariah, or street dog, is usually rufous yellow, but all known dog tints occur, for creole colours now diversify the tawny aboriginal race. Chronic hunger is the central fact of his life, which is one long search for food, and his pastime is another long search for fleas. As a rule he owns himself, but he sometimes selects a master and always belongs to a place. "Why are you so lean, dog? I have to gather my dinner from nine houses."

He is supposed to be valuable as a scavenger, and it is certain that he mostly dines in the night, resembling in this respect his timid cousin the jackal, who usually slinks aside from offal heap or dead carcass as he approaches. The jackal is accused of ghoulish propensities, favoured by the shallow graves dug for their kindred by Muhammadans, but the street dog, if strict truth were told, is almost as great a sinner. He is reported on good authority to frequent the burying-places where Hindus are cremated, and,—but I forbear. Stress of hunger alone leads him to dark deeds which forfeit his claim to human sympathy. It should be remembered in extenuation that he owes little or nothing to a cruelly indifferent humanity, and that he preserves, as we shall presently see, an innate friendliness which no neglect can quite eradicate. He is a street Arab, but he shows preferences for people as well as for places. He follows the cultivator afield and watches the gray bundle of cotton cloth slung to a branch and the hūqqa left under a tree, but I doubt whether he would make any effective defence of them. When the frugal "nooning" of unleavened flapjacks and butter-milk is eaten he wistfully awaits his share at a respectful distance. The children handle and play with him, and go to sleep by his side when tired of rolling in the dust, but when they grow up they cut his companionship.

Most Anglo-Indians have had an experience similar to that related by Bishop Heber in his journal of a sudden and unaccountable attachment on the part of a homeless pariah dog. A scrap of food, a word of notice, or even a look from one accustomed to command dogs wakes a chord in the creature's nature, and he

PLAYFELLOWS

longs to acknowledge a master. There are many instances of street dogs becoming civilised in European hands, and some have become faithful companions and friends. But it is as dangerous for a dog of this kind to leave his kindred as for a high-caste Hindu to cross the sea. Canine caste laws are strict, and a dog from a strange clan venturing into the territories of another tribe is sure of a hot reception. A country story expresses this with pretty irony. Once upon a time a dog ran "all the way from the Ganges" (any long distance) in one day. "How on earth did you come so swiftly, O dog?" "By the kindness of my brethren," is the reply. He had been chivied and chased from village to village as an intruder. A dog who had left his place and family connections for a period could not return with safety. So the pariah is not reluctant to adopt a master without a cause. He is the victim of an implacable socialism, the slave of a sharp-toothed trade union. He would like regular meals, and for their unwonted sake is willing to submit to authority, but what would the other tykes say and do? So he resigns himself to thoughtless freedom, wherefore does his skull remain narrow, his form wolf-like, and his mental character timorous and suspicious; sudden in impotent rage, loud in complaint, and nocturnal in habit; with that strange and long-drawn sympathy with lunar influences which the dog of civilisation has partly learned to forget.

There are many dogs which have an air of vagabondage, but who are owned and in some sort cared for. Yet the general habit of the animal in India is to attach himself to a place rather than to a person. In Europe this trait is often the mark of a high and magnanimous nature, for there dogs are attached to regiments, fire brigades, and other bodies corporate, of which they form an almost essential part, belonging to no one individual, but enjoying a noble sense of comradeship with all. No such honour is allowed to the poor Indian dog. They say contemptuously of a parasite or time-server, the Serai (native inn) dog is friendly with everybody; and the washerman's dog furnishes a saying in universal use. The washerman has a house, but he takes his clothes to the river-bank or ghât to be washed, so of the dog who attends him they say, he belongs to neither house nor ghât. This saying is commonly applied to idle artisans, gadding house-wives, and truant schoolboys. The washerman's dog stands for a person at a loose end, as the oilman's ox for a laborious man or woman. Mr. Quilp said of his dog that it lived on one side of the way and was generally found on the other.

An old gentleman in *Punch* seeing at a railway station a cat without a tail, says to the porter,—"One of the celebrated Manx cats, I suppose?" "No," replies the porter,—"2.30 express." At Indian railway stations dogs are often seen minus a leg or a tail; for in a country where even the railway men have not yet learned that it is dangerous to go to sleep with a head or a leg across the rails, it is scarcely to be wondered at if the dogs are sometimes caught napping. The mutilated member soon heals, and the animal hops cheerfully round the station and learns to meet every train regularly. On the long Indian journeys much food is taken by the passengers, both Native and European, and there are many scraps. So the railway dog is becoming an institution. On the "toy railway," as natives persist in calling the narrow gauge lines, the animals are rather tiresome, for a bound brings them into one's carriage and another takes them out with a cold fowl or a packet of sandwiches in their prompt mouths.

The one ritualistic observance in which the dog takes a part concerns neither Hindus nor Muhammadans, but only the Parsees. It is a practice of the sun-worshippers to bring a dog into the room where a Parsee is lying in the hour and article of death. This, I believe, is the prescribed form, but the practice seems to be to take the dog in to look at the corpse when the spirit has passed away. The rite is as obscure in theory as in practice, and I have never heard or seen a satisfactory explanation of it.

The dog is more frequently eaten than we are apt to believe. In Hindu poetry, innocent low-caste folk are contemptuously spoken of as "dog-cookers." I am assured that there is some ground for the gibe at Sansis and other gypsy tribes,—"When the gypsies come in at one side of the town, the dogs file out at the other." There is a double reason for this retreat, for not only do the Sansis eat dogs, but being in their way sporting characters, they keep dogs of their own, and a dog with never so squalid a man for master is dreaded by the ownerless pariah. An ordinary Indian street dog weighs from twenty to thirty-six pounds, and if he were fed would probably be over forty pounds in weight. Carrion-eating tribes have no prejudices in the matter of food, and the lizard, the jackal, and the rat are favourite roasts. It is manifest that to stomachs of this hardihood a dog would furnish lordly dishes.

There is a nine-word saying among poor folk to express a dilemma, which indicates the possibility of dog's flesh being mistaken for that of the kid: "If I tell, my mother will be beaten, if I don't tell, my father will eat dog's flesh." The story is that a house-wife cooked dog's flesh by mistake, and the small son of the house alone knew what manner of meat was in the pot—an awful weight on the mind of a Muhammadan child. It is by no means necessary, of course, for the currency or force of the saying, that it should be based on an actual incident, for a remote possibility or an impossibility serves just as well.

In some regions dogs are regularly eaten. The Nagas on the Assam frontier have a partiality for a dog who has just been full fed with rice and milk. He is hastily killed and cooked whole,—"*chien farci au naturel.*" It may be that outcaste folk have more toothsome food than we know. It is not proved that the lizard, the crocodile, and the snake are uneatable; indeed, it is probable they are very good. Jackal and fox must be dry and hard, but the stew-pot may reduce them to succulence. Darwin dined on puma in South America and found it like veal. I once accompanied a little company of silent Bhils in a search for field-rats, which were dug out and captured with great dexterity, —plump brown and white creatures, fed on the best of the crops and doubtless of fine flavour; but I did not wait to see how they were cooked over a fire, the kindling for which was carefully borne by a young woman of the party, who had much ado to screen it from the wind blowing over the high downs of the Deccan.

In the foregoing paragraphs the academical or official view of the outcaste dog as regarded by respectable people has been treated. The picture is not pleasing, nor should it be completely convincing to those who know and like the animal. In spite of conventional prejudice the dog, as might be expected, has won his way to a better place than most Europeans know of. The habit of foul and indiscriminate feeding may disgust the Hindu; and the Muhammadan,—most conservative of races,—may cherish his ancient grudge, but both are learning that the dog of good caste is a useful companion and friend. The indigenous canine aristocracy is not large, but it exists. Among the best breeds are the hounds kept by the Banjāris—a caste of half gypsy carriers and traders, referred to elsewhere. These are large and stout animals marked by the Eastern tendency to greyhound form, and are prized both as watch-dogs and for the chase. The Rampur hound is a similar beast, much cherished by sporting Nawabs. English authorities seem to think the greyhound came to Europe from the East. Persian greyhounds are imported and naturalised. Their coats are ragged and the forms lack symmetry, but some of these animals recall Sir Walter Scott's *Maida* of beloved memory. The sheep dogs kept by the Himálayan shepherds are warmly spoken of by their owners, who say that when the mountain paths are hidden in mist, they are infallible guides. On the plains sheep-dogs are seen, but they have none of the dash or vivacity of the British collie, slouching along, head and ears down; companions rather than directors of the sheep. Often, indeed, they may be seen in the middle of the flock. The sulky Tibetan mastiff is a splendid watch-dog, supposed to be capable of killing and eating a thief, and he is sometimes seen in the plains, but his ferocity, ill-temper, and heavy coat will prevent him from becoming popular. The black-tongued, thick-furred Eskimo-looking animal, now a favourite in England, comes to India from Tibet over the hills, and the ordinary village dog of the Himálaya has a strongly-marked tendency to this bushy-tailed, fox-muzzled type. There are also among common pariahs some mongrel variations, including a creature like the turnspit. Bishop Heber, an observer of unusual quickness, was more struck by the variety of colour and breed in native dogs than the unity

T

apparent to his successors, and asks, "Are they indigenous, or is it possible that their stock can have been derived from us?"

Although no Eastern writer has said much in favour of the dog, there are a few stories current among the people which testify to an appreciation of his faithfulness. A Punjab tale recalls the pitiful fate of Gelert over which so many English children have grieved. A Pathan gave a Hindu banker some money to keep for him and lent his dog to guard the banker's house. One night the thieves came and the dog barked, trying in vain to rouse the sleeping usurer. Failing in this, the clever beast watched the thieves and saw where they hid the spoil. In the morning he led the banker to the spot, scratching the ground to show where to dig. The money was recovered, and the grateful banker tied a letter round the dog's neck and sent him to the Pathan. But the latter, being hasty and irascible, struck off the animal's head for deserting his post, finding too late by means of the letter that the poor beast had been faithful to his trust. Even the pariah dog enjoys some popular respect as a watch-dog.

British influence, however, is the main factor in a slow but indubitable revolution now taking place in favour of the dog. A modern philosophical writer says the British Empire in India is but "a romantic episode" destined to pass away and leave no recognisable trace. This utterance would be worth respecting if trustworthy documents existed on which so large a forecast could be reasonably based. But in the present state of our knowledge of the country, and of the tendencies of the popular mind, it can be nothing more than one of the superficial profundities of smart journalism. That the form which Indian political institutions will eventually assume may differ materially from the intentions and anticipations of those who have planted them is an elementary consideration beyond which no plain man will now care to travel. Whatever may be its results in a political sense, the "romantic episode" will leave a notable imprint on some physical aspects of the land. Traces of the Briton will long survive in the animal as in the vegetable world. The dog and the horse accompany us everywhere, for it is part of our insular vanity to declare that no other dogs or horses are half so good as ours. Packs of fox-hounds are regularly imported; the subaltern, the private soldier, and the civilian bring bull-dogs, mastiffs, and terriers of every degree. Spaniels, retrievers, and greyhounds accompany sportsmen; the great Danes are occasionally seen, while ladies bring such pets as Maltese, Skyes, Dandie Dinmonts, and dachshunds.

This canine immigration has been going on for a long time. Sir Thomas Roe brought a present of British mastiffs to the Great Mogul,—the Emperor Jehanghir. One jumped overboard to attack the porpoises diving near the little ship; another on the way up-country seized an elephant. These little traits of pugnacity endeared them to the Emperor, who provided them with servants, carriages, and palkis in which to take the air, and had silver dishes and tongs made in order that he might feed them with his own royal hands. Probably they were fed to death, but haply some of their descendants are now slinking round the slums of Delhi or Agra trailing nerveless tails in the hot dust and yapping at the travelling Briton as a foreign intruder.

The English dog has come to stand as a high-caste

animal of respectable birth. Our domestic life is jealously shut off by the people from contact with their own, but the inmates of the prison-house have learned that the dog is a valuable domestic friend. Native ladies see that European animals are unlike the unclean creatures of the street, and are anxious to adopt them. Already English names are naturalised and Persianised after the liquid Oriental manner. The *punyár* is the spaniel, which used to be thought most highly of, probably from its silky unlikeness to the pariah, but its coat is too heavy for the climate. The bull-dog, vulgarly spoken of as the *gūldānk*, is highly prized as a watch-dog, while its fighting instincts commend it to the increasing class which takes delight in sport. A dog of an English breed sometimes receives an English name from its native master, as Eespot for "Spot." A servant of ours once contributed to a family debate on the name to be given to a puppy the remark that Fanny (both vowels very long) was the best possible name for a dog. "Bully" is a favourite Indo-Anglian dog-name.

In recent years the clever and amiable fox-terrier, who withstands the great heat of the plains better than any other breed, has come to the front and promises to be the dog of the Indian future. The pariah, like the sound patriot he is, appears to know this, and waylays the English animal as bands of street-boys in the West waylay a strayed public-school boy. A new science, the care and lore of dogs, picked up by menial servants from their English masters, is being formed and spreads upwards among the people.

So, though we may pass away and be forgotten, the dogs we loved will remain as permanent colonists. But it appears to be a fact that the creole dog, born in India of imported parents, develops some of the characteristics of the indigenous animal. His head, especially his nose, grows longer and narrower, he loses substance in the neck, chest, and loins ; he stands on higher legs and wags a longer tail than his British-born parents. The climate exerts a deteriorating influence on his moral qualities, and he loses some of the courage, temper, and fine spirits which are the birthright of a good dog in the West.

It is to an influence of this nature, rather than to any reasoning or religious prescription, that we may look for the growth of a humane appreciation of animals in general. There can be no doubt that the English people are more indebted to the humble and sympathetic tutorship of the dog than they are aware of, for such pre-eminence in a recognition of the rights of animals as distinguishes them. You may quote in opposition to the canons, which of set purpose have thrust the ass and the dog beyond the pale of mercy, that wise word of Jeremy Bentham, who said, "The question is not,—can animals speak or reason, but can they suffer ?" But the companionship of a good dog will teach more effectively than the words of any philosopher. Nor is the lesson uncongenial to the Indian people, although for many generations they have allowed a practice of neglect and indifference and a multitude of superstitious beliefs to obscure the real kindliness of their nature.

It is a good omen when a fox shows his face, so a sympathetic saying runs, "The fox gives luck to everybody, but himself is thinking of the dogs all the time." A sly fellow is called a fox in India as elsewhere, and the animal plays a part in some stories. But the jackal is the true Mr. Reynard of Eastern folk tales, the great original of the best of our fox stories ;—sweet-toothed, mischievous, lurking ; and as full of resource as Brer' Rabbit.

The jackal's night-cry,—the wild chorus with which the band begins its hungry prowl, is of evil omen, which is wonderful, seeing that in nearly every town and village of the vast continent it is heard about the same hour of the evening ; but it is believed that when the cry is raised near the house of a sick person, it is a sure presage of death, and that jackals scent coming dissolution, much as sharks are said by sailors to scent death on a ship. There are endless stories in favour of this belief.

The jackal's chorus is so sudden and shrill a clamour, so importunate and ear-filling, that one daily marvels at its equally sudden cessation. The air ought to go on vibrating with these fearsome yells, but it abruptly shuts down on them, still as a sleeping pond. And you resume your talk or work, but the creature with that one imprecation has sworn himself to hours of silence. Thereafter he goes dumbly to a night of hungry and often ghoulish research, for his sanscrit-born name is "greedy." But when going on a morning journey, the distant cry of one jackal (besides being rare) is lucky, as says a North-West Provinces rhyme, translated by Mr. Crooke in his valuable *Agricultural Glossary* : "A donkey on the left, a jay (the roller is meant) on the right, and a jackal howling in the distance—all omens of wealth and happiness. Go, and bring home four bags of gold." A jackal crossing the road to the left is lucky, to the right, unlucky.

Very many stories of the jackal are to be found in old books and folk-lore, but in the talk of to-day he scarcely takes the high place to which his classic reputation entitles him, being used as much as an object of derision as a model of cleverness. Most modern native humour, however, takes the form of irony. His talents are acknowledged in a saying which classes him with that busy and important person, the barber: "The jackal is the sharpest among beasts, the crow among birds, and the barber among men." The barber of India is, in fact, a clever Figaro; news-bearer, matrimonial agent, surgeon, and busybody in general. The painted jackal who fell into the dyers' vat and set up as king on the strength of his fine colour, has strayed from the Panchatantra into modern life, and you may hear of "painted jackals" being elected to the honours of a municipal "Kemety" (committee). "The jackal fell into a well,—I think I will rest here to-day, said he"—is a charming way to express the making the best of a downright bad job. "The jackal born in August says of the September flood, I never saw so much water in all my life," is a popular snub for youthful conceit. So also is, "The horse and the elephant are swept away, and the jackal asks—Is it deep?" "The jackal fell into the river and cried, The deluge has come and all the world is drowning!" recalls the American "Thinks the bottom has tumbled out of the universe because his own tin-pot leaks," or the drunken English skipper, who, when fished out of London dock, went dripping to the cuddy and gravely wrote in his log-book, "This night the ship went down, and all hands were drowned but me." He is supposed to be the friend and guide of the tiger, so the hangers-on of powerful persons are known as jackals. Boy and jackal have the same name in the North-West Provinces, and neither has much right to complain. "The jackal slips away and your stick jars on the ground," is a saying of obvious meaning.

Not that a stick would be of much avail against a jackal, for they say, no matter how savagely he may be beaten, he will pick his sore body up when left to die, and slink away to resume a life of crime. I once saw a large Irish retriever do all he knew to kill a jackal, and at last, in despair of the efficacy of his teeth, he dragged him at a hint from his master to a pond and drowned him fit for any coroner.

IN FLOODTIME

The jackal afflicted with rabies is a deadly creature, and more common than one likes to think.

Menu, the wise Hindu law-giver, was consistently brutal to women, and after classing wives as "marital property" with cows, mares, she-camels, slave-girls, she-goats, and ewes, he says the wife who violates her duty to her husband is disgraced in this world, and after death she enters into the womb of a jackal and is tormented by diseases! There is a hateful monotony in the abuse bestowed on women. Nowadays no one greatly cares for Menu, but in the East, as in the West, the baser sort habitually call their women folk by the name of the female dog.

India is probably the cradle of wolf-child stories, which are here universally believed and supported by a cloud of testimony, including in the famous Lucknow case of a wolf boy the evidence of European witnesses. And there are many who firmly believe in the power of magicians to transform themselves into wolves at will. But though the wolf is probably the parent of all dogs, he is, as a wild beast, beyond the narrow scope of this sketch.

CHAPTER XII

OF CATS

"If you want to know what a tiger is like, look at a cat; if you want to know what a thug is like, look at a butcher," is a common Hindu saying, but only half of it is quite true. The thug is, or let us hope, was, capable of many disguises, and his favourite semblance was that of the Brahman and the religious mendicant. Victor Hugo has expressed the tigerishness of the cat in his own swaggering fashion: "*Dieu a fait le chat pour donner à l'homme le plaisir de caresser le tigre.*" There are not many Indian sayings about cats in men's talk, but probably sensitive women have more than we know of. Cats are not so much petted here as in England, and have a stronger tendency to run wild. Generations of devoted cat-lovers in Europe have not been able to quite overcome this tendency, and many a gamekeeper can tell you of cats which during the day are models of saintly propriety, and at night are "just prowling tigers." No creature is more independent than the cat. Its more complete domestication in the West is in reality merely due to its love of warmth. For the sake of comfort it will tolerate humanity and blink amiably at the fireside, but a serene selfishness is the basis of cat character. The Indian domestic cat is not bound to the family circle by the need of warmth; there is no fireside to speak of, and it lives its own life.

Nor are household breakages attributed so freely to the cat, because there are so few things to break in an Indian household, and the customs of the country do not include pantries and the storing of flesh food. It is sometimes, however, slung in a net, so they say of a windfall, "Cat's in luck, the net broke!" Care does not kill the Eastern cat, nor has she nine lives nor nine tails, but she is used in a frequently-quoted saying about doubtful matters. "If the Punchayet (village council) says it's a cat, why, cat it is." This saying *may* be built on a story, but it is certain that a little story is built on the saying. A grocer one night heard sounds in his shop, and, venturing into the dark, he laid hold of a thief. The marauder mewed like a cat, hoping the grocer would let go. But the grocer only gripped tighter, saying, "All right, my friend; if the Punchayet in the morning says you're a cat, you shall be a cat and go; but meanwhile I'll lock you up."

A proverb about setting a cat to watch uncovered milk pans shows the Indian cat to be as fond of milk as the English. "I wasn't so angry at the cat stealing the butter, as at her wagging her tail," is a saying of obvious application. Of the great Sepoy mutiny they say, "The cat (the English) taught the tiger (the Sepoy), till he came to eat her." Of a hypocrite: "The cat, with mouse tails still hanging out of her mouth, says—Now I feel good, I will go on a pilgrimage to Mecca." The Indian cat *miyaus*, which is better by a syllable than the English *mew*; so they say to child or servant: "What! my own cat, and *miyau* at me!" "The cat does not catch mice for God" has obvious applications.

An odd bit of observation, acknowledging in a mistaken fashion the exquisite nervous sensibility of the cat, is shown in, "When the cat is ashamed, it scratches the wall." The idea is that when a cat is noticed it becomes afflicted with self-consciousness, and "to make itself a countenance," as the French say, it scratches the wall. But cats scratch the wall to keep their claws in order, just as tigers and leopards do. I venture to see in the saying an evidence of the Oriental dislike of the mood of embarrassment or shyness. A well-brought-up Oriental is remarkable, as a rule, for his want of *mauvaise honte.* Quite small boys are calm and self-possessed, with full control over eyes, fingers, and limbs, in situations where English children would be writhing in nervous embarrassment. In Capt. R. C. Temple's edition of Fallon's *Hindustani Proverbs* it is an angry cat that scratches the wall in impotent rage. I have heard it "ashamed" as above. The scratching, moreover, is a tranquil performance, usually ensuing after a yawn and stretch, and in nowise suggests rage. Probably both versions are current. "Even a cat is a lion in her own lair," is a saying used when mild people flare up in self-defence.

The cat seems to have no particular walk in Hindu mythology, nor are there many folk tales like our Whittington, and Puss in Boots. The jungle wild-cat is a poor relation of the domestic pussy, and poor relations are apt to compromise the most respectable people and prevent them taking their proper place in society. The Persian cat is prized as a family pet, and numbers are brought down from Kābul by the Povindahs, a tribe of Afghan dealers who bring camel caravans with various kinds of produce into the Punjab every winter.

Cats are frequently kept in the courts and purlicus of Muhammadan mosques which serve as rest-houses for religious persons. If you make friends with a mosque cat and talk with the Mutwalli or sacristan, its owner, you will probably hear of Abû Harera (father of cats), one of the friends of Muhammad, who had as great a fondness for cats as Théophile Gautier, and with whom the Prophet conversed on the subject, saying,—" I love all who are good to cats for your sake." Though this is a merely popular legend, sanctioned by no authoritative tradition or *hadîs*, it seems to have secured good treatment for the cat at the hands of most Indian Muhammadans. From Cairo, when the annual procession of the Kiswa goes to Mecca, cats are always sent on the camels; formerly they were accompanied by an old woman known as the Mother of the Cats, and it has been suggested that this may be a survival of the ancient Egyptian reverence for cats which has so often made readers of Herodotus smile. But the legend of Abû Harera shows that we need not look so far back for an explanation of the honour in which Puss is held. The sympathy of the Prophet with his friend's predilection seems to be confirmed by the pretty story of his cutting off the skirt of his coat rather than disturb the sleeping cat, his pet.

I told that story once to a Kashmiri Muhammadan, when urging on him the advantages of treating animals kindly, and was answered as prosy preachers deserve to be. "Yes," said my friend, the leader of a gang of *kahars* or porters, "the sahib spoke the words of truth, it is wrong to ill-use creatures whom God has made. Once before it was my fortune to listen to similar talk from a sahib who also knew of the Prophet. That sahib was a model of virtue, he also would not allow mules or ponies to be beaten, and his regard for men was such, that he insisted on paying them double the usual daily rate, while to me,—such was the virtue of that sahib,—he gave a handsome present." This little speech was beautifully delivered, but it ought to be Englished in the Irish tongue to give it due effect.

A sneering saying is, "In a learned house even the cat is learned." A sly man is said to look like a drowned cat; a live cat is said to be better than a dead tiger, as a living dog is better than a dead lion; a stealthy tread is, of course, catlike; and it is easy to imagine occasions when one might say of a human creature, "The cowed cat allows even a mouse to bite its ears." In nature a cowed cat is as rare as a silent woman, but a proverb has not necessarily much concern with nature. We say, "Even a worm will turn." In India the cat is considered so gentle, they say, "Even a cat, hard pressed, will make a fight for it." To an idle girl a mother will say, "Did the cat sneeze, or what?" (that you drop your work). To her child, too, the mother will point the cat cleaning her face and fur as an example of cleanliness, saying the cat is a Brahmani, nice and clean.

In Kashmir they say, "If cats had wings, there would be no ducks on the lake." Cats are credited with an occult sympathy with the moon, on account of their contracting eyes and nocturnal habits. You may hear cats spoken of with mistrust for this peculiarity, for natives dislike being abroad at night. They take lanterns, go in companies, and sing to keep their courage up; but they hate and fear the dark, thickly peopled with ghosts, demons, and imaginary evil folk of flesh and blood. So we need not see in the ascription of the cat to the moon an echo of its ancient Egyptian dedication. A cat's moon is a Kashmiri expression for a sleepless night. Old-fashioned English rustics talk of a man "as lazy as Ludlam's dog that leaned his head against the wall to bark." In Kashmir, says the Rev. J. H. Knowles, they speak of Khokhai Mir's idle cat that scratched the ground on seeing a mouse, as who should say, "You may catch it, master, if you like." The sensitiveness of the cat's eye is noticed, but they do not pretend, like the Chinese, to tell the time by looking at its pupil.

Among a vast number of omens the cat takes a place. A cat crossing the path of a native going out on business would turn him back at once, for it is most unlucky. Orientals are terribly superstitious. Yes, but here is a verse by an English poet,[1] writing from first-hand knowledge of hard-headed Whitby fisher folk,—

"I'm no way superstitious as the parson called our Mat,
When he'd none sail with the herring fleet, 'cause he met old Susie's cat.
There's none can say I heeded, though a hare has crossed my road,
Nor burnt the nets as venomed, where a woman's foot had trode."

[1] *On the Seaboard and other Poems*, by Susan K. Phillips.

CHAPTER XIII

OF ANIMAL CALLS

"The beasts are very wise,
Their mouths are clean of lies;
They talk one to the other,
Bullock to bullock's brother,
Resting after their labours,
Each in stall with his neighbours.
But man with goad and whip,
Breaks up their fellowship,
Shouts in their silky ears
Filling their souls with fears.
When he has tilled the land
He says,—'They understand.'
But the beasts in stall together,
Freed from yoke and tether,
Say, as the torn flanks smoke,
'Nay, 'twas the whip that spoke.'"—R. K.

IN English we say "Puss puss" to a cat. "*Pooch pooch*" is sometimes used in India, but "*koor koor*" is a more frequent word to dogs, cats, and domestic pets. "*Toi-toi*" is a call of the same kind. "*Ti-ti*" is a Kashmir call to fowls and ducks. "*Ahjao!*" the first syllable long drawn out, is the usual cry to fowls for feeding, and faqirs living in woodland places thus call peacocks and monkeys to a dole of grain. Though not a tail is visible at first, plaintive cries like those of lost kittens come faintly from aloft and afar in response, gradually growing louder. Then, one by one, slinging onward and downward, the creatures arrive with their leader. "*Ah ah ah!*" is also a common fowl and pigeon call. The sacred crocodiles in the Rajputana lakes are invited to dinner by the Brahmans with "*Ao bhai!*"—Come, brother! Elephants have quite a small dictionary of their own. There are separate words for—go quickly, sit, kneel with front legs, with hind legs, with all four, lie down and sleep, go slowly, lift a foot, rise, move backwards, stand still, break off branches, put me up with your trunk, make a salaam, and possibly more. All these are understood. A good mahout, too, is always talking to his beast, like the ploughman and ox-cart driver. When riding on an elephant those who have the knack of self-effacement and appearing to take no notice may hear quaint things sometimes, naïve comments on themselves and odd phrases of reproach and encouragement to the beast. One might, indeed, from these soliloquies, ascribe more faith in animal intelligence to the Oriental than he really cherishes. Many natives habitually talk to themselves by way of beguiling the tedium of a long road; and old women of the rustic class, when walking alone, frequently rehearse their family quarrels or bargainings with dramatic gestures.

Camels have but a limited vocabulary, nor do they seem to have brought with them the Arabic "*tss, tss,*" which is the "woa" of the beast throughout his Western home from Morocco to Hadramaut. "*Hoosh*" is the Biloch driver's command for sit, but in the Eastern Punjab plain they say "*jai.*" For go on they use the heavily aspirated word for shout, "*hānkh,*" which is also a great ox-word; whence comes "*hānkh,*" a drive of wild animals. In Anglo-Indian slang there are Government servants who have to be "*hānkhed*" or driven to their work.

"*Hiyo!*" is a cow cry, but with none of the fine note of the English north-country "How up!" nor is there a pretty call like the "Cūsha! cūsha!" that Miss Ingelow has used so effectively in her beautiful poem, "A high tide on the coast of Lincolnshire." And as "Whitefoot" and "Lightfoot" are called to come up to the milking shed, so Indian cows are summoned by their names, often those of the days of the week, Tuesday (Mangal) being especially lucky. A deep, guttural, cork-drawing tock, very different from the English carter's click, and hard to learn, is much used for oxen, with a variety of tones of anger, encouragement, and remonstrance in the chest-deep "*hān.*" When in a hurry or stuck in a rut, Indian carters produce noises that the most skilful ventriloquist would find hard to imitate. They rumble like a rusty tower clock in act to strike, they gurgle, grunt, click, moan, and shout strange words known only to oxen, punctuating every period with blows. "*Cheeo, Cheeo*" is said to oxen drinking, and as they are released from labour, and must be a welcome word.

Animals also hear just the same foul and senseless abuse of their female relatives that their masters bestow on each other. The constantly heard "*Sala*" (brother-in-law) is the key-word to this loathsome line of talk. Among caressing epithets in use are young one, son, father, mother, darling, and daughter; sometimes *my* child, etc. The interjection of surprise of ordinary life "*aré!*" is often heard as a sort of "Would you, now?" Horses are calmed and stopped by the kissing chirrup with which we stimulate them in Europe, as a new-comer learns with surprise when his steed stops dead at a sound meant to make him go faster. Bird-catchers and jungle-folk at large imitate all bird and animal cries with surprising skill. Quails, however, are lured to the net by a mechanical call, produced by the finger-nail on a stretched skin. On thieving excursions the notes of the jackal, owl, and other creatures are used as signals by burglars and cattle-stealers.

On the whole Indian country cries and songs are harsh and unpleasing. But there are exceptions to this rule. In Hindustan and parts of the Bombay Presidency where oxen, walking down an incline, haul up water, the drivers accompany their work with songs clear in note, musical in cadence, and pathetic in effect.

CHAPTER XIV

OF ANIMAL TRAINING

INDIA,—land of waning wonders,—has a great name for the training of animals, a pursuit in which the people are popularly believed to attain marvellous success by reason of special aptitudes and faculties. In the yellow-backed romances of the boulevard Orientalism in which the French indulge, Indian princes and princesses are habitually attended by trained leopards and tigers, while English writers dwell on the skill of the trainers. But seen from near and compared with what has been done and is now done in other countries, the wonder pales a little. Nothing half so squarely attempted and completely accomplished as the modern European and American training of wild beasts in performances foreign to their nature and habits has ever been thought of in India. It should be noted, to begin with, that only persons of low caste ever engage in this pursuit, which demands peculiar qualities of hand, will, and temper, and cannot be learned as easily as wood-sawing. These people have a wonderful knowledge of woodcraft, and are fearless with the creatures they know so well. They can catch and tame, but, at the risk of falling into the pestilent error of hair-splitting, I venture to discriminate between taming and training. The first is the most important part but not nearly the whole of the latter, and it is the first only which is well done.

But as to training as indicated, for example, in the deservedly popular works of the late Rev. J. G. Wood, it may be worth while to look a little nearer. This authority wrote that "in India trained otters are almost as common as trained dogs." But they are not used throughout Hindustan, nor in Central India, nor in the Punjab, where they are found in great numbers, and in the regions where they help in fishing they are never seen out of the hands of their owners, obscure river-side tribes. They are only employed in the back waters of Cochin, in part of Bengal, and on the Indus river. All that we see of the otter in Britain is a poor little beast desperately fighting for its life against murderous crowds of dogs and men; but in reality there are few animals of more amiability, talent, and docility. A Scottish gamekeeper once trained one to go with dogs, and used to say it was the best cur in the pack. They are effectually tamed in India, which is an easy matter, and they practise for the benefit of the fisherman the art to which they are ordained by nature. The cormorant and the pelican are also used by the Indus boatmen as in China for fishing. The pelican, though furnished by nature with the finest game-bag or creel ever carried by angler, is inferior to the cormorant (*Graculus carbo*) as a fisherman. Both these birds, like the otter, fish by nature, nor could Buckland or Cholmondeley-Pennell teach them a turn of their craft. It is certainly interesting to see the hooded cormorants on the fishermen's house-boats and the otters tethered to stakes near, playing with the no less amphibious children and behaving like the playful, intelligent water-cats they are. But both this sight and the knowledge that they are used in this wise are distinctly *un*common and out of the range of the people of India at large.

The same writer also descants on the great powers of Orientals in training the cheetah or hunting leopard (*Felis jubata*). In this instance the only point where real skill comes into play is in the first capture of the adult animal, when it has already learned the swift bounding onset,—its one accomplishment. The young

A HUNTING CHEETAH

cheetah is not worth catching, for it has not learned its trade, nor can it be taught in captivity! The Christian Missionary is occasionally asked to state exactly how he proposes to convert the heathen man, and he sensibly concludes, as a rule, to begin with the child. The problem of how to catch uninjured so powerful and active a beast as the hunting leopard seems as difficult as the conversion of the heathen adult. In practice, however, it is simple. There are certain trees where these great dog-cats (for they have some oddly canine characteristics) come to play and whet their claws. The hunters find such a tree, arrange deer-sinew nooses round it, and await the event. The animal comes and is caught by a leg, and it is at this point the trouble begins. It is no small achievement for two or three naked, ill-fed men to secure so fierce a captive and carry him home on a cart. Then his training commences. He is tied in all directions, principally from a thick grummet of rope round his loins, while a hood fitted over his head effectually blinds him. He is fastened on a strong cot bedstead, and the keepers and their wives and families reduce him to submission by starving him and keeping him awake. His head is made to face the village street, and for an hour at a time several times a day his keepers make pretended rushes at him and wave cloths, staves, and other articles in his face. He is talked to continually, and women's tongues are believed to be the most effective anti-soporifics. No created being could resist the effects of hunger, want of sleep, and feminine scolding, and the poor cheetah becomes piteously, abjectly tame. He is taken out for a walk, occasionally, if a slow crawl between four attendants, all holding hard, can be called a walk, and his promenades are always through the most crowded bazaars, where the keepers' friends are to be found. The street dog snarls and growls from a safe distance at the little procession, and occasionally a child, suddenly catching sight of the strange beast, breaks into a frightened cry; but the people on the whole are rather pleased than otherwise to see the Raja's cheetahs among them.

It is difficult to give a just idea of the curious intimacy with animals that exists in India among those who have charge of them. The cheetah's bedstead is like that of the keeper, and when the creature is tamed, leopard and man are often curled under the same blanket. When his bedfellow is restless, the keeper lazily stretches out an arm from his end of the cot and dangles a tassel over the animal's head, which seems to soothe him. In the early morning I have seen a cheetah

A RESTLESS BEDFELLOW

(Copyright 1891, by J. Lockwood Kipling)

sitting up on his couch, a red blanket half-covering him, his tasselled red hood pushed awry, looking exactly like an elderly gentleman in a night-cap as he yawned with the irresolute air of one who is in doubt whether he will rise or turn in for yet another nap. Of actual training in the field there is little or none. So it is not wonderful that the cheetah loses its natural dash and is often left behind by the antelope. At the wedding festivities of a Punjab chief the other day (March 1886) the guests were shown this sport, and the cheetah caught and killed a black-buck. But it was found that the Raja's servants, by way of making quite sure, had first hamstrung the poor antelope!

The ordained procedure is that the hooded leopard is taken afield on a cart driven near a herd of black-buck, shown the game, and slipped. In a few bounds he reaches and seizes it, is rewarded with a draught of blood, or a morsel of liver in a wooden spoon, and put on his cart again; but there is a large proportion of failures. And the creature is not practising a feat he has been taught, but is merely let loose to perform an act he learned in a wild state, which his keepers cannot teach, and for which, in fact, their teaching seems to unfit him. I fail, therefore, to see where the "wonderfully perfect training" of which the Rev. J. G. Wood speaks comes in.

In some hunting pictures by Indian artists, the cart that bears the cheetah and his keeper is drawn by a pair of black-buck antelopes, and you often hear of the Nilghai also being trained to the yoke for Indian Princes. Nay, there are Englishmen who have tried to harness these fine animals to the buggy and the dog-cart. But though confidently reported, you may go far before meeting with an authentic case of successful antelope-harnessing. An Oriental hears vaguely of things of this nature, and promptly accepts them as common and indubitable facts. In official life, speaking with Europeans, he is learning to say, "I have *heard*," but in private he is as cock-sure as a London literary man who has found a fallacy repeated in five books.

Still less capacity is shown in the training of animals

for street performances. The bear, the monkey, the goat, and sometimes the bull, are led abroad to fairs by men of low caste. The gray bear (*Ursus isabellinus*) and the common black bear (*Ursus labiatus*) are most docile creatures, and would repay good teaching. But

A BEAR LEADER

the bear-leader is a man of few and chance-hap meals, and though starvation and the stick make his creatures gentle enough, he has not the wit to teach them well. Some bear-leaders buckle a leather apron round their bodies and, thus protected, pretend to wrestle with the poor beast; but a paralytic dance on his hind legs, cadenced by jerks on his chain and blows with the staff, is the usual depressing performance. No more complete picture of misery can be imagined than that presented by a dancing bear on a hot day in a town in the Plains, where there is no escape from the pitiless sun.

A goat and two or three monkeys are the actors in a little play that goes on unceasingly all over India.

PERFORMING MONKEYS AND GOAT

Their leader is a picturesque tatterdemalion who wanders far in search of audiences and is suspected of picking up more than alms. The goat kneels as a salaam; sometimes he stands with all four feet carefully adjusted on a pile of hour-glass-shaped blocks of wood, and he serves as charger to the monkeys, who put on caps and coats and are jerked to and fro by their chains in a sort of dance, their hungry eyes intently watching the crowd for something to eat. They are Rajas going to court, they are Lord Generals-in-Chief going to fight, they are champions and swordsmen ; and they do everything with sad indifference to the accompaniment of a droning mechanical patter intoned with an air of profound boredom. While confessing that this performance always makes me melancholy, I must admit that children, for whom it is intended, and who ought to be good judges, are delighted by it. To some generations of Anglo-Indian children as well as countless hosts of native little ones it has given a vast amount of gratification.

Dogs are so entirely neglected that the ordinary fetch-and-carry tricks of an English spaniel or retriever are looked at with astonishment, and you are listened to with polite incredulity when you describe the performances of a good collie with sheep.

I have mentioned the elephant in another place, but while cordially acknowledging that Indian mahouts have a complete and most intimate mastery and knowledge of their own peculiar beast, I would point out that it is naturally docile and gentle, and that American and English circus trainers make the creature do more than the most skilful mahout has taught.

It is seldom in Northern India that the bulls led about by the *quasi*-religious mendicants known as "Anandi" do more than shake their heads or kneel at a sign of command. With a clever *boniment* or patter even this much might be made entertaining, but the patter is seldom clever. In Southern India a bull and a cow are sometimes made to enact a quarrel and a reconciliation, but there is not a showman in Europe who would consider the animals taught to any purpose. So little contents an audience of rustic Indian folk, and when you call your bull Rama, and your cow Sita, and they are, to begin with, sacred and most cherished objects, there is obviously no need for elaborate performances.

As to horses, they are not so much trained as constrained, with the often cruel constraint of a timorous hand. No animal throughout India is brought to that wonderful pitch of education shown by the horses

A PERFORMING BULL (MADRAS)

(Copyright 1891, by J. Lockwood Kipling)

employed in railway shunting yards in England, where trains are made up. At a word these fine animals put forth a measured strength to set a carriage in motion, at a gesture they stop or turn ; they seem to know the intricate points of the rails as well as the signalman ; and, their service done, they take up of themselves their own place in the labyrinth of iron, standing unmoved while the locomotives go roaring and screaming past.

No, the Oriental is not a first-rate animal trainer. With almost boundless patience, he has no steadfastness of aim, nor has he sufficient firmness of hand and will to secure confidence and obedience.

Yet, while the art of training may not be very thoroughly understood, the tribes which have to do with jungle life are often wonderful trackers and highly skilled in woodcraft. Many English sportsmen in their talk, and some sporting writers in their books, fail to do justice to the courage and skill of the unarmed assistants on whom they depend for success. There are many chases in which the honours ought to go to the bold and patient trackers who mark down the game day after day, and manage to drive it up to the guns of the well-fed English gentlemen, waiting serene and safe with a battery of the best weapons London gunsmiths can provide. This mistake in taste and judgment is not made by such masters as Sir S. Baker and Mr. Sanderson, who show a friendly sympathy with their assistants.

CHAPTER XV

OF REPTILES

"And death is in the garden awaiting till we pass,
For the krait is in the drain-pipe,
The cobra in the grass."
Anglo-Indian Nursery Rhymes.—R. K.

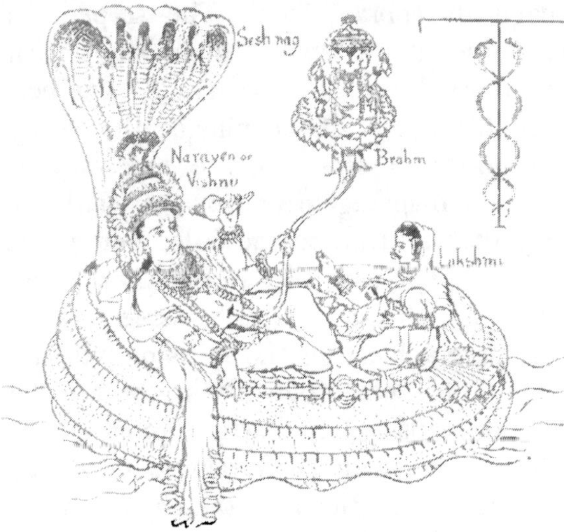

VISHNU RECLINING ON THE SERPENT
(FROM AN INDIAN LITHOGRAPH)

THE serpent has swallowed up the rights of the rest of the reptiles in Indian lore and talk. As Adi Sesha Seshnâg or Ananta, the nâg or cobra is a sacred eternal creature on whom the world rests. He is also a couch to Vishnu, and the hoods of his thousand heads are clustered like the curls of a breaking wave in a canopy over the form of the Creator. In rustic ceremonies, survivals of the antique prime, before sowing or reaping, the village Brahman's first care is to find in which direction the great world-supporting serpent is lying, while the peasants wait, awe-stricken, half fancying they hear the stir of his slow uncoiling. The beloved Krishna, too, India's cerulean Apollo, is often represented in modern bazaar pictures standing on the head of the great black snake he slew and dragged from the river Jumna. He bruised its head with victorious heel, but in the pictures he stands at ease, tranquilly blowing his pipe and attended by Lamia Gopis or milkmaids.

Then there are still beliefs in serpent folk and serpent transformation, and legends and chronicles of dynasties of naga or cobra kings. The serpent of Scripture who "was more subtil than any beast of the field which the Lord God had made" has perhaps conveyed to the minds of the nineteenth-century Europeans some notion of what snake legends may be like. But it is no disparagement to the faith of Christians to say that in Europe the Eden serpent is vague. When we do not (like Dr. Adam Clarke) injuriously suspect him of being an ape, he serves mainly as a metaphor, a mere vehicle for the spirit of evil, and we are too far off to make out his scales, his flat triangular head, and his quick darting tongue. In India he is alive,—alive with swift powers of death, and always very near. In the roof thatch, the stone wall, the thorn fence, the prickly pear thicket, the well-side, or coiled on the dusty field path, he waits his appointed hour to strike.

He takes part in a thousand tales of mystery and wonder, and is wiser and more wicked than all the sons of men. There are several fabled Indian jewels; that in the Elephant's brow, in the lotus of Buddhism, in the head-dress of the princely Bodisat or Buddha-to-be; but the jewel in the cobra's head evokes a livelier faith than the rest. It is not infected with the serpent's guilt, but is an antidote to poison and a sure remedy for pain. Fortune waits on its possessor, and he will never bear a heavy heart. But it is not easily come by, for they say, "A chaste woman's breasts, a serpent's jewel, a lion's mane, a brave man's sword, and a Brahman's money are not to be handled till they are dead."

Serpent tales are too numerous to be told at length. In some, a young Prince accidentally swallows a snake which feeds on his vitals. Many involved turns of the story-teller's art follow after this beginning. In one an anxious Princess, watching by her afflicted husband's side as they are journeying in search of health, sees the snake emerge from his mouth as he lies asleep, and overhears a conference with another snake which guards a treasure. They reveal the charms by which they may be subdued, and the Princess restores her husband to health and gives him illimitable wealth. This is also an old European superstition, for Gerald of Barri says that a young man, grievously afflicted by reason of having swallowed an adder, went to all the shrines of England for relief in vain, but found at last health and peace in Ireland, where no snake may live. Physiologists could tell us what would really happen to a snakelet exposed to digestive processes. That snakes guard treasure is a modern Italian superstition.

Lamia stories are common. A peasant meets a lovely disconsolate woman in the woods, brings her home, and makes her his wife. A holy man passes that way and repays his entertainment by instructing the peasant how to detect and destroy the monster woman snake.

So the now suspicious husband prepares for dinner a salt curry, having previously broken the drinking water vessels. As he lies by her side, pretending to sleep, her beautiful head rises from the pillow, the neck slowly, slowly lengthens, the forked tongue plays in feverish thirst as the serpent curves and twines round the hut seeking the door. Then, with sinuous stretch, it glides out and away, and he hears the lapping of water on the distant river brink, while the fair body by his side is cold and still. Then it returns, coil on coil shortening and settling noiselessly down, until at last a lovely woman's head is laid on the pillow with a soft sigh of content. The next day, while his industrious and beautiful wife is busy at the oven outside, the peasant thrusts her into its glowing depth and piles on wood till she is utterly consumed, even as the holy man instructed him. In some varieties of the tale the *pâras*, or philosopher's stone, which turns all it touches into gold, is found in the oven after the burning, and other adventures ensue.

The worship of the serpent may not everywhere survive in official form, and there are, I believe, no temples entirely consecrated to Nâgas, but it is still practised as a domestic ordinance in Southern India, and everywhere the true Hindu reverences the fateful creature that carries pure death in its fangs. *Sarpa homa* is the name given to the somewhat elaborate ceremony of snake-worship. But in everyday life, when the women of a household hear a cobra chasing rats or mice in the ceiling or roof, they will pause in their work and put their hands together in silent adoration. *Nâg panchami* is the serpents' fête-day—a holiday throughout India. In the south models of the five-hooded cobra are made in terra-cotta, brass, or silver, so contrived that the centre coil forms a socket for a cup in which an offering of milk is put and the whole is worshipped.

In poetry it is easy to talk of a thousand heads; the sculptor and the painter content themselves with five, so modern folk say that in old days the cobra had five heads, but in this iron age he has deteriorated. In Ceylon, and possibly in the extreme south of India, the snake is often an almost familiar member of the establishment, seen daily and regularly fed and worshipped. Nor is it wonderful that the cobra should be reverenced when his attributes are taken into account. He is the necklace of the Gods, he can give gems to the poor, he is the guardian of priceless treasures, he can change himself into manifold forms, he casts his skin annually and thus has the gift of eternal youth, he can make milk, fruit, bread and all innocent food stark death when he chooses to pass over them, he is of high caste, he is in the confidence and counsel of Gods and demons, and when the great world was made he was already there.

In rustic life the serpent has peculiar reverence as the appointed guardian of the village cattle; in this capacity he is regarded as an incarnation of some ancestor, and is generally named by a colour, as the Red, Black, or Blue snake, and becomes in a sort a tutelary divinity. Poisonous snakes kill scores of cattle, therefore they are in India accounted the natural protectors of cattle.

The Government pays large sums annually for the destruction of poisonous snakes, but it will be many a year before a respectable Hindu will willingly kill one. This is not surprising when we reflect that an ordinance not yet obsolete decrees that when a snake is killed the Hindu shall perform mourning ceremonies of a like ritual to those in honour of a dead relation. This, of course, is not often done, but the snake's skin is frequently burned as an atonement to its outraged spirit. They call him Raj-bansi, royal scion, as an honourable name, and generally seek to propitiate as we to destroy the pest.

A Financial Commissioner of the Punjab told me that once, when walking through fields with the son of a village Lambardar or head-man, he raised his stick with the Englishman's instinct of killing a cobra crossing the path, but the young man laid a hand on his arm, saying: "Nay, sir, do not strike, the snake also has but one little life,"—an unusual act, from which the lad's father would probably have refrained, partly in deference to a high officer of the Government, and partly from the Hindu habit of minding his own business and letting other people alone. But it shows the ingrained respect for serpent life.

It is possible, however, to show mercy to many generations of serpents and yet to know little about them. When a snake has a musk-rat in his mouth he is considered to be in a terrible dilemma. If he swallows it he becomes blind, if he vomits it he becomes leprous. The way out of it is for him to go into the water. I have never been able to understand the how or why of this escape, but it is accepted as a triumph of serpent cunning. No need to say that the snake, having swallowed the rat, brings the dislocated gearing of his jaws together and thinks no more about it, or that the musk-rat is just as welcome to him as any other.

Sayings which treat the snake as purely noxious may be guessed to be mainly Muhammadan, but the Hindu is not prevented by a sense of veneration from speaking his mind, as the numerous gibes at Brahmans show. "The snake moves crookedly as a rule, but to his own hole he can go straight enough," is a reflection on a Brahman or a cunning and selfish person. "In a council of snakes tongues play fast," is a reproach to those who talk much and do little. The silent play of the serpent tongue, however, scarcely suggests talk. "Even the breath of a snake is bad" is a common saying. I have noticed an evil odour in the breath of a python, the only creature of the race I have ventured to be intimate with, and it may be this is based on observation.

"The gadding wife sees a snake in the roof of her own house" is a wise word for India, but inapt for England, where the customs of modern good society have elevated gadding into a duty and a fine art and falsified the folk-talk of ages. "Kill the snake but do not break the stick," is sensible advice often given to over-eager people; and to those who miss opportunities, "The snake is gone, beat the line of his track." To appreciate this it should be remembered that over the greater part of India is a layer of dust on which the track left by a snake is plainly imprinted. The hopelessness of snake-bite is acknowledged in "Bitten by a snake, wants no water," *i.e.* will not live to drink it. The snake's bite goes in like a needle but comes out like a ploughshare, is an expressive phrase used in Bengal. A rhyming saying might be Englished "After snake-bite sleep, after scorpion weep." In the first case the sleep of course is eternal. Of the deadly little Kupper snake they say in Western India, "Its bite begins with death." Another contrast with the relatively harmless scorpion is a saying applied to rash and foolish persons, "Doesn't even know the spell for a scorpion, but must stick his finger in a snake's mouth." "Even in a company of ten the serpent is safe," they are all so much afraid of it is the inference. "One serpent can frighten a whole army" is an expansion of the same notion. But there is something worse than even snake-bite: "You may survive the cobra's fang, but nothing avails against the evil eye," says popular superstition.

There is a popular belief that to see a couple of snakes entwined together, as on the wand of Esculapius and the caduceus of Hermes in classic sculpture, is a most fortunate event. It is certainly rare, and a friend of mine who saw a pair of cobras thus engaged says this encurled dalliance is a surprising and beautiful sight. A single cobra reared in act to strike stands high, but a pair twisted together and full of excitement rear up to a great height. The heads with expanded hoods are in constant movement, and the tongues play like forked lightnings. Then he fetched his gun and shot them both dead. A Hindu would have folded his hands in adoration and considered himself made lucky for life by this auspicious sight.

The Secretary of State for India is anxious that more should be done by the Indian Government towards the extirpation of poisonous snakes and deadly wild animals. From the smooth pavements of London town the task doubtless appears easy. In reality nothing is more difficult, for in addition to the protection of Nature is the no less powerful protection of superstitious respect and deeply-rooted apathy on the part of the people. This last quality, by the way,—absolutely incomprehensible in Europe,—is an immense factor in Indian affairs which Governments and eager reformers are apt to overlook.

The Indian Government has done its best, but is

inclined to despair in the face of an increasing mortality in all Presidencies except Bombay, and is now minded to recommend that the system of rewards for dead snakes should be discontinued, and that increasing care should be given to the clearing of the scrub and jungle round villages. With a diminishing staff of English civil officers it will probably be found as difficult to carry out this wise precaution as to provide for the improved sanitation which is the most urgent need of the time. Native subordinate officers are to be directed under the orders of the Sanitary Board of each Province to destroy cover for snakes near villages. But thorn-heaps, prickly pear thickets, jungle growth and clumps of tall sedge are as cherished traditions of the village outskirt as are the noisome ponds from which drinking water is drawn ; and there is not one Oriental in a thousand to whom they appear in their true light as nurseries of vermin and disseminators of disease. Lord Lansdowne quoted at the opening of the Allahabad water-works a translation of a native couplet,—

> "A confounded useless botheration
> Is your brand new nuisance, sanitation—"

and expressed a hope that it was a libel on the more thoughtful and intelligent part of the community. But that is only a microscopic part, after all. The average native hates sanitation as the devil hates holy water, and worse.

The offer of rewards for dead snakes has naturally developed a new and remunerative industry—the rearing and breeding of snakes by outcaste jungle folk ; excepting, it would seem, in the Bombay Presidency, where large numbers are killed at a cheap rate, and where the death-rate from snake-bite is decreasing.

During the last eleven years Rs.237,000 (say £20,000) have been spent on rewards for destroying snakes, and evidently to very little purpose, for the mortality of man from snake-bite shows over the greater part of India no diminution, but on the contrary is increasing.

The outlook is not in the least encouraging, nor can any one who really knows the country honestly hold forth a hope that the Government by any agency it can command will be able to tread out the deadly snake. The people will not allow it for many a year to come.

It may be worth while to quote a few figures from the last Government report on the subject. In the Bombay Presidency in 1889, 400,000 snakes were killed and only 1000 human deaths from snake-bite were recorded. In the Punjab, 68,500 snakes died; in Bengal, 41,000; in the North-West Provinces and Oudh (the greater part of Hindustan proper), less than 26,000. In Bengal 10,680 persons are reported to have died from snake-bite, and in the North-West Provinces 6445. But not every death ascribed to the snake is really caused by him. Many a murder and poisoning case is passed off as snake-bite, for the murderer is just as ingenious in India as elsewhere.

The creatures to which mortality is mainly due are the Cobra (*Naja tripudians*), the Krait (*Bungarus ceruleus*), Russell's Viper (*Daboia Russellii*), and the Echis (*Echis carinata*), to which may be added in Western India the Kupper snake, and in Assam the Hamadryad (*Ophiophagus elaps*).

Snake-bite seems likely to remain incurable until some more fortunate Dr. Koch of the future discovers a fluid which on injection will counteract the horrible decomposition of the blood that snake-poison causes. In India there are many antidotes in which the people put their trust, but probably all are worthless. A German Missionary recently claimed that a nostrum, to which he gave a pretty name from Persian poetry, was efficacious, but it seems to have been no better than the rest. The snake-stone,—a porous piece of calcined bone, pumice-stone, or something of that nature,—is the sheet-anchor of many, and in the year of grace 1890 an enlightened native gentleman of Hyderabad gave several hundred rupees for one. The theory is that when the snake-stone is placed on the bitten part it adheres and swiftly extracts the poison, dropping off when the virus is absorbed. It is reasonable enough that any absorbent, even the lips of her "who knew that love can vanquish death," if applied promptly enough, may prevent a mortal dose of the poison from entering into the circulation; but once mixed with the blood, all the snake-stones and quack nostrums in creation cannot avail to withdraw it. Yet even nonsense of this kind has its use. The Briton who spends thirteenpence-halfpenny on cholera pills and the Indian noble who spends a few thousand rupees on a snake-stone do not utterly throw away their money. They buy confidence and courage, most valuable commodities. The hope that springs eternal in the human breast is the innocent first cause of the quack.

One of the unalterably fixed beliefs in the native mind is that the mongoose knows a remedy for snake-bite,—a plant which nobody has seen or can identify, but which, when eaten, is an antidote so sure that the mere breath of the animal suffices to paralyse the snake. The gem in the head of the serpent itself is a no less potent remedy. No human being has seen that gem, but it must be there, since generations of Hindus have written and talked of it. The mongoose has only its quickness of attack and its thick fur for safeguard, and once fairly bitten, goes the way of all flesh into which the deadly poison is poured. But no Oriental of high or low degree will believe this, and you are made to feel like an infidel scoffing at serious things if you assert it.

Having thus incidentally met the mongoose or ichneumon, we may pause to say a word on its tamability. Few wild animals take so readily to domestic life as the Indian mongoose, who has been known to domesticate himself among friendly people; first coming into the house through the bath-water exit in chase of snake or rat, and ending, with a little encouragement, by stealing into the master's chair and passing a pink inquisitive nose under his arm to examine a cup of tea held in his hand. This is the footing on which pets should be maintained. A creature you put into a cage, or tie up with string or chain, is no pet, but a prisoner who cannot but hate his keeper.

There is one person of Indian birth to whom the sanctity of the cobra is a joke; a cynic who dallies with the crested worm, disarms him of death, and makes him dance to the tune of a scrannel pipe; who breeds him for sale to Government officers, that he may receive the sixpence officially set on his beautiful hood, and knows all his secret ways. The Indian snake-charmer of to-day is a juggler, and often a very skilful one. He belongs to a caste to which all things are pure and clean, and is, in consequence, more dirty than all the rest, and yet he is not proud of his superiority to Levitically bonded souls.

Most animals have their peculiar masters,—or servants. The horse owns an imposing retinue of princes, nobles, soldiers, and grooms all over the world, to say nothing of the slaves of the betting ring; the cow and the ox have an humbler following; a peculiar public is devoted to the dog; elephants and camels have their body-servants and *attachés*; in Europe even the rat has an incubus who lives scantily on his murder; but it is only in India that the reptile under the rock has retainers. There are snake, lizard, and crocodile eaters, and those who, with no assumed madness like that of Edgar in *King Lear*,—"eat the swimming frog, the toad, the tadpole, the wall-newt and the water; . . . swallow the old rat and the ditch-dog; drink the green mantle of the standing pool; who are whipped from tithing to tithing, and stock-punished, and imprisoned." In our days, however, the scorn and oppression of the upper classes fall lightly on these outcastes, although, according to the most admired code of Menu, their life is worth less than that of the creatures they devour. From one of these numerous clans comes the snake-charmer. One would like to believe that he exercises a special occult influence over his snakes, but, like the mongoose, he owns no more than his nimbleness, possesses no charm more potent than knowledge of his subject, and it is to be feared that he can only draw that snake out of its hole which but now was secretly put by his own hand. A fair theosophist, describing the conditions under which the early miracles of her curious creed were wrought, declared in print that for their due performance it was necessary that the miracle-workers should "know the place and have been there, the more recently the better." If this is true of discovered brooches, broken tea-cups, or cigarette papers, it is also true of cobras. All the snake-charmer asks is to know the place and to have been there recently, and you shall have your snake without fail.

But there are theosophists who declare that in

A SNAKE-CHARMER

(Copyright 1891, by J. Lockwood Kipling)

watching a snake-charmer's tricks we are witnessing manifestations of occult mysteries. "Then is the moon of ripe, green cheese compact." Yet is he connected with the Gods by one article of his equipment. The *dauru*, a small, hour-glass-shaped drum-rattle of fearsome noisiness (drawn in the forefront of my sketch), is the badge of all his vagrant tribe, and also of the great God Siva, who bears it slung on his trident in many pictures, and will one day rattle it furiously to usher in the destruction of the world, which will be set afire by the flame of the midmost of his three eyes.

The amphisbæna, because it appears to have two butt ends, is believed by some to have a head at each, while others, with a scientific turn, say that for six months its head is at one end and for other six at the other. And it is universally known as the *do mûnhia*—two-faced one. The delightful Sir Thomas Browne seems, in his *Vulgar Errors*, inclined to accept this double-headed serpent, but at last he "craves leave to doubt." The era of doubt is not yet reached in India.

The large lizard, *varanus dracæna*, which is perfectly innocuous, like all Indian lizards, is called the bis-cobra by some, though the name really belongs, according to others, to a different creature, and is counted highly dangerous, while it is believed to be so strong that Sivaji, the renowned Marathi chief, escaped from a fortress wherein he was confined by being dragged up the wall by one of these creatures, and some say they are habitually used by burglars for this purpose. I used to keep one of these harmless animals, and even while holding it in one hand I have been assured by natives of its vast strength and deadliness. The cry of the small house lizard, a kind of gecko, is unlucky in certain conditions. In Southern India, where lizards are numerous and are perpetually falling from the thatched roofs, there is a marvellously elaborate code of omens drawn from the varying circumstances, the parts of the body, house utensils, etc., upon which they drop. Less attention seems to be paid to lizards in the North, but even there they say, "A lizard has fallen on you, go and bathe."

Crocodiles are occasionally regarded as sacred, one cannot say kept and periodically fed. *Muggur pir* near Karachi is a pond full of these creatures, which are often fed for the amusement of visitors. There is a legend of a British officer who crossed this pool, using its inhabitants as stepping-stones in his daring passage. In some of the lakes in Rajputana they are cherished and come to the Brahman's call; not one may be visible at first, but there is first a ripple, then a slow, hideous head protrudes, then another, till the water is alive with crocodiles.

Some outcaste river-side tribes are in the habit of eating tortoises and crocodiles. Of one of these castes a current Punjab gibe says the crocodile can smell a Mor when he passes on the river bank, and truly no very delicate nose is necessary for this feat.

General Sir Alex. Cunningham has identified ancient sculptured representations of the tortoise as meant to indicate the river Jumna—an ascription of which modern Hinduism takes no account. Describing sculptures at Udayagiri he writes: "The figures of the Ganges and Jumna are known by the symbolic animals on which they stand—the crocodile and the tortoise. These two representative animals are singularly appropriate, as the Ganges swarms with crocodiles, and the Jumna teems with tortoises. The crocodile is the well-known *vâhan* or vehicle on which the figure of the Ganges is usually represented; but the identification of the tortoise as the *vâhan* of the Jumna, though probable, was not certain until I found, amongst the Charonsat Jogini statues in the Bhera Ghât temple, a female figure with a tortoise on the pedestal and the name of Sri Yamuna inscribed beneath." Much graceful and significant symbolism of this nature seems to have been dropped in recent times, and a tortoise is now a tortoise and no more. In a Hindu temple at Volkeshwar, Bombay, they were kept and worshipped within the last thirty years, perhaps even now. They say of low-born people that "their words are like a tortoise's head," to be put forth or withdrawn according to circumstances. But no saying reflects on the infamous tyranny of ages that has made the low-caste man a timid time-server and a sneak.

CHAPTER XVI

OF ANIMALS IN INDIAN ART

MORE has been said and written on Indian art than is justified by a right appreciation of its qualities and defects. In architecture alone can it be said to claim the highest distinction. The plastic art of the country at its best was inferior to that of other lands, and the spirit of its artistic prime has been dead for centuries. Among the Indian collections in European museums we see casts and photographs of ancient buildings side by side with representations of the life and customs of to-day, nor is it until we have lived in India and carefully sought out the truth that we learn how dead the characteristic art of a vivid faith and life may be while the faith still lingers and the outward aspect of the life is but slightly changed. There is a considerable distance between the art of an Italian town of to-day and that of the Augustan age, but a still greater gulf between that of a modern Hindu and the Sanchi topes, the Gandhāra and Amravati sculptures. But the Italian himself has changed far more than the Hindu. In India the ancient sculptures are still alive and walk the streets, while if you confront a group of modern Italians with the personages on a Roman sarcophagus you see at a glance that the marble has but little concern with the living man. This persistence of certain elements of Indian life has led some writers to attribute immutability to all. To those who know the country it is obvious, on a little reflection, that artistic India is just as liable to change as the rest of the world, and that in fact there is no country where foreign influences have been more actively at work. To some it is unnecessary to hint truisms of this kind, but in Europe it seems to be believed that the Indian people of to-day have the same artistic endowments and should be required to practise the same style of art as their long-forgotten ancestors.

But though it would be pleasant to plough the infertile sands of art criticism (on whose Indian horizons there are some brave mirages), we have our own row to hoe, and must turn from dreams of what might or ought to be to that which has been and is in our narrow field.

A comparison of the figures of animals shown on the Sanchi topes and in the Ajanta Caves with those of a modern Indian draughtsman shows at once how much difference there is between then and now. The work of the ancient Hindu painter and sculptor is full of life and variety. Monkeys and elephants are always good, while buffaloes come next for truth and naturalness. Lions, tigers, peacocks and swans are conventionalised according to a somewhat restricting but still consistent decorative canon with great propriety and admirable effect. Nothing can exceed the freedom and facility with which elephants are drawn and painted in the Ajanta Cave frescoes, in every conceivable action. The wonderful suppleness and acrobatic capabilities of the beast have never since been so skilfully indicated. Sir Emerson Tennent's book on Ceylon has pictures of bound elephants wildly struggling after capture, but they give an impression of contortion rather than of the india-rubber litheness of the animal in action. In Europe generally, the mere bulk of the beast is all that is represented, for the old notion that "the elephant hath joints, but none for courtesy; his legs are legs for necessity, not for flexure" still survives to some extent. The ancient Hindu artist saw this also, and there are striking representations of the creatures standing like monumental mounds among the forest trees.

In old Hindu temples as at Hallibeed and Khajuraho, friezes of sculptured animals occur in regular sequence. Near the base of the building are elephants, then lions or tigers, over these horses, then cows, then men, and lastly, winged creatures. (In India people habitually talk of "winged things" for birds, a proof, it may be, that more flying creatures than birds are believed in.) The sequence indicates an elemental scheme in which Hindus see more than strikes a European observer. The elephant supports the world, lions and tigers inhabit the jungles of it, the horse is a tamed wild creature, and the cow, next to man, is his benefactor and half a divinity, while the bird courses fly above his head, parrots first, and then swans. The swan (or wild goose) is an accepted image of the soul, hence its high honour among Hindus, although Brahma, with whom it is officially associated, is no longer an object of popular worship. It is not the tame goose however, that is meant, but the flying wild fowl seen far aloft winging its way to some distant and unknown bourne. A Hindu saying goes, "The swan (the soul) flies away and none can go with it." A Western poet has well expressed the sense of solitary flight with definite aim through—

> "The desert and illimitable air,—
> Lone wandering, but not lost."

And it is natural that the piety of Hindus should crystallise in its own fashion the thought in Bryant's mind when he wrote—

> "He who from zone to zone,
> Guides through the boundless sky thy certain flight,
> In the long way that I must tread alone,
> Will lead my steps aright."

So we are presented with the under world, the earth, the air, and a hint of the distant heaven beyond all.

Some Hindus insist that this sequence is invariable. In purely Hindu countries this may be the case, but in regions where contact with Islam and other influences have modified Hinduism it is not followed, and indeed is almost unknown. The elephant's place at the base is a post of honour, but he ascends also, and is shown in pairs with uplifted trunks pouring waters of lustration over the adorable Lakshmi or Saraswati, Goddess of learning, from sacrificial vases. Nothing could be more spirited and natural than the elephant sculptures, while the friezes above them are merely decorative and no more like life than are the leopards and wyverns of European heraldry. The birds have superb tails of fretted foliage faintly recalling some details of late Gothic sculpture. In an architectural sense nothing is lost by the want of veracity, but it is curious that the elephant should be treated with so much feeling for nature, while the equally familiar horse and ox are always wooden in character.

On the face of the rock-hewn Buddhist temple at Karli, on the Western Ghauts, three elephants affront the spectator, and support the hill-side rock on each side of the entrance, with a calm air of competence for their task. In gold, silver, brass, ivory, clay, and wood, elephants serve a hundred purposes, and are drawn and painted everywhere. In such modern work as the tomb of Maharaja Jai Singh at Jeypore, where every detail is treated in a conventional way, and the

MODERN ELEPHANT SCULPTURE, FROM THE TOMB OF SOWAI JAI SINGH, MAHARAJA OF JEYPORE

creature's ears are fluted as regularly as scallop shells, there is still a strong sense of his shape and action. A small pen sketch here given may show this. Centuries had closed down on the ancient freedom, and the Muhammadan canon forbidding the representation of life, though never thoroughly accepted in India, had repressed the plastic instinct. You may hear, when going over palaces in Rajputana, of elaborate carvings in stone, which on a threatening hint from the iconoclastic court at Delhi, were hastily covered up with plaster. In other parts of India recent research has unearthed remains of richly-carved Hindu work, sometimes lying in heaps of broken fragments and bearing traces of fire. But though you expel nature with a pitchfork or shut it up like a jack-in-the-box, it is not to be wholly repressed. Even the Muhammadans

BORAK. CALIGRAPHIC PICTURE COMPOSED OF PRAYERS

themselves do not always obey the law; the Persian Shiahs have never considered themselves bound by it, and modern Indian art is mainly Persian.

For pious Muhammadans it has long been a practice of Oriental penmen, who are often artists, to weave the fine forms of Persian letters into the outlines of animals or birds. I give an example of the Prophet's mystic horse, Borak, which contains a whole litany of prayers. An elephant on the cover, a tiger on the dedicatory page, and the birds over the monogram of the publishers of this book, are also woven in words of prayer. Every creature alive can be thus represented, and the piety of the inscription covers the profanity of the picture. Muhammadanism, like more religions, is full of ingenious little compromises and transactions after this kind. A more frank defiance of the laws by which at the supreme moments of their lives they profess themselves bound, is characteristic of Christians—

> "Whose life laughs through and spits at their creed!
> Who maintain Thee in word, and defy Thee in deed!"

A curiosity of the time is the way in which those who now follow the craft of the Persian limner and often boast Persian descent, have adopted Hindu notions in their work, though still remaining Muhammadan. Some of the best representations in the popular lithographs sold at fairs of the many-armed Hindu divinities are the work of Muhammadan draughtsmen. So in the time of the Mogul power the Court chroniclers were often Hindus who complacently wrote of the pillage and wreck of the temples of their own faith as triumphs over idolatrous infidels and officially lauded the deeds of Muhammadans in phrases of unctuous insincerity.

An official illuminator is attached to most native courts, an artist whose pride it is to work with "a brush of one hair," and to repeat carefully the types he has learned. There is a complete series of portraits of all the dynasties that have ruled at Delhi, Agra, and Lucknow. The persistence of the types is curious and interesting. The long nose of the Emperor Aurengzebe and the round face of Nūr Mahal are as familiar and constant as the characteristic features of Lord Brougham or Lord Beaconsfield in volumes of *Punch*. The English gentleman and lady were learned a hundred years ago in high-collared coats, tight pantaloons, frilled shirt-fronts, gigot sleeves, and high-waisted, short frocks. To-day in drawing English people the same pattern is faithfully followed. Animals are similarly sketched in obedience to a strict convention. The tiger is almost invariably of the short-bodied variety. This occurs in India at times, but is much less common than the Bengal tiger proper. In the Kensington Natural History Museum I recognised on a shelf the tiger of the Indian illuminator, and shortly afterwards met Colonel Beresford Lovett, R.E., by whom it was presented, who told me that he shot it in Mazanderan, in Persia. Perhaps it is rash to jump to the conclusion that the Persian artist imported his peculiar beast into a land with tigers of its own, but it is certain that the squareness of the Indian limner's tiger is entirely unlike the typical shape of the Indian animal.

The horse is always fat, with a tremendously arched neck and slender legs, resembling, as has been noted in another place, the horse of the painters of the European Renaissance; but lacking his learned display of loaded muscle. In Dr. Aitkin and Mrs. Barbauld's delightful *Evenings at Home*, a boy attempts a definition of the horse which has always seemed to me to embody very fairly the vague Oriental conception: "I should say he was a fine, large, prancing creature with slender legs and an arched neck, and a sleek, smooth skin, and a tail that sweeps the ground, and that he snorts and neighs very loud, and tosses his head and runs as swift as the wind." Herein, as the instructive book points out, are very few of the vital facts of the animal, but they have sufficed without much help from actual observation for many generations of Orientals. Carven horses are rare and seldom successful either as ornamental creations or as representations of nature.

The native of India is but now beginning to learn to care for accurate statements of fact, whether in a literary, scientific, or artistic sense. The Education Department, which, after all, is only the stress of the time brought to a point, and represents the will of the upper classes of the people as much as that of their British fellow-subjects, is determined that this reproach shall be removed, and imports the illustrated lesson-books and wall-pictures of Western schools. In all that concerns the well-being of animals and people, improved knowledge cannot but do good, but the extinction of the pictured horses of romance, the pursy steeds of Sohrab and Rustom, of the legendary Raja Rasálu and the fat chargers of many a Hindu Maharaja and Muhammadan Nawab will not be accomplished without regrets. With them will perish the Persian winged horses which have become naturalised among Indian draughtsmen, and there will be no place for the Yālis and other fantastic creations in which horse forms are traceable. Sūrya, the sun-god, is always represented in a chariot drawn by horses, invariably in profile: one horse being completely drawn and a long row indicated behind with a few repeating lines. Very admirable design is possible under these conditions, but few modern pictures of the Indian Phœbus are admirable either in suggestion or accomplishment.

On a very humble level are the little animals made in clay by the women of a household and often by potters for certain Hindu anniversaries. I write "humble" mechanically, but it must be said in fairness that the rustic classes in Europe do not produce for their amusement anything so good. We once had an elderly servant of serious demeanour, respectable appearance, first-rate testimonials as to character, and hopeless incapacity for his work. One evening, with all the shyness of a youthful artist, he invited me to see a little "picture" he had prepared in the court of the servants' quarters. I was delighted by a charming model of a fort with walls and bastions complete, in which there were camel-riders, dragoons, generals, colonels, and Rajas, all modelled in clay and painted; little lamps were lighted round the mimic scene, the children sat gazing in rapt admiration, and from the dark background of the yard sympathetic murmurs echoed my words of praise. The "bearer's" triumph was complete when his mistresses came to see and admire, but if he had been very wise he would have been content with the master's approval. For during the rest of the time he afflicted us I was often reminded that he had missed his vocation, and would be better employed in modelling soldiers, elephants, and camels, which he did well, than in trimming lamps, making beds, dusting furniture, and blacking boots in a half-hearted and wholly inartistic manner.

Figures of horses and cattle like the gingerbread "gee-gees" of country fairs in Europe, are all that are strictly required for these rustic celebrations, which are probably of great antiquity, representing the worship of domestic animals as part of the family prosperity in a pristine age, or the setting forth of the army of Rama, with an interweaving of obscure legends. But when the artist is clever the subject is naturally expanded and embroidered upon. When you see Mr. H. M. Stanley paraded as Guy Fawkes in London streets it is easy to

SMALL WARES IN METAL

understand how, with themes of a far more vague and shadowy character, Oriental fancy has free play.

A regular part of the potter's business in many regions is the fashioning of toy animals in terra-cotta, gaily painted by his women folk for fairs and festival days. At Delhi, by way of compliment to the chief civil authority, the potters there have at times made small statuettes of the Commissioner and Deputy-Commissioner. These portraits were often amusingly like the originals. There is a legend indeed, that one distinguished officer was so much more than flattered by his clay images that he bought up the whole baking to be broken up. Fantail pigeons, peacocks, parrots, and the generic bird of Indian domestic decoration, akin to the "dicky-bird" of the British child's slate, are made as toys in great numbers. Crows and poultry seldom appear.

Birds and animals are often fashioned in metal, and always with purely decorative intent. The resolute conventionalism of the Indian artisan is shown in the silver mouse from Muttra here sketched with half a dozen small wares, and in the brass owl from Bengal. The parrot and the peacock are old and constant types, but the brass bison is the work of a jungle artist, who from direct observation has learned that a bison's horns meet and join over its brow. And there his lesson ended.

A Muhammadan artist who is skilful in Hindu mythology and produces many lithographs and illustrations, has been kind enough to sketch for me half a dozen birds as they are rendered to-day—a peacock, a pigeon, a heron, a partridge, a parrot, and a bird which he describes by the word we use for wild duck, but which is evidently a water-fowl of another kind. In coloured work the forms would be carefully filled up and finished, but the outline would remain the same, and speaks here for itself. All are *yek chashm*,—one-eyed,—the Persian draughtsman's idiom for in profile.

A full face picture is *do chashm*, two-eyed; but birds are never shown full front. In illuminations for poems and romances the yellow mango bird, the hoopoe, and the maina are occasionally shown, but the distinctive differences lie more in the colouring than in the form.

BIRDS BY AN INDIAN DRAUGHTSMAN

A pair of cranes stands as in Chinese and Japanese pictures (*e.g.* the willow pattern plate) for an emblem of the souls of lovers. A pair of Brahminy ducks sporting in the water, or a pair of pigeons, serves the same purpose. The bird of ancient myth, *Garuda*, whose name in Southern India is given to the common kite, is a Hindu conventionalisation of aquiline forms from which eagle character is usually omitted. In bazaar prints he carries three or four elephants as he flies or serves as a steed to Vishnu in one of his forms, and sometimes he appears as half man half bird. He

A PERI ON A CAMEL

is borne in the arms of the Maharaja of Mysore, with whom in heraldic guise is associated the Yali, the strange, horse-like beast that is carved as a ramping corbel or truss on some of the Hindu temples in Southern India.

The name Shikargah (hunting pattern) is given to a diaper or border of antelopes, tigers, and horsemen often combined with foliage. In old work the designs are often beautiful, as on the margins and backs of

KRISHNA ON AN ELEPHANT

Persian MSS., in embroidery, carpets, metal-chasing, and decorative painting. Modern commerce does not encourage this kind of art, but there are still artists capable of good work.

A fantastic but very popular device is to fill up

the outline of an animal with a jumble of various

KRISHNA ON A HORSE

creatures. Three examples are here given from the brush of Bhai Isur Singh, a Sikh designer. Trivialities of this nature scarcely bear description, and, like many more Oriental fancies, are safe from serious criticism. In one a peri rides on a camel compounded of men and beasts. In another, Krishna playing his pipe, is borne on an elephant made up of adoring Gopis in the guise of modern dancing women. In the third the

NANDI OR SACRED BULL

(Copyright 1891, by J. Lockwood Kipling)

god holds a lotus flower, and his adorers are arranged as a horse.

When one considers the sacred character of the cow and bull, and the estimation in which they are held, it is wonderful that cattle forms are usually so vaguely seen by Hindu artists. There are thousands of carved stone bulls in the courts of the temples of Mahadeo, and hundreds of thousands of brazen bulls in domestic shrines, and all might own direct descent from the golden calf of Moses (which must have been a piece of half-learned Egyptian conventionalism), so fixed and negligent of nature is the type. That Hindu artists can see nature clearly at times, is proved by those who practise the modern new craft of modelling figurines in terra-cotta for sale to Europeans. At Lucknow in Oudh, and at Kishnagar in Bengal, cattle are often skilfully rendered in clay. But draughtsmen and painters as a rule keep faithfully to the hieratic type of the stone-cutters, who never make preliminary models. The Jeypore marble-workers, who turn out a large quantity of animal statuettes, excel in buffaloes in black marble, but since the main of their practice is the supply of images for temples, they adhere to the conventional form for Brahminy cows and bulls.

Sir George C. M. Birdwood has kindly lent me from his collection a coloured picture of Krishna and other personages attended, as usual, by cows. A group of cattle from the foreground of this composition is here engraved, and shows an unusual feeling for nature. The popular ideal, which is the hieratic, is shown more truly in the picture broadsides illustrating country romances, and sold at fairs for a pice each. The muzzle is clumsy and bulbous, the brow is round, the shortness of the body is exaggerated, the dewlap is almost ignored or shown by conventional flutings, the clean, thoroughbred legs are made thick and shapeless, while the form of the hump is seldom truly seen.

It is curious that a cow's head, carved separately as an ornament, is seldom seen in old Indian work and never in that of to-day. Much as he loves the cow, a

CATTLE BY AN INDIAN ARTIST

Hindu of the old rock would prefer not to drink from a fountain where the water issued from a carved cow's head,—the first idea to strike an English sculptor as "neat and appropriate." The head of the elephant is frequently used in ornament, that of the horse is a favourite old Rajput dagger pommel in jade and silver, and tigers' and lions' heads are plentiful, but never that of the cow. A steel *garz* or mace with a horned head, occasionally seen in collections of Indian arms, is really Persian, and represents one of their many fabulous beasts. The reason of this exclusion is that technically the cow's mouth is impure. A horse may drink from a vessel and, after the usual sacramental scrub with earth, it is no worse for family use, but a cow defiles anything it touches with its mouth.

Outcastes seldom find their way into pictures, so one of the most important subjects of the Western animal painter is lost to the Oriental limner, for dogs are not respectable enough to be drawn. The story of Yudhishtira and his dog, already mentioned, offers a good subject for illustration, but though the legend is known to educated Hindus, its hero has for centuries ceased to be popular and there are no pictures of him to be found. In illustrations to the popular romance of Leila and Majnūn a dog accompanies the lady, while a parrot perches on the gaunt shoulder of the passion-worn Majnūn. A dog, a staff, and a bottle are the attributes of the black Bhairon, most popular of Hindu divinities. Perhaps the science of dog-breeding or appreciation of the variety of canine races has been developed since St. Roch was canonised. At all events, the same casteless mongrel that waits on this holy man in Continental churches attends on Bhairon and runs after antelopes and tigers in such popular

Indian romances as Raja Rasálu. The Greeks knew more and better, for they loved and classified their dogs, and sculptured them with discrimination of breed.

The *Illustrated London News* and the *Graphic* are foremost in an educational movement unnoted by many observers. In quite out-of-the-way places as well as in the large towns you may see the narrow wall spaces of the shops covered with their pictures, among coloured German lithographs and native prints. Portraits of the Queen and the Royal Family, pictures of the Oxford and Cambridge boat-race, of winners of the Derby, of prize cattle, of the buxom British infant and types of Western beauty, are stuck side by side with the blue Krishna and the black Kali, and nobody sees any incongruity. Some say that European picture papers are fraught with peril for the Indian artist. There is, however, no possibility of keeping them out of the country, so we must be content to wait for a generation or two before we can judge of their evil effects. Meanwhile, it is only fair to say in anticipation that races who for centuries have known how to accept and assimilate a long series of foreign importations and yet to maintain their own individuality of character may be trusted to deal even with the *Illustrated London News* and the *Graphic*.

The boar in art occurs only in a form so highly conventionalised as to be almost unrecognisable, in representations of the Boar *avatar*. There is a superb boar of colossal size at Khajuraho, carved in stone and completely covered over with row upon row of human figures in relief. It has never occurred to a Hindu to draw a pig for its own sake, while a Muhammadan would scorn to look at a pig picture.

In consequence of the popularity of the Monkey-god, Hanumān, the whole tribe has fared well at the hands of the Indian painter. He scarcely ever occurs in ancient carved work, and the sculptures of to-day are horribly rude, but in many pictures there is a first-rate appreciation of monkey character. In a MS. Rāmāyana in the Lahore Museum a pair of monkeys are shown drinking from a stream, and drawn with wonderful delicacy and naturalness. In the Ajanta frescoes there are some well-painted monkeys. Even in the much conventionalised representations of Hanumān, drawn for the poorest classes, there is often a quaint humour and observation, surprising to those who accept the common fallacy that the people of India are destitute of humour. That representations of the Monkey-god have long been admired is clear from the mention of his picture on Arjuna's banner in the ancient Hindu Epic. Rajput chivalry still bears a red Hanumān on the "five coloured" flags peculiar to the race.

One of the futile works of patience which so often take rank as works of Indian Art is a picture of Hanumān, composed of thousands of repetitions of the sacred name Ram. You draw the Monkey-god in pencil and then write Ram all along the lines in minute Hindi characters. Ram, ram, is a common salutation among Hindus, and mere repetition of the word is a sacrament. All sacraments mean more than meets the eye or ear, so we need not find anything absurd in the case of a Hindu personage who, by a curse of the Gods, was condemned to forego the use of the life-giving word. But he was permitted to say Mra, mra. This relieved his despairing soul, for, saying it quickly for an hour at a time, the most vindictive God or demon alive could hear only Ram, ram.

Bears took part in the wars of the Gods, and in

A PUNJAB HEROINE (FROM AN INDIAN LITHOGRAPH)

consequence are sketched with some freedom. A heroine of Punjab romance in more recent times is credited with marvellous exploits in hunting, and a bazaar print, reproduced here in little, gives a favourable idea both of the state of popular art in its humblest form and of the kind of legend in which the masses still delight. Whatever may be thought of the tigers in the upper panel, there is good bear character in the lower, and, as a large sheet bearing four such pictures is sold for a halfpenny, criticism ought to be disarmed. The gains of the artists employed on this kind of work are not large. I remember a friend of mine criticising with some asperity the careless drawing in a full-page cartoon of a vernacular comic paper. The draughtsman took it in good part and listened humbly, but when some of the laborious triumphs of Persian art were brandished before him, he mildly remarked that it was not easy to produce masterpieces at the rate of fivepence per picture, which was all that his Editor allowed.

In Indian Art, as in Indian talk, the only use made of the Ass is to point a curse withal. "Cursed be he that removeth his neighbour's landmark," said the Jews, but the Hindus inscribed their commination, a nameless, shameless horror, on the stone landmark itself. Several of these grotesque abominations now lie in Bombay Town Hall.

ANTELOPES. AN INDIAN ARTIST'S FANTASY

BUFFALO BULLS

CHAPTER XVII

OF BEAST FIGHTS

ALL nature fights. We are nowadays familiar with false phrases such as "unnatural strife" and the like, used in denunciation of one of the central instincts of life, but at heart we acknowledge that war is always natural to man and beast. The next best thing to fighting is to see others fight, says the experience of the world, and India has travelled a well-worn track in its enjoyment of fighting as a spectacle. English readers are already familiar with accounts of the gladiatorial displays and beast fights of the Emperor Akbar and of the Nawab Hyder Ali and Tippoo Sahib. There are many allusions in popular sayings and legends, and in the chronicles of native states, to wager fights between man and man, man and beast, and beast and beast, which show how popular and widespread the practice was. In a comparison between the arenas of old Rome and those of India the latter would come poorly off by reason of the inferiority of Orientals in the faculty of organisation, but in spite of details left to chance and an imperfect *mise en scène,* the Indian shows had much in common with the Roman displays, and the spirit and intention were the same. Wild animals are easily obtained here, and both Princes and people are greedy of sensations, so that it is natural that an arena for beast fights should become a regular appanage of a princely court. Lut'f'ullah in his interesting autobiography describes the populace of Baroda regularly spending its large leisure in the well-known animal yard there, and its wondering interest in the rhinoceros, familiarly known as the "*janwar,*" *the* beast *par excellence.* These arenas are still haunted by the people, and will probably change gradually into Zoological gardens, but there can be no doubt that the beast fight is popular to-day. You may call it brutal if you please, and organise a brand new society for its suppression, but it should be remembered that only yesterday the populations of whole towns (like Birmingham) swarmed to the British bull-ring, and that nature herself set the fashion.

There are indeed beast fights, promoted by men, which are simply developments of the beneficent principle described by modern science as the survival of the fittest. Of these are the spring-time buffalo bull fights treated as solemnities by Indian herdsmen. Once diversions of the pastoral prime, these conflicts are still annually brought off, even in Bombay, within sight of railways and telegraph posts The men say—and doubtless with truth—that they are useful in showing decisively which animal is best fitted to be a sire. Such fights are not always brought about by the herdsmen. One of the most impressive pictures of defeat I ever saw was one evening on a lonely road in the Western Ghauts, when a buffalo bull suddenly appeared against the sunset in labouring flight, rolling as he staggered along like a rudderless ship, his mouth and nostrils foaming, a horn broken, and his black flanks stained with blood. A long way behind him came the conqueror, bearing marks of the fight, but lumbering easily forward, half minded to stop; content that his foe was beaten and flying.

Sportsmen in pursuit of the black-buck antelope have occasionally seen a pair of these beautiful creatures so fiercely engaged in fighting as to take no notice of the intruder with a gun, and the skulls of deer with horns firmly interlocked have often been found as proofs of a fatal struggle.

Whether it is wrong to pit men against beasts, or to employ the natural, noble rage of male animals for conquest to make a holiday for a populace, are questions that may be easily answered, but the reprobation to be meted for the offence depends in some measure upon one's standpoint. From that of civilised Europe nothing could be more reprehensible, but it is not the populace of Europe that gives this answer; else why does the Midland or Northern mechanic lose a day's wage for a dog-fight, why are there bull fights in Spain, imitations of them in Paris, and everywhere an inclination to enjoy similar spectacles which breaks through the illusory crust we describe as civilisation and progress? In India, also, you may find thousands who would agree with the humanitarians of the West, but they keep their moral teaching for their own caste-fellows, and do not incline to damn the sins they have no mind to. In other words, though the natives of India are, as a mass, indifferent to the sufferings of creatures, it is doubtful whether they are intrinsically worse in this respect than the rest of the world. At the same time the age-long popularity of beast-fights shows that they are no better, and that the religious prescriptions of mercy to animals are, like most Levitical ordinances, merely local and ritual in their effect, taking no deep hold on the mind and life.

If it were desirable to pile up horrors, nothing is easier than to tell authentic stories of the cruelties formerly wrought for the pleasure of Indian Princes and their subjects in the arenas where beasts were made to fight. The accessories and accompaniments of these performances are more abhorrent than the fights themselves, for they show a loathsome and cold-blooded persistence in cruelty on the part of the men employed which told in any detail would be revolting. Bishop Heber in his admirable Indian journals has, however, given a description that may be quoted without offence: "We were shown five or six elephants in training for a fight. Each was separately kept in a small paved court, with a little litter, but very dirty. They were all what is called *must*, that is, fed on stimulating substances to make them furious, and all showed in their eyes, their gaping mouths, and the constant motion of their trunks, signs of fever and restlessness. Their mahouts seemed to approach them with great caution, and, on hearing a step, they turned round as far as their chains would allow, and lashed fiercely with their trunks. I was moved and disgusted at the sight of so noble creatures, thus maddened and diseased by the absurd cruelty of man, in order that they might, for his diversion, inflict fresh pain and injuries on each other."

This is an ancient practice; the manner of it is still a part of the mahouts' science, and full of mysteries and absurdities. Among other things they firmly believe that the wax of the human ear is an infallible agent when duly combined with other nasty messes. But it is unnecessary to rake very deeply in this unpleasing subject. Moreover, the worst features of the old fights are now seldom presented. The lives of men are not now lightly risked to please a populace. The elephant, rhinoceros, buffalo, horse, ass, tiger, leopard, camel, dog, wolf, and ram have all been made to fight to death in their time, but even this is seldom now permitted. The encounters between elephants, indeed, are often of a half friendly nature, like those of American boxers; for it is not easy, without setting up a functional disturbance, to get an elephant into a rage. At the word of command he will drub another elephant, much as he would roll a log or lift a cart-wheel, but he has too sweet and amiable a nature to make a real fighter.

In order to give an accurate picture of what takes place at an Indian beast fight to-day, of the slip-shod arrangements and the quaint way in which folk and animals are mingled together, I quote a description of one of these entertainments given at the installation of His Highness the Maharaja of Jammu and Kashmir, done from the life by my son for the Lahore paper in 1886:—

"Two huge water-buffaloes with ropes on their feet and a dozen men at each rope were introduced to each other; the crowd closing round them to within a few feet. Neither animal required any urging, but put his head down at once and butted. The shock of the opposing skulls rang like the sound of a hatchet on wood across the arena. Then both brutes laid head to head, and pushed and grunted and pawed and sweated for five minutes; the crowd yelling madly meanwhile. The lighter weight was forced back into the crowd, recovered himself, butted again, turned sideways, and was again forced back. After a few minutes more, when each animal was setting down to his work with whole-hearted earnestness, the order was given to separate them; and very reluctantly the gigantic creatures were hauled in opposite directions. Then a curious thing happened. A little child ran forward out of the press, and standing on tip-toe, reached up and embraced with both arms the hairy jowl of the beast who had borne himself the most savagely in the fray. It was a pretty little picture—spoilt by the other buffalo suddenly breaking loose and charging down anew. A second shock and yet another struggle followed, and both beasts were eventually led off snorting and capering in uncouth fashion to express their disgust at not being allowed to go on. Two fresh bulls advanced gravely into the middle of the arena, gazed at each other politely, and as politely retired. They must have shared the same wallow together, for fight they would not.

"Next came the fighting rams, spotted and shaven beasts, with Roman noses and rowdy visages straining away from their owners and all apparently 'spoiling for a fight.' Two or three couples were let go together, ran back to gather way, came on and met, ran back, charged again, and repeated the performance till the sound of their foolish colliding heads was almost continuous.

"After the first few minutes, when you begin to realise that neither animal is likely to fall down dead, ram fighting is monotonous. Sometimes a ram runs back for his charge valiantly enough, but midway in his onset loses heart, turns a fat tail to his antagonist, and flees to his master. The adversary, being a beast of honour, immediately pulls up and trots back to *his* master. One light-limbed *dūmba* (the fat-tailed variety) with red spots seems to be the champion of Jummu. His charge generally upsets his antagonist at once, and few care to stand a second.

"As soon as all the rams had been disposed of, certain vicious shrieks and squeals gave evidence that the horses were being got ready, and the police set about widening the ring. Presently a bay galloway and a black pony danced out, dragging their attendants after them at the end of a long rope. The instant they were let go, they ran open-mouthed at each other, then turned tail to tail and kicked savagely for five minutes; the black suffering most. Then, after the manner of horses all the world over, they turned round and closed, each striking with his forefeet and striving to fix his teeth in the other's crest. They squealed shrilly as they boxed, and finally rose on end, a magnificent sight, locked in each other's arms. The bay loosening his hold on the black's poll, made a snatch at the black's near foreleg, which was at once withdrawn. Both horses then dropped to the ground together and kicked and bit at close quarters till the bay fled, with the black after him, through the crowd. The men at the end of the drag ropes were knocked over, scrambled up, and caught at the ropes again, while the two maddened brutes plunged and struggled among the people. About half a dozen were knocked over and shaken, but no one was seriously hurt; and after wild clamour and much running hither and thither both bay and black were caught, blindfolded, and led away to reappear no more. Buffaloes fight like men, and rams like fools; but horses fight like demons, with keen enjoyment and much skill.

"And now twilight had fallen; the wrestlers, who tumbled about regardless of the excitement round them, had all put their man down or had their own shoulders mired. The mob on the double tiers of the amphitheatre dropped down into the arena and flooded the centre till the elephants could scarcely wade through the press.

"Just at this time an unrehearsed and most impressive scene followed. The biggest of the elephants, a huge beast with gold-bound tusks, gold 'broidered jhool and six-foot earrings, had been ordered to sit down for his riders to mount. Before the ladder could be adjusted, he sprang up with a trumpet, turned round towards the palace, uphill, that is to say, and knocked a man over. Then he wheeled round, the mahout pounding at his forehead with his iron goad, to the other end of the arena, where another elephant was going down the incline towards the lower part of the city. He raced across the space, full of people, scattering the crowd in every direction, butted the retreating elephant in the rear, making him stagger heavily; ran back, butted him again, and threw him on his knees near the stone revetment of the earth-work terrace of the palace. Here the mahout re-established some sort of control, swung him round, and brought him back to be taken off roped and chained, in deep disgrace.

"The man thrown down at the beginning was brought up into the palace verandah. He was naturally knocked out of breath and desperately frightened, for the elephant had set a foot on the loose folds of his paejamas. An old woman, overthrown in the charge after the other elephant, lay on the ground for a few minutes, and then hobbled off with the help of a stick. That was the extent of the damage, inconceivably small as it may appear, caused by a vicious elephant rushing through a crowd of some thousands of people. The murmur of fright and astonishment that went up from the crowd after it was seen that the brute was out of hand, was curious to listen to; being a long-drawn A—a—a—hoo which chilled the blood. The sight of the crowd flying in deadly fear of their lives was even more curious and impressive. Most impressive of all was the bulk of the beast in the twilight, and the clang of the silver earrings as it darted,—elephants can dart when they like,—across the ground in search of its enemy.

"With this unique spectacle the sports of the evening closed."

CHAPTER XVIII

OF ANIMALS AND THE SUPERNATURAL

"O Hassan! Saving Allah, there is none
More strong than Eblis. Foul marsh lights he made
To wander and perplex us,—errant stars,
Red, devil-ridden meteors bringing plague—
Deserts of restless sand-drifts,—ice-bound seas
Wherein is neither life nor power to live;—
Bound Devils to the snow-capped peaks;—(These vex
Earth with their struggles,)—lashed undying fire
About the forehead of the tortured hills,
And filled the belly of the Deep with life
Unnameable and awful at his will:—
Sent forth his birds, the owl, the kite, the crow:—
Gray wolves that haunt our village gate at dusk
Made he his horses, and his councillor
The hooded snake;—in darkness wove the grass
That kills our cattle, made the flowers that suck
Man's life like dew-drops,—evil seeds and shrubs
That turn the sons of Adam into beasts
Whom Eblis snatches from the sword-wide Bridge.

"The thing that stung thee and its kind, his hands
Fashioned in mockery and bitter hate,—
Dread beasts by land and water, all are his.
Each bears the baser likeness of God's work,
Distorted, as the shadow of thy face
In water troubled by the breeze."

The Seven Nights of Creation—R. K.

ALL Indian animals are more or less concerned in the Hindu mind with the over or the under world, but certain ideas and beliefs which have not been noticed in the foregoing pages deserve a moment's attention. An enumeration of the fabulous creatures invented by Eastern fancy would be a long business, and, strictly speaking, belongs to another story—to the book some happy pedant, rich in lore and leisure, will one day write on the Natural History of the birds, beasts, and fishes that never were in air or land or sea. Many of them are kin to the strange creatures of the monkish bestiaries of medieval Europe, the herring-gutted menageries of heraldry, and the poetry of all the world. The Rukh, mightiest of eagles; the Huma or Phœnix; the Simurgh or Hippogriff; the buffalo demon or Bucentaur; the Garuda, often shown as a winged man with a bird's head; the Yali, a wonderful horse monster; Jatayu, the Vulture King; with dragons, sea-monsters, and the winged animals of every kind in which Mongolian and Persian imagination is exceptionally prolific, are only a few of a mighty and most fantastic host. Some have plainly grown to their place through the attempts of artists to represent the vague dreams of poets. Rude versions of the Avatars or incarnations of the Gods are accepted as portraits of possible creatures, such as Narsingha, the man-lion, the man-fish, and so forth. To trace the birth, kinships, growth in human esteem, migrations, and uses of these delightful monsters, and to marshal them in historical procession, is a task that has been attempted of old time; but it still remains to link the East with the grotesque pageant, if not to place her contingent at the head.

The ascription of souls and a share in a future state to animals is, however, the most truly supernatural aspect of Eastern notions with reference to them. Even Muhammadans, whose restrained fancy is bitted by the severe injunctions of their creed, have allowed their minds to wander along this line and have opened heaven's gate to mere creatures. Shah Ali's camel, mentioned in another place, was led thither by the angel Gabriel. Abraham's ram is there because when the blindfolded Patriarch had slain, as he thought, his only son Isaac whom he loved, he found, as the bandage fell away from his eyes, his son by his side and the ram bleeding on the altar. Solomon's ant is in Paradise because the wise king preached a sermon on its industry, and because the dutiful insect dragged a locust for an offering up the steps of the lion-sculptured gold and ivory throne; the parrot of Balkis, Queen of Sheba, because it was so wise and eloquent; the ass of Balaam which spoke to the point; Jonah's whale; and for some topsy-turvy reason (perhaps because the passionate worship of it has damned sordid generations to another place), the golden calf of Moses; and Khetmir, the dog of the seven sleepers. According to the best authorities (who display an amazing confidence in these matters), there will be only men and women in our Christian heaven; and many in no irreverent spirit have been inclined to think with the Indians of both the old and new worlds that the celestial courts will be a little dull without a dog. For many dreamers of large leisure and wandering wit have strayed down the blind alley opened by the insoluble question,—do animals possess souls? Hitherto they have brought nothing back, nor can we hope for an answer, though every day we see the interrogation renewed in thousands of wistful animal eyes.

> "That liquid, melancholy eye,
> From whose pathetic, soul-fed springs
> Seem'd surging the Virgilian cry,
> The sense of tears in mortal things."

"Soul-fed," said Mr. Matthew Arnold, and yet he sorrowfully puts his dachshund "Geist" back to a dark place among merely mortal things.

We may not gainsay the conclusion, but surely there are those who will linger and hesitate. It would almost seem that they who most triumphantly read a clear title to their own sky mansions are the most reluctant to spell out a chance for the beast. Was not that sincere and good man, Dr. Johnson, just a little unkind to the worthy divine afflicted with a belief in the immortality of brutes? Boswell describes how the "speculatist with a serious, metaphysical, pensive face," said: "But really, Sir, when we see a very sensible dog, we don't know what to think of him." To which the doctor replied: "True, Sir: and when we see a very foolish *fellow*, we don't know what to think of *him*." And then the great man rolled and shook in contemptuous laughter over his rude and all too easy victory. You must laugh with him, but, the laughter done, it is God that knows, and not Dr. Johnson.

Another link with the supernatural is the power over wild creatures with which Indian ascetics are universally credited. Like many other ideas accounted peculiarly Oriental, this is only a belated European fancy. In Mr. Lecky's *History of European Morals* examples of miraculous power over savage nature are given from the saintly legends of the West, and all might be capped by tales of Indian jogis and faqirs. You can be shown to-day forest shrines and saintly tombs where the tiger comes nightly to keep a pious guard, and you may hear in any Hindu village of jogis to whom the cruel beasts are as lapdogs. In the native newspapers, as in popular talk, cases are reported in complete good faith where a Raja out hunting is endangered by a mad wild elephant or a ferocious tiger. At the critical moment the jogi appears and orders the obedient beast away. There may be some ground for this belief. An anchorite, living in the forest among well-nourished beasts of prey who were plentifully supplied with antelope and wild pig, could come and go unharmed. When wild things are let alone they are not so shy as sportsmen fancy. (At this moment a wild wood pigeon, shyest of birds, is nesting unnoticed by the thousands who pass her in Kensington Gardens.) And when one considers the awful *ennui* of a life given up to religious meditation and abstraction,—mental feats of which not more than twenty strong souls in a generation are capable,—it is conceivable that a bored hermit, weary of stretching after the unknowable, might amuse himself with the easy feat of taming a wild animal; but here, surely, the miracle would begin and end.

A case occurred in Lahore within the last five years which seems to show that though faith survives, it is now a dangerous anachronism. A Mussulman faqir, visiting the beast garden, deliberately thrust his arm through the bars of the cage in which Moti, our tiger, was confined. Moti ought to have fawned on the sacred limb, but instead of worshipping as the faqir intended, he began to dine, and the arm was torn from its socket before the poor man could be dragged away. At first there seemed a chance that he would survive the dreadful mutilation, but after lingering two or three days, bearing himself with great serenity and composure, he died in hospital. A native would tell you that this was not a fair trial. Moti was a demoralised, denationalised tiger, for he was captured when a few days old, and brought up by the officers of a British regiment, and it was only to be expected that he should make a mistake.

That mere faith is a potent charm is shown by another little story in which Moti was concerned. Once he escaped from his den and there was a wild alarm. The Jemadar or headman of the gardens, a man of great personal courage, ran across the road to Government House demanding an official order from the Sircar for the arrest of the truant. Somebody gave him a large official envelope with a big seal, and thus armed the Jemadar went in chase. Moti was found on the public promenade or Mall, very much alone, as might be expected. The keeper hurried up to him, displaying the Lord Sahib's order, and shaking it in his face, rated him in good, set terms for his black ingratitude in breaking from the care of a Government that fed him regularly and used him well. Then he unwound the turban from his head, and having tied it round the beast's neck, haled him to his den, gravely lecturing as he led. Moti went like a lamb. Some years after, it is sad to say, the Jemadar was killed by a bear who had not the tiger's respect for official authority. Which things are an allegory of Empire as well as a true tale.

In his turn Moti also died, and his skin, now in the Lahore Museum, being carelessly removed, does scanty justice to the memory of a beautiful beast—the only animal of my acquaintance that really liked tobacco. The smoke of a strong Trichinopoly cheroot blown in his face delighted him ; he would sidle, blink, stretch, and arch his mighty back with the ineffable satisfaction that all cats find in aromatic odours.

An ancient superstition of world-wide currency, and

still firmly rooted in India, is the belief that some men and women can assume at will the form of animals. This theme is obviously capable of infinite variations. One of the most popular of a hundred tales accounts for a man-eating tiger of unusual bloodthirstiness. Once upon a time he was a man, who by traffic with demons had acquired a charm which enabled him to change to a tiger. His wife, being as curious as the rest of the daughters of Eve, begged to be allowed to witness the transformation. Very reluctantly he consented, and entrusted her with a magic root to be given to him to restore him to his real estate. But when the tiger appeared before her, the poor woman lost her head and ran away in terror, and before she could recover the villagers saw him and set out in chase. She never had another chance of meeting her husband. So she died of grief, and he in rage and despair revenged himself on humanity at large. Tales of this kind should be told, as in India, in the evening shadows under the village pipal tree, suggestively whispering of ghost-land overhead, while the vast background of the outer dark beckons the fancy to a far travel. Under these circumstances the absurdity of animal transformation assumes a dignity and reasonableness impossible to convey in print.

We have mostly forgotten in Europe the meaning of the marks printed on men and animals, though there are signs of a revival of the trivial nonsense among those who profess to foretell the future. As the sutures of the skull are supposed to print in God's own undecipherable Arabic the fate of each soul, so many another imprint gives signs which only the very wise may read. And there are pleasant popular fancies of the more obvious animal marks. Thus Buddha gave the cobra the characteristic spectacle-shaped markings on the back of his hood as a protection against Garuda, the kite,—a somewhat futile invention, for they would seem made to attract a kite. Rather should they have been the prints of the hands of the Gods, who used him as a churn string when the sacred mountain was the churn-stick and the sea was stirred to the wondrous tune of creation. The stripes on the Indian squirrel are the marks of Hanumān's thumb, seizing the little creature in haste to fill up the last gap in the bridge he built between India and Ceylon. Muhammad has left a thumb-mark on the neck of the Arab horse, much as St. Peter thumb-marked the John dory when he took from its gills the providential tribute money; and all the Christian world knows how the sign of the cross was imprinted on the shoulder of the ass.

. . . .

That supernatural beliefs should sit so lightly on the souls of men is a phenomenon as wonderful as the beliefs themselves. There are a few in all lands to whom their creeds are vital, others on whom they press only at the urgent crises of their lives; but the vast bulk of humanity is content to mutter an indifferent acquiescence. If we did not daily see by how slack a hold the faiths of the West control its life, we might marvel at the indifference of the East to the sufferings of animals whose bodies are believed to be tenanted by human souls.

Printed by R. & R. Clark, Limited, *Edinburgh.*